Black American Literature

Roger Whitlow

1974

LITTLEFIELD, ADAMS & CO.

Totowa, New Jersey

Black

American

Literature

A Critical History

*With a 1,520 - title bibliography of works
written by and about black Americans*

Published 1974 by
LITTLEFIELD, ADAMS & CO.
by arrangement with Nelson-Hall Company
Copyright © 1973 by Roger Whitlow

Library of Congress Cataloging in Publication Data

Whitlow, Roger
    Black American Literature
    (A Littlefield, Adams Quality Paperback No. 278)
    1. American literature — Negro authors — History and criticism.   2. American literature — Negro authors — Bibliography.   3. Negroes—Bibliography.   I. Title. II. Title: Black Americans.
[PS153.N5W45 1974]   810'.9'896073   74-10582
ISBN 0-8226-0278-4

"I Shall Return" and "Harlem Shadows" from *Selected Poems of Claude McKay*. Copyright 1953 by Bookman Associates. Used by permission of Twayne Publishers.

From *On These I Stand* by Countee Cullen: "Yet Do I Marvel," Copyright, 1925 by Harper & Row, Publishers, Inc., renewed 1953 by Ida M. Cullen; "To Certain Critics," Copyright, 1929 by Harper & Row, Publishers, Inc., renewed, 1957 by Ida M. Cullen. Reprinted by permission of Harper & Row, Publishers, Inc.

From *The World of Gwendolyn Brooks*: "People who have no children can be hard." Copyright, 1949 by Gwendolyn Brooks Blakely. Reprinted by permission of Harper & Row, Publishers, Inc.

"Harlen," Copyright 1951 by Langston Hughes. From *The Panther and the Lash*, by Langston Hughes. Reprinted by permission of Alfred A. Knopf, Inc. "The Negro Speaks of Rivers," Copyright 1926 by Alfred A. Knopf, Inc., renewed 1954 by Langston Hughes. From *Selected Poems*, by Langston Hughes. Reprinted by permission of Alfred A. Knopf, Inc.

"Between the World and Me," from *White Man, Listen!* by Richard Wright. Copyright © 1957 by Richard Wright. Reprinted by permission of Doubleday & Company, Inc.

Selections from "Middle Passage" by Robert Hayden from *Selected Poems*. Copyright © 1966 by Robert Hayden. Reprinted by permission of October House, Inc.

Selections from "For My People" by Margaret Walker. Copyright © 1942 by Yale University Press. Used by permission of Yale University Press.

Selections from "I Am a Cowboy in the Boat of Ra," by Ishmael Reed used by permission of the author.

"Preface to a Twenty Volume Suicide Note," © 1961 by LeRoi Jones. Reprinted by permission of Corinth Books/Totem Press.

"The True Import of Present Dialogue, Black vs. Negro," "Nikki-Rosa," and "My Poem" reprinted from *Black Feeling, Black Talk/Black Judgement*, by Nikki Giovanni, © 1970. Used by permission of William Morrow & Company, Inc.

For Miriam, Betha, and Stephen

Contents

Acknowledgments   xi
Preface   xiii

I.   Folklore: Humor, Endurance, and the Mask   1

        Origins
        Tales of Exaggeration
        Blues and Spirituals
        Work Songs
        Legendary-Men Tales
        Slave Stories
        Animal Tales
        Minstrel Shows and Vaudeville
        Folk Tradition in Black Literature
        Contemporary Folk Forms

II.   1746-1825: Looking Toward Religion   15

        Lucy Terry: First Black Writing

II.   1746-1825: Looking Toward Religion (continued)

Jupiter Hammon: First Published Black Literature
Phillis Wheatley
Gustavus Vassa: The Slave Narrative

III.   1825-1890: Early Themes of Protest   27

George Moses Horton: Early Protest Poetry
James M. Whitfield
Frances E. W. Harper
The Maturity of Black Autobiography
Frederick Douglass
William Wells Brown: First Black Fiction and Drama
Frank J. Webb
Martin R. Delany

IV.   1890-1920: Developing Artistic Consciousness   53

Paul Laurence Dunbar
Charles Waddell Chesnutt
James Weldon Johnson
W. E. B. DuBois

V.   1920-1940: The Harlem Renaissance and Its Influence   71

Alain L. Locke: Explanation of the "New Negro"
Claude McKay
Jean Toomer
Countee Cullen
Langston Hughes
Nella Larsen
End of the Harlem Renaissance
George S. Schuyler
Arna Bontemps
Zora Neale Hurston

VI. 1940-1960: Urban Realism and Beyond   107

Richard Wright
Richard Wright as Poet
The Wright School
Ann Petry
Dorothy West
William Demby
Ralph Ellison
James Baldwin
Gwendolyn Brooks
Robert Hayden
Margaret Walker
Paule Marshall
Lorraine Hansberry

VII. 1960 to the Present: Satire, the Past — and Themes of
Armageddon   147

Satire in Drama and Fiction
Ossie Davis
Kristin Hunter
Ishmael Reed
William Melvin Kelley
Return to the Twenties and Thirties
Sarah E. Wright
Robert Deane Pharr
Themes of Armageddon
Etheridge Knight
Imamu Amiri Baraka (LeRoi Jones)
Nikki Giovanni
John A. Williams

Conclusion   185

Notes   189

Black American Literature: A Bibliography of Folklore, Poetry,
Autobiography, Fiction, Drama, Anthologies, Literary Criticism
and Bibliography, and Social and Historical Comment   197

Index   273

Acknowledgments

While the dozens of sources which contributed to the compilation of the bibliography are far too numerous to mention, I should like to acknowledge the following especially helpful works, used both to supply previously undiscovered titles and to confirm spellings, dates, etc. left uncertain by other sources: Doris E. Abramson, *Negro Playwrights in the American Theatre 1925-1959*, 1969; Robert A. Bone, *The Negro Novel in America*, 1965; Frank Deodene and William P. French, *Black American Fiction Since 1952*, 1970; James V. Hatch, *Black Image on the American Stage: A Bibliography of Plays and Musicals 1770-1970*, 1970; Howard University, Departments of English and Afro-American Studies, "The Literature of the American Negro: A Selective Bibliography"; Alain Locke, *The New Negro*, 1925; William H. Robinson, *Early Black American Poets*, 1969; Arthur B. Spingarn, annual bibliography of recent works published, in February issues of *The Crisis;* Darwin T. Turner, *Afro-American Writers*, 1970; and Maxwell Whiteman, *A Century of Fiction by American Negroes, 1853-1952*, 1955.

Preface

During the last five years many learned people—some of them specialists in American literature—have been astonished to learn that black American literature has existed for two and a quarter centuries; that much of it is excellent literature produced by gifted writers; and that the work of many of these writers, such as Claude McKay, Langston Hughes, Richard Wright, Ralph Ellison, and James Baldwin, has been translated into more than a dozen languages and has been, in fact, often treated with greater respect by foreign readers and critics than by their American counterparts.

There are many reasons why all but a handful of black writers are virtually unknown to readers, white and black, and why until recently only two or three—usually Wright, Ellison, or Baldwin—were studied in literature classes. This situation can be explained, in part, by pointing out that many pieces of black writing were originally published in small editions and by obscure publishers, and that, until rather recently, the reading public interested in black writing was quite small. However, the most obvious reason, certainly related to those already mentioned, for the obscurity of many of these writers is the unfortunate notion on the part of many literate Americans that black writers could not actually produce "first-rate literary art" and that to offer courses in black literature is to succumb to coercion from "black power" groups.

In some ways, of course, the social activism of the 1960s led many to the discovery of this body of writing, too long overlooked. But the important fact is that now that these writings have been discovered and recognized as valuable contributions to the canon of American letters, most colleges and universities and many high schools in the United States offer study in black literature. And well they must, for the contributions of black Americans in the fields of folklore, poetry, autobiography, fiction, drama, and the essay can no longer be overlooked.

I have endeavored in this book to present and to explain the history and development of black American literature, moving from the earliest form of black cultural expression, the oral folk tradition, through the major periods, movements, themes, works, and authors, to the present. Among the numerous purposes of such a presentation, one is the attempt to make the reader more conscious of the range and depth of the black literary heritage. Another is to illustrate that, because it is largely reflective of cultural experiences that have been consistently separated, by law and prejudice, from the mainstream of American culture, black literature has developed its own traditions, periods, and movements, which only rarely correspond to (and, far more often, run counter to) the traditions, periods, and movements of American literature generally.

For this reason black writing can best be understood and appreciated when studied separately from other American literature. The influences that produce most black writers and their literature, and the implications of that literature, can seldom be grasped when individual pieces of black writing are thrust, without considerable preparation, into their chronologically appropriate positions in general American literature courses.

I offer my gratitude to graduate assistant Miss Mary-Nance Olds and to Mrs. Cathy-Lynn Shelton and Mrs. Evelyn Johns, whose patience and diligence in typing and proofreading the manuscript made my task a much easier one.

R.W.

I. Folklore: Humor, Endurance, and the Mask

Origins

Before discussing the written literary forms of the black American, one must consider the oral tradition of his cultural expression, his folklore, the rich body of stories and songs that has served as the source of much of his cultural inspiration as well as the source of much of his writing. Recent study of black folklore reveals that, contrary to early explanations that nearly all black American folklore is descended from African oral traditions, there is no such direct path from Africa to the American plantation. Folklorist Richard M. Dorson, for example, points out that many of the well-known animal stories are European in origin and that many of the thousands of other tales can be traced to England, the West Indies, and to white American folk traditions.[1]

Even tales which originated in other lands were "Americanized" soon after they were transported by slaves to the southern plantation, where their themes and characters were modified to reflect more accurately the new black experience. In the introduction to *Book of Negro Folklore*, Arna Bontemps, who together with

Langston Hughes edited the collection, explains the "Americaniza-
tion" of the animal tales which came from Africa:

*In the African prototypes of the American Negro tales the heroes
were generally the jackal, the hare, the tortoise, and the spider. The
African jackal survived as the American fox, the African hare as
the American rabbit, and the African tortoise as the American dry-
land turtle or terrapin. The spider came only as near as the West
Indies, where it reappeared in the Anansi tales of Jamaica. As a
villain the African hyena was replaced by the American wolf, but
that role is sometimes assigned to the fox or the bear in the American tale. The rest of the cast of characters, the lions, leopards,
tigers, and monkeys, was safely transported.*

In America the already established oral tradition was reinforced by laws, especially harsh in the nineteenth century, forbid-
ding the teaching of reading or writing to slaves—sometimes to
blacks generally, slave or free.[2] In introducing his book *American
Negro Folktales*, Richard Dorson says of this oral expression:

*Only the Negro, as a distinct element of the English-speaking
population, maintained a full-blown storytelling tradition. A separate Negro subculture formed within the shell of American life,
missing the bounties of general education and material progress,
remaining a largely oral, self-contained society with its own un-
written history and literature. In 1880 a portion of this oral
literature for the first time became visible to the mass of Americans
with the publication by Joel Chandler Harris of* Uncle Remus: His
Songs and His Sayings.

Between 1880 and 1918 Harris published eight additional collections of Uncle Remus tales and thereby generated the widespread
interest in black folk culture that still exists.

The folklore of the black American reveals a great deal about the way that he viewed—and views—himself and others, about the ways that he has amused himself and sustained himself in an often hostile culture, and about the ways that he has disguised his actual feelings and opinions from white society. Found among the thousands of black folktales and folk songs are stories of experiences in heaven and hell, of bargains made with God and the devil; stories about Biblical characters; explanations of the causes of natural events such as thunder, lightning, rain, and snow; ghost stories; preacher stories; stories about why animals and people are formed as they are and why they are the colors that they are; courting tales; exaggerated tales of the meanest man, the quickest man, the ugliest man, the dirtiest man, and so on; stories about the relationship between the sexes, why men are stronger (weaker), more intelligent (less intelligent) than women; the ubiquitous animal and bird tales; witch-riding stories; hard-work stories; accounts of spiritual suffering and salvation; and legendary-men tales.[3]

Tales of Exaggeration

Many of the folk stories are designed sheerly as lightheartedly absurd accounts of people who, because of the exaggerated circumstances in which they are placed or the exaggerated feats which they perform, are the subjects of a form of tall-tale humor which at times is little short of hilarious. One such story, a "courtship/ fastest-man" tale, is found in Zora Neale Hurston's collection, *Mules and Men* (1935):

"Youse in de majority, now Shug," B. Moseley said, seeing Bennie asleep. "Le's hear 'bout dat man wid three women." Shug said:

Naw, it was three mens went to court a girl, Ah told you. Dis was a real pretty girl wid shiny black hair and coal black eyes. And all dese men wanted to marry her, so they all went and ast her pa if they could have her. He looked 'em all over, but he couldn't decide which one of 'em would make de best husband and de girl, she couldn't make up her mind, so one Sunday night when he walked into de parlor where they was all sittin' and said to 'em, "Well, all y'all want to marry my daughter and youse all good men and Ah can't decide which one will make her de best husband. So y'all be here tomorrow mornin' at daybreak and we'll have a contest and de one dat can do de quickest trick kin have de girl."

Nex' mornin' de first one got up seen it wasn't no water in de bucket to cook breakfas' wid. So he tole de girl's mama to give him de water bucket and he would go to the spring and git her some.

He took de bucket in his hand and then he found out dat de spring was ten miles off. But he said he didn't mind dat. He went on and dipped up de water and hurried on back wid it. When he got to de five-mile post he looked down into de bucket and seen dat de bottom had done dropped out. Then he recollected dat he heard somethin' fall when he dipped up de water so he turned round and run back to de spring and clapped in dat bottom before de water had time to spill.

De ole man thought dat was a pretty quick trick, but de second man says, "Wait a minute. Ah want a grubbin' hoe and a axe and a plow and a harrow." So he got everything he ast for. There was ten acres of wood lot right nex' to de house. He went out dere and chopped down all de trees, grubbed up de roots, ploughed de field, harrowed it, planted it in cow-peas, and had green peas for dinner.

De ole man says, "Dat's de quickest trick. Can't nobody beat dat. No use in tryin'. He done won de girl."

De last man said, "You ain't even givin' me a chance to win de girl."

So he took his high-powered rifle and went out into de woods about seben or eight miles until he spied a deer. He took aim and fired. Then he run home, run round behind de house and set his gun down and then run back out in de woods and caught de deer and held 'im till de bullet hit 'im.

So he won de girl.

Blues and Spirituals

Only occasionally lighthearted, and reflective of the serious concern of the black American for maintaining a sense of dignity in often nearly impossible circumstances, are the blues and spirituals, the work songs, and the legendary-men stories. In the blues, especially, is found the will to endure, to relate to singer and listener alike the shared suffering of race or poverty, or of lost love—to repeat the suffering in the hope of making the distress more tolerable through the knowledge that it is understood and experienced by all. The spirituals convey feelings of both oppression (from a sense of sin) and elation (from the sense of spiritual salvation); it is notable that the sense of oppression is usually universal, not racial, as it applies to all "sinners," hence all human beings.

Observe, for example, the following lines from religious songs collected and discussed by Odum and Johnson (*The Negro and His Songs*):[4] "The Lord is a listenin' all the day long/Bear yo' burden, sinner"; "O sinner man, you better pray/For it look-a like judgment every day"; "Oh, what a hard time! Oh, what a hard time/Oh, what a hard time—all God's children have a hard time." The sense of elation is found in such lines as, "I'm so glad, so glad, I'm so glad, so glad/Glad I got religion, so glad," and others like these which express the new-found peace and courage of "knowing Jesus" and "being held in Jesus' arms."

Work Songs

More futile than the blues and spirituals are the work songs, often sung with a rope-pulling or hammer-swinging cadence

which implies that the work will never cease, that the worker will
never free himself from the rope or the hammer. One of the most
famous of the work songs is "Hammer Song":

Well she ask me—hunh—
In de parlor—hunh;
And she cooled me—hunh—
Wid her fan—hunh;

An' she whispered—hunh—
To her mother—hunh:
"Mama, I love dat—hunh—
Dark-eyed man"—hunh.

Well I ask her—hunh—
Mother for her—hunh;
And she said she—hunh
Was too young—hunh;
Lord, I wished I'd—hunh—
Never seen her—hunh;
And I wished she'd—hunh—
Never been born—hunh.

Well, I led her—hunh—
To de altar—hunh;
And de preacher—hunh—
Give his command—hunh—
And she swore by—hunh—
God that made her—hunh;
That she'd never—hunh—
Love another man—hunh.[5]

While there may be success in love, in "Hammer Song" and in many other work songs, that love is incessantly interrupted and diminished—in the composition of the song and in lives of the lovers—by the never-ending intrusion of the labor itself, the pulling of the rope, the swinging of the hammer.

Legendary-Men Tales

The legendary-men stories, a source of both amusement and endurance, are less indigenously black in origin than the blues, spirituals, and work songs. There are, of course, those black men of legend such as Stagolee and Eddy Jones, both of "bad nigger" (pistol-, razor-, and dice-wielding) fame, who are apt subjects for black folklore because, in their own vernacular, they "don't take no shit" from anyone, black or white. Many who have related their stories undoubtedly have taken comfort from telling of their exploits in fighting, gambling, loving, and living in general—especially because they engage in these exploits "on their own terms," something American blacks generally have seldom had the luxury of doing.

Many of the legends of famous folk heroes, however, have their roots in white American—especially nineteenth-century railroad and outlaw—folklore. Among the most famous of these heroes are John Henry, Casey Jones, and Frank and Jesse James. While these heroes no doubt serve the same amusement function for blacks as for decades they have for whites, their adoption by blacks is significant because these heroes are invariably underdogs in conflict with powerful adversaries. Just as Stagolee and Eddy Jones are in conflict with urban social and legal conventions, John Henry is in conflict with the indefatigable machine, virtually the entire age of technology; Casey Jones is in conflict with the power of the locomotive which he thinks that he, as engineer, can control;

and Frank and Jesse James, in the Robin-Hoods-of-the-West role in which they are cast, are in conflict with the inequitable economic standards of the "gilded age."

An interesting fact about the folk stories of these men is that, while their deaths form the climax of the tales and are explained in elaborate detail, their demise does not represent failure. In fact, the strength of the legends—and undoubtedly the source of inspiration for many of the black Americans who have again and again retold them—lies in the realization that, given the overwhelming odds that the heroes face, the heroes' deaths are deferred as long as they are. There is in the tales, then, a sense of awe for the survival-power of the heroes, a recognition that a man who labors at what he knows to be a futile but necessary task, if he labors with courage and dignity, is indeed a noble man—a man whose nobility can be spiritually assumed by those who for generations tell and hear his story.

Slave Stories

The question of dignity appears also, though less obviously, in the slave stories and the animal tales so abundant in black folklore. In these forms the slave (or his oppressed but crafty counterpart in the animal lore, often Br'er Rabbit) by "wearing the mask," the impassivity of expression, the harmlessly lethargic behavior, secures his safety in a culture in which both custom and law decree him an object hardly deserving of respect. Also, through his wiles, he gains such luxuries as hoarded wealth, the pleasure of being anonymously responsible for his master's being beaten or cheated, or the even greater pleasure of being responsible for his master's death. Probably the most famous of the slave-story characters is Old John. In the dozens of stories about Old John,[6] the sly slave, while outwardly humble and shuffling, manages to secure his own land, accumulate a fortune from fortune-telling, convince Massa to leap into the river in a tied sack (thus drowning himself), and, most important, achieve his freedom.

Animal Tales

Old John's counterpart in the animal tales is often Br'er Rabbit, a relatively weak and oppressed creature who through his cunning and determination escapes work and out-maneuvers his more powerful antagonists, chiefly Br'er Wolf, Br'er Bear, and Br'er Fox. Although many generations of plantation masters and whites generally were familiar with these characters, they did not recognize them as white substitutes who, while powerful and oppressive, could nonetheless be tricked. One of the hundreds of such tales, titled "The Bear in the Mudhole,"[7] illustrates the nature of the animal narratives:

Well, Mr. Bear he was hungry. He goes gets in the mudhole and lays down flat on his back, to make them think that he was bogged up to his neck. He starts hollering, "Help, help, help." Mr. Rabbit looked around him and sees Mr. Bear in the mudhole.

"Mr. Rabbit can you help get me out, can you pull me out?"

"No, I can't pull you out by myself, I'll run to get the boys." Mr. Rabbit gets Mr. Turtle, Mr. Terrapin, Mr. Possum, Mr. Coon, and Mr. Fox, and brings them all back.

Mr. Bear said, "Let me catch hold of your tail, Brother Rabbit."

Rabbit said, "No no, my tail is skinned. Brother Bear, catch hold of Brother Turtle's tail; Brother Turtle, catch hold of Brother Possum's tail—he's got a long tail and that will put him way out on the ground." (The possum ain't much of a swimmer.) "Mr. Possum, catch hold of Mr. Coon's tail; Mr. Coon, catch hold of Mr. Fox's tail. Well, we ready to go?" (Rabbit was the bossman.) "Haul away! Hiya coming, Mr. Bear?"

"Oh, you moved me three or four inches."

"Well, let him rest a little—don't worry about that, Mr. Bear, we'll get you out. Okay, ready to go! Haul away! Feel yourself coming any, Mr. Bear?"

"Oh yeah, I come about three feet, but I'm stiff and sore through."

"Well, let the boys rest again—we'll git ye this time. Don't worry. We'll make it snappish and let's get him out this time, boys. Haul away."

Well, they got him about five feet and he's out on the ground. Rabbit say, "How you feel, Mr. Bear?"

"Oh I feel sore and stiff from this mud—rub my legs a little bit. Oh that's good, rub my shoulders a little bit."

Brother Rabbit says, "We're going to get you so you're well in a day or two—you'll be well."

So when they rub his shoulders the Bear says, "Oh, rub my neck, that's where I been laying on it, it's so sore, rub my neck." When they got rubbing his neck he grabbed Mr. Rabbit. Brother Turtle he soaked down in the mud (he was a mudturtle). Brother Terrapin he went off to the woods and lay down side of a log—he was so slow he didn't wait till the Rabbit got through rubbing. Up jumped Mr. Rabbit, he went to running too. So Brother Bear caught Brother Rabbit.

Rabbit said, "Oh, you know if you say your prayers before you eat me you'll have something to eat all the time—that's what the Good Book says." Well, Mr. Bear shut his eyes and returned thanks. When he opened his eyes Brother Rabbit was gone.

Minstrel Shows and Vaudeville

An unfortunate use of the early black folk humor came, incidentally, with the appearance, in the late nineteenth and early twentieth centuries, of the minstrel show and vaudeville. Both of these entertainment forms depended upon brief, light humor, and performers in both found a storehouse of brief stories and quips in the established tradition of black folklore. What is distressing about the use of black folk material in this way is that blacks telling humorous stories about blacks to blacks is a very different matter from whites (even whites disguised as blacks) or blacks telling the same stories to whites who have paid to hear humor which does not abrade their own social standards, or prejudices. And, of course, because white audiences almost entirely missed the double meanings of many of the tales, especially the slave stories with their often threatening undertones, and thereby accepted the surface image of the shuffling, childish, and lazy darky, the "plantation" stereotypes were perpetuated through still additional American institutions.

Folk Tradition in Black Literature

In addition to the exaggerated tales of humor, the blues, spirituals, work songs, and legendary-men stories, and the slave and animal tales, there has grown out of the black folk tradition a large and valuable body of written expression, from the poetry of Paul Laurence Dunbar and the short stories of Charles W. Chesnutt; through the poetic novels of Jean Toomer and Zora Neale Hurston; to the novels, short stories, and poetry of Langston Hughes, Claude McKay, George W. Henderson, Margaret Walker, Ernest Gaines, and Sarah E. Wright. Langston Hughes, for example, transplanted black folk narrative style into Harlem in his "Simple" sketches, tales of the day-to-day experiences and attitudes of Jesse B. Simple as discussed with an unidentified narrator in five volumes published by Hughes between 1950 and 1965. Observe in the opening of the sketch "Feet Live Their Own Life"[8] the sense of timelessness in Simple's tale, the sense of its all having been, in one variation or another, said, felt, shared countless times before:

"If you want to know about my life," said Simple as he blew the foam from the top of the newly filled glass the bartender put

before him, "don't look at my face, don't look at my hands. Look at my feet and see if you can tell how long I been standing on them."

"I cannot see your feet through your shoes," I said.

"You do not need to see through my shoes," said Simple. "Can't you tell by the shoes I wear—not pointed, not rocking-chair, not French-toed, not nothing but big, long, broad, and flat—that I been standing on these feet a long time and carrying some heavy burdens? They ain't flat from standing at no bar, neither, because I always sets at a bar. Can't you tell that? You know I do not hang out in a bar unless it has stools, don't you?"

"That I have observed," I said, "but I did not connect it with your past life." . . .

"When I was a wee small child," said Simple, "I had no place to set and think in, being as how I was raised up with three brothers, two sisters, seven cousins, one married aunt, a common-law uncle, and the minister's grandchild—and the house only had four rooms. I never had no place just to set and think. Neither to set and drink —not even much my milk before some hongry child snatched it out of my hand, I were not the youngest, neither a girl, nor the cutest. I don't know why, but I don't think nobody liked me much. Which is why I was afraid to like anybody for a long time myself. When I did like somebody, I was full-grown and then I picked out the wrong woman because I had no practice in liking anybody before that. We did not get along."

"Is that when you took to drink?"

"Drink took to me," said Simple. "Whiskey just naturally likes me but beer likes me better. By the time I got married I had got to the point where a cold bottle was almost as good as a warm bed, especially when the bottle could not talk and the bed-warmer could. I do not like a woman to talk to me too much—I mean about me. Which is why I like Joyce. Joyce most in generally talks about herself."

"I am still looking at your feet," I said, "and I swear they do not reveal your life to me. Your feet are no open book."

"You have eyes but you see not," said Simple. "These feet have stood on every rock from the Rock of Ages to 135th and Lenox. These feet have supported everything from a cotton bale to a hongry woman. These feet have walked ten thousand miles working for white folks and another ten thousand keeping up with colored. These feet have stood at altars, crap tables, free lunches, bars, graves, kitchen doors, betting windows, hospital clinics, WPA desks, social security railings, and in all kinds of lines from soup lines to the draft. If I just had four feet, I could have stood in more places longer. As it is, I done wore out seven hundred pairs of shoes, eighty-nine tennis shoes, twelve summer sandals, also six loafers. The socks that these feet have bought could build a knitting mill. The corns I've cut away would dull a German razor. The bunions I forgot would make you ache from now till Judgment Day. If anybody was to write the history of my life, they should start with my feet."

Contemporary Folk Forms

The most recent descendant of black folk material is the monologue comedy of such entertainers as Flip Wilson, Godfrey Cambridge, Dick Gregory, Jackie "Moms" Mabley, and Bill Cosby.[9] One finds, for example, in Flip Wilson's "Rev" tales a contemporary version of the old "preacher" stories and in Bill Cosby's "Weird Harold" and "Fat Albert" sketches a modern variation of the old anecdotes about the fastest-man, the ugliest-man, and so on.

This recent form of comedy, related mostly by blacks to audiences of blacks and whites, reflects a new maturity in the American racial climate. Now a black comedian can point in humor to the foibles of both blacks and whites and expect his mixed audiences to get pleasure from laughing at the foibles themselves, without feeling the need to identify the foibles racially as "theirs" or "ours" and feeling smugly pleased or defensive about what they hear. Note, for example, the opening of "Moms" Mabley's sketch "Little Cindy Ella,"[10] in which light-handed references are made to the anathema of many whites, that "time-payment" Cadillac, to the White Citizen's Council, and to the Ku Klux Klan, all subjects that until recently were usually treated with contempt:

I want to read you one about Little Cindy Ella. You-all call her Cinderella in that book you-all got. Anyhow, way down South lived a little girl. She had long black hair, pretty brown eyes, pretty brown skin. Well, let's face it—she was colored! Little Cindy Ella dressed very shabby because she had to use her money to pay the notes on her boy friend's Cadillac.

She worked for a mean, mean, mean old woman with her two ugly daughters. Ugly—UG-U-G-L-Y! They were so ugly until they had a dishonorable discharge from The White Citizen's Council. *One day the mean old woman and her ugly daughters got an invitation to a prom dance. It was the biggest dance of the season. That was the time that they usually picked "Miss Ku Klux Klan."*

This recent comedy has by no means replaced the earlier forms of black folk expression—tall tales, blues, spirituals, work songs, legendary-men tales, animal stories, and the many others. All of these forms continue to exist not only in the rural South where they were born or adapted, but also in the northern and southern urban centers,[11] where they have been transported by generations of migrating black Americans and where they continue to provide amusement and cultural inspiration.

II. 1746-1825: Looking Toward Religion

Lucy Terry: First Black Writing

The first known piece of literature written by a black American is a short doggerel titled "Bars Fight," which was written in 1746 by a sixteen-year-old servant girl named Lucy Terry (1730-1821). Not published until 1893, the poem, far more important for its role in history than for its obviously weak literary merit, is the account of a Massachusetts Indian raid witnessed by Miss Terry:

August 'twas, the twenty-fifth,
Seventeen hundred forty-six,
The Indians did in ambush lay,
Some very valient men to slay,
The names of whom I'll not leave out:
Samuel Allen like a hero fout,
And though he was so brave and bold,
His face no more shall we behold;
Eleazer Hawks was killed outright,

Before he had time to fight,
Before he did the Indians see,
Was shot and killed immediately;
Oliver Amsden, he was slain,
Which caused his friends much grief and pain;
Simeon Amsden they found dead,
Not many rods off from his head;
Adonijah Gillet, we do hear,
Did lose his life, which was so dear;
John Saddler fled across the water,
And so escaped the dreadful slaughter:
Eunice Allen see the Indians comeing,
And hoped to save herself by running,
And had not her petticoats stopt her,
The awful creatures had not cotched her,
And tommyhawked her on the head,
And left her on the ground for dead;
Young Samuel Allen, oh! lack-a-day,
Was taken and carried to Canada.[12]

At the time that she wrote her poem, Lucy Terry worked for Ebenezer Wells of Deerfield, Massachusetts. Ten years after the Indian raid described in the poem, in 1756, she was given her freedom by Wells in order that she might marry a free black named Abijah Prince, by whom she had six children. Prince became the owner of considerable land and was one of the founders of Sunderland, Vermont, where he and his family moved from Massachusetts.

The account of the lives of the Princes sounds, except for occasional experiences of racial discrimination, much like that of many nonblack Colonial New Englanders. It is surprising to many, whose images of early American blacks are often couched in settings of brutal nineteenth-century slave existence, that, especially in New England, many blacks, slave and free, were quite well educated, that many free blacks were successful artisans and planters, and that some themselves owned slaves. In short, blacks were generally better treated in the eighteenth century than in the nineteenth, partly because of the influence of religion in the northern colonies, where it was generally held that blacks should be educated at least enough to understand Christianity. This condition was very different from those conditions of the nineteenth century in which brutal forms of punishment awaited blacks and whites alike who attempted to teach blacks to read or write.

The new national idealism felt by many during the Revolutionary Period also tended to moderate the treatment of blacks, and as a result many blacks played significant roles in the Revolution itself. Especially notable were Lemuel Haynes, a Minuteman, and Crispus Attucks, one of the first to die in the initial skirmish of the war. And during the Revolution, because it was felt by many that all Americans should be united against the British (and, it should be noted, because of the widespread fear, partly justified, that the British might themselves enlist the assistance of disgruntled blacks), there were efforts to enlist blacks in the Revolutionary Army as well as efforts to bring slavery to an end in nearly all of the colonies.[13] Unfortunately, however, at the Constitutional Convention of 1787 the racial scenario was written largely by proslavery advocates. The antislavery forces, like their counterparts a century later during Reconstruction, were eager to get on with the building of the new government and had lost much of their zeal concerning the ever-present problem of slavery. Because major compromises were made, the nearly one million American blacks were, for the purpose of representation in government, granted three-fifths the status of whites. Thus the stage was set for the turbulent and repressive racial climate which would come in the nineteenth century.

It is not surprising, then, that the black writers of the eighteenth century, most of whom were located in New England, where they did not experience the hardships of southern plantation life, chose to write relatively little on the subject of race and virtually nothing which corresponded in subject or intensity to the black protest writing of the nineteenth century. Nor is it surprising, given the still intense religious climate of New England in the eighteenth century, that religious themes should dominate the work of the two blacks, Jupiter Hammon and Phillis Wheatley, who were among the first to publish their work.

Jupiter Hammon: First Published Black Literature

Jupiter Hammon (1718?-1806?), the slave of Henry Lloyd of Queens Village, Long Island, published altogether some half dozen works, poems and essays. His poem "An Evening Thought: Salvation by Christ with Penetential Cries" was published as a broadside in 1760 and was the first known work to be published in America by a black. It begins:

Salvation comes by Christ alone,
The only Son of God;
Redemption now to every one,
That love his holy Word.
Dear Jesus we would fly to Thee,
And leave off every Sin,
Thy tender Mercy well agree;
Salvation from our King;
Salvation comes now from the Lord,
Our victorious King.
His holy Name be well ador'd,
Salvation surely bring.
Dear Jesus give thy Spirit now,
Thy Grace to every Nation,
That han't the Lord to whom we bow,

The Author of Salvation.
Dear Jesus unto Thee we cry,
Give us the Preparation;
Turn not away thy tender Eye;
We seek thy true Salvation.
Salvation comes from God we know,
The true and only One;
It's well agreed and certain true,
He gave his only Son.[14]

Hammon's poem has little to commend it as valuable literature. It is the conventional stuff of hymns, the principal source of his poetic instruction. Its alternating iambic tetrameter/iambic trimeter meter, its often forced a-b-a-b rhyme scheme, and its trite religious imagery combine to insure its sing-song mediocrity. In addition to the problem of such vague expressions as "preparation" and "tender eye," apparently used as a convenience to the rhyme scheme, such hackneyed abstractions as "Salvation," "Redemption," "Spirit," and "Grace" relegate the poem to the position of most Christian hymns still sung today (many of which, incidentally, are eighteenth-century in origin), that is, they must gain from "inspiration" what they lack in originality.

Less acceptable, by contemporary social standards, than Hammon's willingness to overlook the obvious evils of slavery in favor of seeking "true Salvation" were the poet's attempts to view the institution of slavery as the "glorious" means by which otherwise heathen Africans were brought into the Christian fold. Such is the subject of his second published poem (1778), which Hammon prefaced "An Address to Miss Phillis Wheatly [*sic*], Ethiopian Poetess, in Boston, who came from Africa at eight years of age, and soon became acquainted with the gospel of Jesus Christ." The poem, similar in type to "An Evening Thought," begins:

I

O come you pious youth! adore
   The wisdom of thy God,
In bringing thee from distant shore,
   To learn His holy word.

II

Thou mightst been left behind,
   Amidst a dark abode;
God's tender mercy still combin'd,
   Thou hast the holy word.

III

Fair wisdom's ways are paths of peace,
   And they that walk therein,
Shall reap the joys that never cease,
   And Christ shall be their King.

IV

God's tender mercy brought thee here;
   Tost o'er the raging main;
In Christian faith thou hast a share,
   Worth all the gold of Spain.[15]

It should be noted that Hammon was not oblivious to the inequities of slavery; but while in his last published work, an essay titled "An Address to Negroes in the State of New York" (1787), he is mildly reproving of the "peculiar institution," he hastens to add, "though for my own part I do not wish to be free."

Phillis Wheatley

For the most part sharing Hammon's attitudes toward slavery and religion, though a more talented poet than Hammon, was Phillis Wheatley (1754?-1784), the African-born servant of John Wheatley, a Boston tailor. Miss Wheatley, because of her

obvious intelligence, was given many of the same educational opportunities that Mr. Wheatley's daughters received and was thereby
well-versed in the Bible and in the English classics, especially Dryden and Pope. She was granted her freedom in 1772 and shortly
afterward married a ne'r-do-well, John Peters, by whom she had
three children, all of whom died in infancy, and by whom she was
deserted. After Peters' disappearance—with, it is thought, his wife's
unpublished manuscript of poems, still undiscovered—Miss
Wheatley worked in a decrepit Boston boardinghouse until her
death, at approximately age thirty, in 1784.

Altogether Miss Wheatley published nearly fifty poems:[16]
some half dozen political pieces, such as "To His Excellency
General Washington" and "Liberty and Peace"; nearly twenty
elegies; and the rest religious poems of various kinds. Her only
book-length collection, *Poems on Various Subjects, Religious and
Moral*, was published in London in 1773. Miss Wheatley was, in
the popular catch-all critical idiom, "imitative"; that is, she was
schooled in the poetic styles of Dryden and Pope, especially the
latter, and she used those styles herself. Her work clearly reflects
her schooling in the imagery and diction of the Bible. Her debt
to Pope is apparent in her first published poem, an elegy, "On
the Death of the Rev. Mr. George Whitefield, 1770," which reads:

Hail, happy saint, on thine immortal throne,
Possest of glory, life and bliss unknown;
We hear no more the music of thy tongue,
Thy wonted auditories cease to throng.
Thy sermons in unequall'd accents flow'd,
And ev'ry bosom with devotion glow'd;
Thou didst in strains of eloquence refin'd
Inflame the heart and captivate the mind.
Unhappy we the setting sun deplore,
So glorious once, but ah! it shines no more.

Behold the prophet in his tow'ring flight!
He leaves the earth for heav'n's unmeasur'd height,
And worlds unknown receive him from our sight.
There Whitefield wings with rapid course his way,
And sails to Zion through vast seas of day.
Thy pray'rs, great saint, and thine incessant cries
Have pierc'd the bosom of thy native skies.
Thou, moon, hast seen and all the stars of light,
How he has wrestled with his God by night.
He pray'd that grace in ev'ry heart might dwell,
He long'd to see America excel;
He charg'd its youth that ev'ry grace divine
Should with full lustre in their conduct shine;
That Saviour, which his soul did first receive,
The greatest gift that ev'n a God can give,
He freely offer'd to the num'rous throng,
That on his lips with list'ning pleasure hung.

"Take him, ye wretched, for your only good,
"Take him, ye starving sinners, for your food.
"Ye thrifty [sic]*, come to this life-giving stream,*
"Ye preachers, take him for your joyful theme;
"Take him, my dear Americans," he said,
"Be your complaints on his kind bosom laid;
"Take him, ye Africans, he longs for you,
"Impartial Saviour is his title due;
"Washed in the fountain of redeeming blood,
"You shall be sons and kings, and Priests to God."[17]

The formal style of her iambic pentameter couplets, like that of virtually all of Pope's imitators, falls short in what Pope called the "correctness" of diction and meter, that near-perfect choice of word and measurement and weighing of syllable. Her lines contain an occasional intrusive half-foot; her diction (her vocabulary, one must add without apology, was not Pope's) is sometimes "bent" to fit the couplet pattern; and her images, in a manner common to much eighteenth-century verse, are consistently vague. All in all, though, her poems are a clear cut above Jupiter Hammon's hymn-lyric verse and are, in fact, more important for their themes, what she felt about the people and the religious attitudes of her age, than for the style in which they are written.

One finds in her religious poems much the same Christian apology for slavery as found in Hammon's work, the same justification used by many whites attempting to blend into moral harmony the seemingly disharmonious institutions of enforced human servitude and the Christian ethic of universal brotherhood. In her most anthologized poem, "On Being Brought from Africa to America," Miss Wheatley produces the forced moral harmony which was used as the most widespread eighteenth-century argument in favor of slavery:

Twas mercy brought me from my Pagan land,
Taught my benighted soul to understand
That there's a God, that there's a Saviour too:
Once I redemption neither sought nor knew.
Some view our sable race with scornful eye;
"Their colour is a diabolic dye."
Remember, Christians, Negroes, black as Cain,
May be refined, and join the angelic train.[18]

Here Miss Wheatley apologizes for her heritage ("my *Pagan* land") and at the same time unwittingly confirms the view of "some" toward blackness ("diabolic dye") by pleading—in a manner reminiscent of that of William Blake in "The Little Black Boy" ("I am black, but O! my soul is white")—that *even* blacks "May be refined" through Christianity.

Gustavus Vassa: The Slave Narrative

The last author to be treated from this earliest period of black American writing is Gustavus Vassa (1745-1797?). Vassa's only known work, his autobiography, *The Interesting Narrative of the Life of Olaudah Equiano, or Gustavus Vassa, the African,*[19] was published in London in 1789 and soon became a best-selling favorite among American and English abolitionists. His work was not the first "slave narrative," the name given to a form of black writing which, for more than a century, was exceedingly popular in both America and England. The first such narrative was written by Briton Hammon in 1760 (not related to Jupiter Hammon, who published his first poem that same year) and was titled *A Narrative of the Uncommon Sufferings and Surprising Deliverance of Briton Hammon, a Negro Man*. The second was published in London in 1785 by John Marrant and was called *A Narrative of the Lord's Wonderful Dealings with J. Marrant, a Black*. Marrant's central theme, like those of Jupiter Hammon and Phillis Wheatley, is that man is sinful but is nonetheless the recipient of the ever-present mercy of God.

The most important slave narrative to come into print prior to the mid-nineteenth-century publication of the autobiographies of Frederick Douglass and William Wells Brown was clearly, how-ever, that of Gustavus Vassa. Vassa's vision of the world and of himself is substantially broader than the vision of either Briton Hammon or John Marrant. In his narrative he recounts his child-hood experiences, dress, customs and religion as the son of an African chieftain; his capture and transportation to America at about age ten; his experiences in bondage on the Virginia planta-tion of his first slavemaster; his sea voyages aboard the ship of his second master; and his life with the Quaker slaveholder, his third and last master from whom Vassa purchased his freedom in 1766. In addition, Vassa discusses his sea travels as a freeman, and, most important, his conversion to Christianity and effect upon his life. The best synopsis of Vassa's religious views is the twenty-eight-stanza poem, found in his narrative, titled "Miscellaneous Verses; or Reflections on the state of my mind during my first convictions, of the necessity of believing the Truth, and experiencing the inestimable benefits of Christianity." Vassa closes the poem:

Bless'd be thy name, for now I know
I and my works can nothing do;
"The Lord alone can ransom man—
For this the spotless Lamb was slain!"

When sacrifices, works, and pray're,
Prov'd vain, and ineffectual were—
"Lo, then I come!" the Saviour cried,
And bleeding, bow'd his head, and died!

He died for all who ever saw
No help in them, nor by the law:
I this have seen: and gladly own
"Salvation is by Christ alone!"[20]

While Vassa was considerably more firm in his assault upon the institution of slavery than most of his contemporaries, he was, in the final analysis, as conservative a Christian as Jupiter Hammon or Phillis Wheatley. Like them, he appears to have been oblivious to the intellectual ferment which was the hallmark of his age, the rationalist rebellion of "the Enlightenment." This attitude of Christian acceptance of one's social role would, before the middle of the nineteenth century, come under attack by more and more Americans as Christianity increasingly became a padded bludgeon used to keep dissatisfied blacks loyal to a system that even the Christian apologists found harder and harder to justify.

III.   1825-1890: Early
Themes of Protest

The first quarter of the nineteenth century produced a new climate of tension in American race relations which affected the course of black writing for the next hundred years. The "heathen-saving" argument for slavery which had been used by Christian apologists for a century and a half was, by the early 1800s, being spurned openly by many blacks and whites. It was giving way to the even more sinister notion that the inherent inferiority of those of the Negroid race justified their being used often as beasts by their Caucasian "superiors."

The Bible was gradually replaced as the "final authority" on the disposition of blacks by various forms of "science" which alleged to prove, based upon "studies" of such things as hair texture, skull formation, and length of limbs, that blacks were indeed an inferior species. With the Christian arguments fading from popularity, the conception of blacks as potential Christians—a conception which was largely responsible for what decent treatment blacks had experienced until that time—no longer was a viable deterrent to the new forms of brutality which soon were heaped upon blacks. Such brutality was especially evident in the Deep South, where Christianity for blacks, while not taken seriously by most whites, had been an instrument for demanding, from slaves especially, obedience to their white masters in order that they "please God."

The reaction to this increased cruelty was swift and predictable and ranged in forms from subtle insubordination to actual slave insurrections and threatened insurrections.[21] It came as well in the form of urban public outrage, expressed by frequent race riots, and through newly formed abolitionist societies, speeches, pamphlets, periodicals, and newspapers. Symbolic of the new black response to American race relations was the insurrection planned in 1800 by Gabriel Prosser, a slave in Henrico County, Virginia.[22]

Gabriel's plan, the first of such magnitude, was to march into Richmond with his army of some one thousand armed slaves and to kill all whites encountered, except Frenchmen, Methodists, and Quakers. The insurrection failed, however, because on the day it was to have occurred, a record-breaking rainstorm sent flood waters rampaging across the countryside, and the march, then impossible, was called off. In the meantime, Gabriel was betrayed by another slave, was captured, and, with approximately thirty others, was tried and hanged.

The widespread news of Gabriel's plan set off two forces which affected southern thinking until the Civil War. On one side was an intense uneasiness—growing to proportions of paranoia in many—among whites who grew more and more to feel, with considerable justification, that the slaves in whose midst they lived, and by whom, in many places, they were vastly outnumbered, would like nothing better than seeing them dead. On the other side were many blacks, and some whites, who took heart at the rumors that they heard about Gabriel and others like him and who concluded that, given the right circumstances, they might try the same. One such plan, Boxley's Conspiracy, was planned by George Boxley, a white, in 1816, for the purpose of freeing the slaves of Virginia by attacking Fredericksburg and Richmond. While Boxley's plan failed (it was betrayed by a slave woman), Boxley was never captured.

Then there was Vesey's Plot, elaborately planned by the free black Denmark Vesey in 1922 for the purpose of attacking Charleston, South Carolina. It, too, was betrayed by a slave, and Vesey and some thirty-five others were executed. The best-known revolt was Nat Turner's Rebellion[23] in Southampton County, Virginia, in 1831, which brought death to some sixty whites before Nat and his followers were tracked down, tried, and hanged. And, finally, the legendary John Brown Raid on the Federal Arsenal at Harpers Ferry, Virginia. Brown intended to supply arms to the slaves in hopes of generating a national slave uprising. The slaves, however, did not arrive to receive the arms; the arsenal was soon surrounded by troops; and Brown was captured, tried, convicted of treason, and hanged.

During these same years of the nineteenth century, other, less violent forces were taking up the abolitionist cause. In 1817 Charles Osborn began publication of the abolitionist newspaper *The Philanthropist* in Ohio, and two years later he founded *The Manumission Intelligencer* in Tennessee. In 1821 the Quaker Benjamin Lundy founded in Ohio what proved to be the most successful anti-slavery paper of the decade, *The Genius of Universal Emancipation*. In 1827 the first black newspaper, *Freedom's Journal*, began publication in New York City; and in 1831 the most famous of the abolitionist newspapers, William Lloyd Garrison's *The Liberator*, was founded in Boston. In addition, by 1830 more than fifty black antislavery societies had been formed in the United States.

Given this social intensity, it is not surprising that nearly every black writer who published between 1825 and 1890—including the three most notable poets of the period, George Moses Horton, James M. Whitfield, and Frances E. W. Harper—wrote in the spirit of protest.

George Moses Horton: Early Protest Poetry

George Moses Horton (1797-1883), whose collection of poetry *Hope of Liberty* (1829) is considered one of the first works devoted largely to themes of protest, was born a slave near Chapel Hill, North Carolina. He was later rented by his master, a planter named Horton, to the University of North Carolina to serve as a janitor. Always interested in poetry, Horton took advantage of the academic environment both to read the English classics and to compose his own poems. The claim that Horton was the first professional black author, that he was the first to earn a living from his writing, is only loosely true. While it is true that he received small sums from the students for composing "personal" pieces, especially love poems, and that he published a second volume, *Poetical Works of George M. Horton, the Colored Bard of North Carolina* (1845), he was nonetheless, through his hire, the property of the university until freed by Union soldiers in 1865, the same year that his last volume, *Naked Genius*, was published.

The protest found in Horton's first work, *Hope of Liberty* (later reprinted as *Poems by a Slave*) is somewhat milder than that found in the poet's later work and much milder than that found in the most bitter of the nineteenth-century protest poets, James M. Whitfield. The supplicating tone and vague images of oppression of Horton's early work diminish much of the strength of protest that the poet sought to convey.[24] Typical of this first volume is "The Slave's Complaint," which reads:

Am I sadly cast aside,
On misfortune's rugged tide?
Will the world my pains deride
                    Forever?

Must I dwell in Slavery's night,

And all pleasure take its flight,
Far beyond my feeble sight,
                    Forever?

Worst of all, must hope grow dim,
And withold her cheering beam?
Rather let me sleep and dream
                    Forever!

Something still my heart surveys,
Groping through this dreary maze;
Is it Hope?—then burn and blaze
                    Forever!

Leave me not a wretch confined,
Altogether lame and blind—
Unto gross despair consigned,
                    Forever![25]

Here the "complaint" becomes, for the most part, a poetic exercise: The images "rugged tide," "Slavery's night," "cheering beam,"
"dreary maze," and "gross despair" create so little sense impression
in the reader that slavery, the sinister institution that Horton is
condemning, appears little more than a somewhat unpleasant
condition.

Another of Horton's poems, "On Liberty and Slavery," while
composed of similarly vague images and a hymn meter like that
found in the poetry of Jupiter Hammon, reveals a tone which, in its
growing bitterness, is more reflective of the social (racial) climate
in which Horton wrote. The poem reads:

Alas! and am I born for this,
    To wear this slavish chain?

Deprived of all created bliss,
  Through hardship, toil and pain!

How long have I in bondage lain,
  And languished to be free!
Alas! and must I still complain—
  Deprived of liberty.

Oh, Heaven! and is there no relief
  This side the silent grave—
To soothe the pain—to quell the grief
  And anguish of a slave?

Come Liberty, thou cheerful sound,
  Roll through my ravished ears!
Come, let my grief in joys be drowned,
  And drive away my fears.

Say unto foul oppression, Cease:
  Ye tyrants rage no more,
And let the joyful trump of peace,
  Now bid the vassal soar.

Soar on the pinions of that dove
  Which long has cooed for thee,
And breathed her notes from Afric's grove,
  The sound of Liberty.

Oh Liberty! thou golden prize,
  So often sought by blood—
We crave thy sacred sun to rise,
  The gift of nature's God!

Bid Slavery hide her haggard face,

And barbarism fly:
I scorn to see the sad disgrace
  In which enslaved I lie.[26]

A few black poets avoided racial themes altogether—poets such as Daniel A. Payne (*Pleasures and Other Miscellaneous Poems*, 1850), and the New England writers Ann Plato (*Essays; Including Biographies and Miscellaneous Pieces, in Prose and Poetry*, 1841) and Henrietta C. Ray (*Poems*, 1887). Most, however, made those themes the reason for their writing as well as their speaking. Several of the most famous of the nineteenth-century poets delivered their usually didactic verse publicly before church congregations, abolitionist societies, and even saloon audiences. Among the best-known of these poet-orators were James M. Whitfield (*America and Other Poems*, 1853), Frances E. W. Harper (*Poems on Miscellaneous Subjects*, 1854), Elymas P. Rogers (*The Fugitive Slave Law*, 1855), James Madison Bell (*Triumph of Liberty*, 1870), and Albery A. Whitman (*Not a Man and Yet a Man*, 1877). Of these authors, the most deserving of study are Whitfield and Mrs. Harper.

James M. Whitfield

James M. Whitfield (1823-1878), born in Exeter, New Hampshire, was reared in Buffalo, New York, where he spent most of his life as a barber, a poet, and an organizer for a black American colonization program which never materialized. A man of great energy and great anger, Whitfield was convinced that the United States would never, in spite of major black contributions to American economic and cultural life, offer blacks respect or even humane treatment. He concluded, therefore, that the black American's only hope for economic and social betterment lay in migration from the United States. He proposed on his lecture tours that blacks colonize in what he and others (the novelist Martin Delany also held this

view for several years) felt to be the more receptive atmosphere of
Central America. It was, in fact, on a colonization venture to Central America that Whitfield died in 1878.

His poetry, especially that collected in his only published
volume, *America and Other Poems* (1853), represents the culmination of nineteenth-century black anger in verse. The title poem
begins:

America, it is to thee,
Thou boasted land of liberty,—
It is to thee I raise my song,
Thou land of blood, and crime, and wrong.
It is to thee, my native land,
From which has issued many a band
To tear the black man from his soil,
And force him here to delve and toil;
Chained on your blood-bemoistened sod,
Cringing beneath a tyrant's rod,
Stripped of those rights which Nature's God
Bequeathed to all the human race,
Bound to a petty tyrant's nod,
Because he wears a paler face.
Was it for this that freedom's fires
Were kindled by your patriot sires?
Was it for this they shed their blood,
On hill and plain, on field and flood?
Was it for this that wealth and life
Were staked upon that desperate strife,
Which drenched this land for seven long years
With blood of men, and women's tears?
When black and white fought side by side,
*   Upon the well-contested field,—*
Turned back the fierce opposing tide,
*   And made the proud invader yield—*

When, wounded, side by side they lay,
   And heard with joy the proud hurrah
From their victorious comrades say
   That they had waged successful war,
The thought ne'er entered in their brains
That they endured those toils and pains,
To forge fresh fetters, heavier chains
For their own children, in whose veins
Should flow that patriotic blood,
So freely shed on field and flood.
Oh, no; they fought, as they believed,
   For the inherent rights of man;
But mark, how they have been deceived
   By slavery's accursed plan.
They never thought, when thus they shed
   Their heart's best blood, in freedom's cause,
That their own sons would live in dread,
   Under unjust, oppressive laws:
That those who quietly enjoyed
   The rights for which they fought and fell,
Could be the framers of a code,
   That would disgrace the fiends of hell![27]

Whitfield's purpose, quite different from Horton's, is to register publicly his *rejection* of American society. The poet is not asking for humane treatment; he has already concluded that such a request is futile. His images more concrete than those of Hammon, Miss Wheatley, Vassa, and Horton, Whitfield juxtaposes the illusion ("Thou boasted land of liberty") with the reality, as viewed from the black perspective ("Thou land of blood, and crime, and wrong"). He thereby sets up the tension which gives the poem its momentum. This tension is climaxed by the irony that those Americans who "quietly enjoyed" those human rights gained through the sacrifices of the Revolutionary War should be the ones to refine the

plan of slavery that would persecute the descendants of those blacks
who had participated in the war which gave the nation its freedom.

Frances E. W. Harper

Certainly as vocal as Whitfield, though much less intense, was
Frances Ellen Watkins Harper (1825-1911), a poet, essayist, and
novelist whose protest themes were not limited to racial concerns.
Born free in Baltimore, Frances Watkins attended a school for free
blacks administered by her uncle, William Watkins. After a brief
experience as a "domestic," she moved to Ohio where she taught
school and became interested in a variety of reform movements,
chiefly those of abolition, women's rights, and temperance. (She
later lectured for the Women's Christian Temperance Union.) A few
of her didactic verses were published in newspapers during the
1850s, and her first collection, *Poems on Miscellaneous Subjects*,
was published in 1854.

Following the rapid succession of events in her life in the early
1860s—her marriage to Fenton Harper in Cincinnati in 1860, the
birth of their only child, a daughter, and her husband's sudden
death in 1864—Mrs. Harper devoted almost all of her energy to
the reformist causes that are reflected in her writing. She became a
very successful platform orator on the issues of abolition and temperance, and she lectured throughout the North and the South, in
spite of frequent threats to her safety. In addition, she wrote for
newspaper publication a torrent of letters, essays, and poems of the
kind which she often read while lecturing.

Mrs. Harper's literary efforts were aimed at the mass audience,
were—unlike those of Whitfield—highly melodramatic, and were,
by all accounts, very popular. Typical of her emotional style, which
in many ways resembles that of Harriet Beecher Stowe, is her most
widely known poem, "The Slave Auction":

The sale began—young girls were there,
    Defenceless in their wretchedness,
Whose stifled sobs of deep despair
    Revealed their anguish and distress.

And mothers stood with streaming eyes,
    And saw their dearest children sold;
Unheeded rose their bitter cries,
    While tyrants bartered them for gold.

And woman, with her love and truth—
    For these in sable forms may dwell—
Gaz' on the husband of her youth,
    With anguish none may paint or tell.

And men, whose sole crime was their hue,
    The impress of their Maker's hand,
And frail and shrinking children, too,
    Were gathered in that mournful band.

Ye who have laid your love to rest,
    And wept above their lifeless clay,
Know not the anguish of that breast,
    Whose lov'd are rudely torn away.

Ye may not know how desolate
    Are bosoms rudely forced to part,
And how a dull and heavy weight
    Will press the life-drops from the heart.[28]

In addition to her public efforts on behalf of abolition and temperance, Mrs. Harper exerted much energy in the cause of women's rights and was, in fact, one of the first American women to attack openly the already infamous "double standard" in sexual morality. Taking the role of the narrator in her poem "A Double Standard," Mrs. Harper concludes by indicting the injustice of a social structure which demands the destruction of the "fallen" woman while remaining oblivious to the male participation in the "fall":

Yes, blame me for my downward course,
  But oh! remember well,
Within your homes you press the hand
  That led me down to hell.

I'm glad God's ways are not our ways,
  He does not see as man;
Within His love I know there's room
  For those whom others ban.

I think before His great white throne,
  His throne of spotless light,
That whited sepulchres shall wear
  The hue of endless night.

That I who fell, and he who sinned,
  Shall reap as we have sown;
That each the burden of his loss
  Must bear and bear alone.

No golden weights can turn the scale
  Of justice in His sight;
And what is wrong in woman's life
  In man's cannot be right.[29]

Mrs. Harper's later work consisted of three volumes of verse, *Moses: A Story of the Nile* (1869); *Poems* (1871); and *Sketches of Southern Life* (1872), a series of accounts of Reconstruction life in the South. Her only novel—the first published by a black American woman—*Iola Leroy; or Shadows Uplifted* (1892), is the account of an exceptionally virtuous octoroon who refuses what would be very easy "passage" into white society and chooses instead to devote her energies to the "uplift" of the black race.

The Maturity of Black Autobiography

During the same period that George Horton, James Whitfield, and Mrs. Harper were publishing their early volumes of verse, black autobiography was reaching its maturity and black fiction was born. Nearly thirty autobiographies—or slave narratives, as most of them were—were published by black Americans during the nineteenth century prior to the Civil War.[30] Those few deserving mention are William Wells Brown's *Narrative* (1847), Josiah Henson's *The Life of Josiah Henson* (1849) (thought to have supplied many of the incidents used by Harriet Beecher Stowe three years later in *Uncle Tom's Cabin*), Henry Box Brown's *Narrative* (1849), Sojourner Truth's *Narrative* (1850), Solomon Northup's *Twelve Years a Slave* (1853), Samuel Ringgold Ward's *Autobiography of a Fugitive Slave* (1855), and William and Ellen Craft's *Running a Thousand Miles for Freedom* (1860). In a category by itself, however, is the autobiography of Frederick Douglass. It was originally published as a slave *Narrative* in 1845, was expanded as *My Bondage and My Freedom* in 1855, was expanded still further as *Life and Times of Frederick Douglass* in 1881, and was expanded and refined one last time in 1892, under the same title, into one of the most important historical and literary documents of its period in American letters.

Frederick Douglass

Frederick Douglass (1817-1895) was born in Talbot County, Maryland, the son of a white father and slave mother. He escaped from slavery in 1838 and later became an advisor to President Lincoln and served in the office of United States Marshal in the District of Columbia and as Recorder of Deeds in the District of Columbia. In 1889 he was appointed by President Harrison to serve as Minister Resident and Consul General to the Republic of Haiti. Douglass was married twice, first in 1838 to Anna Murray, a free black by whom he had five children, and again in 1882, after the death of his first wife, to Helen Pitts, a white some twenty years younger than himself.

More important than Douglass's political successes and family history, however, are the insights, found in the more than 600 pages of his autobiography, into the critical events occurring in nineteenth-century America during the seventy-eight years of his "life and times." His work, unlike most of the autobiographies of this period, transcends the experiences of the individual about whom it is written. While most of the slave narratives—extensions of the folktale tradition in that they reveal and repeat common cultural experiences—recount similar tales of the horrors of slavery, cruel overseers, repeated floggings, inhuman auction blocks, separation of black family members, and sexual abuse heaped upon black women by their white masters, *Life and Times* is a perceptively written view of an entire age in American history. Its opening paragraph promises the lively, colorful, and detailed cultural interpretation which is indeed forthcoming:

> *In Talbot County, Eastern Shore, State of Maryland, near Easton, the county town, there is a small district of country, thinly populated, and remarkable for nothing that I know of more than for the worn-out, sandy, desertlike appearance of its soil, the general*

dilapidation of its farms and fences, the indigent and spiritless character of its inhabitants, and the prevalence of ague and fever. It was in this dull, flat, and unthrifty district or neighborhood, bordered by the Choptank River, among the laziest and muddiest of streams, surrounded by a white population of the lowest order, indolent and drunken to a proverb, and among slaves who, in point of ignorance and indolence, were fully in accord with their surroundings, that I, without any fault of my own, was born, and spent the first years of my childhood.

From here Douglass discusses his childhood in Maryland, with his first awareness of slavery and of black squalor amid the white opulence represented by the "big house"; his learning to read and write and his early religious instruction; his plan for escape, his betrayal, capture, and imprisonment; and his successful escape from slavery in 1838. At this point the autobiography expands its scope as Douglass begins assessing the many ramifications of American political, economic, social, and religious institutions. He analyzes the entire abolition movement and those figures, like John Brown and Harriet Beecher Stowe, who were prominent in the movement. He notes, too, the evolution of his own thinking on the state of America, including his gradual decision that the American religious conscience would never bring an end to slavery:

From this night spent with John Brown in Springfield, Mass., 1847, while I continued to write and speak against slavery, I became all the same less hopeful of its peaceful abolition. My utterances became more and more tinged by the color of this man's strong impressions. Speaking at an antislavery convention in Salem, Ohio, I expressed this apprehension that slavery could only be destroyed by bloodshed, when I was suddenly and sharply interrupted by my good old friend Sojourner Truth with the question, "Frederick, is God dead?" "No," I answered, "and because God is not dead

*slavery can only end in blood." My quaint old sister was of the
Garrison school of non-resistants, and was shocked at my sanguin-
ary doctrine, but she too became an advocate of the sword, when
the war for the maintenance of the Union was declared.*

Douglass continues by analyzing the Southern Secession; the
events and implications of the Civil War; what Douglass viewed as
the turning point in the history of black Americans, the Emancipation Proclamation issued by President Lincoln in September, 1862;
Lincoln's death and its impact on the nation; his impressions of the
Presidents who followed Lincoln; and his interpretation of the legal
and illegal barriers blocking black progress, including the infamous
Supreme Court decision of 1883 which ruled the Civil Rights Law
of 1875 unconstitutional.

Far more than the story of one man's life, *Life and Times* is
the story of nineteenth-century America, told with warmth and
sometimes anger, with seriousness and sometimes humor. (When
asked, "How do you feel when you are hooted and jeered on the
street on account of your color?" Douglass replied, "I feel as if an
ass had kicked, but had hit nobody.") But, most important, it is a
story told with the perception of a man who knew his age well and
wished to capture its events, its difficulties, even its smells and
flavors, in the belief that all of these ingredients must be understood and sensed by those who would want to know what one of
the nation's most volatile periods was all about.

William Wells Brown: First Black Fiction and Drama

The birth of black fiction came in the 1850s with the publication of three novels, one by a runaway slave and two by free blacks.
The first novel was written in 1853 by William Wells Brown
(1816?-1884) and was titled *Clotel: or, The President's Daughter.*
Brown was born near Lexington, Kentucky, the son of a white

father and a mulatto slave mother who was rumored to be the daughter of Daniel Boone.[31] As a young man, Brown, who was known only as William until after his escape from slavery, moved with his master to Missouri where he was assigned the task of house servant and where he was later rented to the St. Louis publisher Elijah P. Lovejoy. In his autobiography, *The Narrative of William Wells Brown* (1847), Brown recounts his experiences before and after his escape from slavery. One of the most memorable and bitter is the escape attempt made by Brown and his mother while Brown was still a teenager:

> *As we travelled towards a land of liberty, my heart would at times leap for joy. At other times, being, as I was, almost constantly on my feet, I felt as though I could travel no further. But when I thought of slavery with its Democratic whips—its Republican chains—its evangelical blood-hounds, and its religious slave-holders—when I thought of all this paraphernalia of American Democracy and Religion behind me, and the prospect of liberty before me, I was encouraged to press forward, my heart was strengthened, and I forgot that I was tired or hungry.*

Brown's anger was intensified, after the escape failed, by his mother's being "sold South," that is, sold to a slavetrader taking slaves to the deep South where plantation conditions were consistently more harsh than those in the upper or border states.[32]

All of Brown's memories are not grim, however. Many of his experiences as an intimate in the Missouri household, for example, because of the slave's perception of the peculiarly hypocritical events which occurred there, are especially amusing. One such event involves the common practice of family devotions:

> *My master had family worship, night and morning. At night, the slaves were called in to attend; but in the mornings, they had to*

be at their work, and master did all the praying. My master and mistress were great lovers of mint julep, and every morning, a pitcherfull was made, of which they all partook freely, not except-ing little master William. After drinking freely all round, they would have family worship, and then breakfast. I cannot say but I loved the julep as well as any of them, and during prayer was always care-ful to seat myself close to the table where it stood, so as to help my-self when they were all busily engaged in their devotions. By the time prayer was over, I was about as happy as any of them.

Brown's successful escape came in 1834, while he was on a riverboat excursion with his master. At an Ohio wharf the slave simply walked off the boat and continued walking North. The run-away slave was aided during his escape by an Ohio Quaker named Wells Brown, whose name he adopted as his own. As William Wells Brown he reached Cleveland which, for a short time, he made his home.

While in Cleveland, Brown for the first time saw an abolition-ist newspaper, Benjamin Lundy's *Genius of Universal Emancipa-tion*, and, shortly afterward, took up the antislavery cause. He became, like many of the other black literary figures of the period, a traveling lecturer, and he soon joined the Massachusetts Anti-slavery Society, where he replaced Frederick Douglass, whose mili-tant attitude was costing him popularity among the moderates who dominated the society.

Brown lectured in England on behalf of the society for several years and was in London when he wrote and published *Clotel* in 1853. He later wrote three plays, the first written by a black American: *Miralda; or, The Beautiful Quadroon* (1855)[33]; *Experi-ence; or, How to Give a Northern Man a Backbone* (1856)[34]; and *The Escape; or, A Leap for Freedom* (1858). None of the plays is extant, nor, as far as can be learned, were any ever produced. Newspaper accounts of Brown's lecturing activities suggest that Brown read excerpts from the plays to his abolitionist audiences.

Clotel was published in three later versions: in 1860-61 as *Miralda; or, The Beautiful Quadroon*; in 1864 as *Clotelle; or A Tale of the Southern States*; and in 1867 as *Clotelle; or, The Colored Heroine*. The three later versions were published in the United States, and with each successive revision names and locations are changed and the tone becomes more moderate. The first and most important version, *Clotel*,[35] is based upon the legend of Thomas Jefferson's quadroon children and focuses upon the misfortunes of Currer, the alleged housekeeper-mistress of Jefferson, and her—and Jefferson's—two daughters, Clotel and Althesa, who are described early in the novel in a slave auction announcement: "mulatto girls of rare personal qualities: two of them very superior." Brown closes Chapter I, after Clotel has been sold for fifteen hundred dollars, by saying: "Thus closed a negro sale, at which two daughters of Thomas Jefferson, the writer of the Declaration of American Independence, and one of the presidents of the great republic, were disposed of to the highest bidder!"

From this point Clotel becomes the property and mistress of Horatio Green, a Virginia politican whose new wife cruelly mistreats Clotel's child and sells Clotel "South." Clotel escapes slavery, makes her way to the safety of Cincinnati, then returns to Virginia determined to free her daughter. Unfortunately Clotel chooses as a time to return to Virginia the same time that Nat Turner's Rebellion is being put down, and, along with many other innocent blacks, she is jailed in Richmond. From there she is taken to Washington, D.C., to a slave prison which, symbolically enough, "stands midway between the capitol at Washington and the president's house." After escaping from the prison she finds herself trapped on Washington's Long Bridge where she resigns herself to death before capture:

On came the profane and ribald crew, faster than ever, already
exulting in her capture, and threatening punishment for her flight.
For a moment she looked wildly and anxiously around to see if
there was no hope of escape. On either hand, far down below, rolled
the deep foamy waters of the Potomac, and before and behind the
rapidly approaching step and noisy voices of pursuers, showing
how vain would be any further effort for freedom. Her resolution
was taken. She clasped her hands convulsively, and raised them, as
she at the same time raised her eyes towards heaven, and begged for
that mercy and compassion there, which had been denied her on
earth; and then, with a single bound, she vaulted over the railings
of the bridge, and sunk for ever beneath the waves of the river!

Brown's novel is most of the things that it has been criticized
as being: melodramatic, digressive, propagandistic, "conventional."
For all of that, it is a warmly readable work, rich in details about
slave life and social and political hypocrisy, as well as rich in the
idiom of nineteenth-century prose style which modern readers,
with their constant diet of spare naturalistic prose, seldom experience. If it is melodramatic and propagandistic, it is so intended.
Brown was a man dedicated to the ideal of social justice, as were
such diverse authors as Dickens, Hardy, Sinclair, and Steinbeck.
His purpose, like theirs, was to shake into wakefulness a mass
human conscience which had slumbered far too long. Within those
somewhat limited bounds, the book is successful.

Frank J. Webb

The second novel written by a black American is *The Garies*
and Their Friends, published in London in 1857 by Frank J. Webb,
an important author about whom nothing appears to be known
beyond the exceptionally sketchy description provided by Harriet

Beecher Stowe in her preface to the novel. Says Mrs. Stowe, "The author is a coloured young man, born and reared in the city of Philadelphia."

A considerably more conscious artist than William Wells Brown, Webb gives careful attention throughout the novel to the use of excellent metaphoric detail. The first chapter begins:

> *It was at the close of an afternoon in May, that a party might have been seen gathered around a table covered with all those delicacies that, in the household of a rich Southern planter, are regarded as almost necessaries of life. In the centre stood a dish of ripe strawberries, their plump red sides peeping through the covering of white sugar that had been plentifully sprinkled over them. Geeche limes, almost drowned in their own rich syrup, temptingly displayed their bronze-coloured forms just above the rim of the glass that contained them. Opposite, and as if to divert the gaze from lingering too long over their luscious beauty, was a dish of peaches preserved in brandy, a never-failing article in a Southern matron's catalogues of sweets.*

From here Webb unfolds a moving story about two American families, the Garies (Mr. Garie, a wealthy white southerner, his mulatto wife, and their two children) and "their friends," the Ellises, black and wealthy northerners.

At the request of Mrs. Garie, whom he had purchased at a Savannah slave auction ten years earlier for two thousand dollars, Mr. Garie agrees to leave his native Georgia and to move to Philadelphia, where, Mrs. Garie has heard, the "coloured people" have a "pleasant social circle" which she would like to be a part of. In addition, there are the children to think about, their education, their social development. And so, the Garies move to the North, where, to their surprise, they face, in addition to a consistent pattern of racial hypocrisy to which they are unaccustomed, the open hostility of the immigrant classes, especially the Irish. (Webb is the first black author to explore northern ethnic prejudice directed at blacks.) Eventually the Garie home is attacked by a racist mob screaming, "Down with the Abolitionist—down with the Amalgamationist." Mr. Garie is murdered, and Mrs. Garie, hiding in the cold woodhouse with her children, dies during the night in premature childbirth.

There is something quite personal about Webb's narrative technique. By intruding in the plot, like Scott or Dickens ("And now, my reader, whilst they are finishing their meal, I will relate to you who Mr. Winston is, and how he came to be so familiarly seated at Mr. Garie's table"), Webb creates the illusion that a play is being performed and that he, cognizant of background details the audience cannot perceive upon first viewing, has graciously consented to serve as interpreter of this, his painfully illuminating drama.

Martin R. Delany

The third black American novel, *Blake; or The Huts of America*, is the only work of fiction produced by its author, Martin R. Delany (1812-1885). Delany was born in Charlestown, Virginia, of a slave father and free mother. Assuming by birth his mother's freedom, he, as a young man, moved with his mother to Pennsylvania, where he began his adult life as a barber in Pittsburgh. He later, in 1848 and 1849, served as editor to Frederick Douglass's abolitionist newspaper, *The North Star*. During his many-faceted career, he studied medicine at Harvard and became a physician; he became actively involved in abolitionist and black nationalist politics; he espoused, before Booker T. Washington, vocational education for blacks; he lived in Canada; he urged black American colonization in Central America and Africa; he was commissioned an officer in the Union Army during the Civil War; he was an agent for the Freedmen's Bureau and was active in South Carolina politics during Reconstruction; and, despite the often stormy life that he lived, he died quietly surrounded by his family in Ohio in 1885.[36]

Delany's important writing consists of two books. In addition to his novel *Blake*, he published in 1852 an ideological work, *The Condition, Elevation, Emigration, and Destiny of the Colored People of the United States, Politically Considered*, in which, like James Whitfield, he advocates Central American colonization for American blacks. The novel *Blake* had a rather unusual publication history: The first twenty-six chapters appeared serially in *The Anglo-African Magazine* between January and July, 1859. No additional installments were published until the entire novel was carried serially between November, 1861, and May, 1862, in *The Weekly Anglo-African*, in which William Wells Brown's *Miralda* had been published the year before.

Delany's novel, more militant than the novels of Brown or Webb, has as its protagonist Henry Blake (Henrico Blacus), the son of a wealthy West Indian manufacturer, who went to sea as a sailor and who was sold as a slave by his own captain upon reaching the shores of the United States. The novel, set mostly in Mississippi and in Cuba (the latter setting making it virtually unique in black fiction), begins in the United States with Blake's decision to cause a slave uprising of unheard of proportions throughout the entire South and Cuba. Amid scenes of flogging and torture of blacks, Blake moves clandestinely throughout the South, among the "huts [slave quarters] of America," preaching insurrection. He then carries his scheme to Cuba where plans for a general rebellion are carefully laid among the oppressed black population; and the novel, as it now exists, closes on the eve of the Cuban insurrection.

The novel, like Brown's, contains periodically inserted didac-

tic poems and songs which add little to the plot of the work. An
example is the parody of "America" sung by rebellious black
Cubans:

O Cuba! 'tis in thee
Dark land of slavery,
    In thee we groan!
Long have our chains been worn,
Long has our grief been borne,

Our flesh has long been torn,
    Even from our bones!
The white man rules the day,

He bears despotic sway,
    O'er all the land;
He wields the tyrant's rod,
Fearless of man or God,
And at his impious nod,
    We fall or stand!

      Another major weakness is Delany's dialogue. Blake's instruc-
tions to his slave subordinates much of the time have the polish of
the New England sitting room. For example: "I now impart to you
the secret, it is this: I have laid a scheme, and matured a plan for
a general insurrection of the slaves in every state, and the successful overthrow of slavery!" or "Keep this studiously in mind and
impress it as an important part of the scheme of organization, that
they must have money, if they want to get free." Even worse is the
speech of a young armless slave, presumably illiterate: "I am compelled to pick with my toes, a hundred pound of cotton a day."

      For all of its technical weaknesses, though, the novel reveals
an informed political consciousness. Delany obviously knew well

the economics of the slave trade, from the financial manipulations among African chieftains and the "practical" decisions that were made on the infamous "middle passage" to the official and unofficial political maneuvers in both the United States and Cuba which maintained the economic health of the "peculiar institution" against which the greatest part of black American writing during Delany's age was directed.

IV. 1890-1920: Developing Artistic Consciousness

By the last decade of the nineteenth century, the social and literary climate for black Americans had changed considerably. The period between 1890 and the start of the Harlem Renaissance of the 1920s was the first in which virtually all of the important black writers were free born. Also this period was the first to produce writers who, in spite of oppressive racial conditions, were able to maintain in their writing significant artistic detachment from those conditions. It was, in short, the beginning of serious artistic consciousness in black literature.

By 1890 race relations, especially in the South, were at an all-time low. The South had, twenty-five years earlier, experienced humiliating defeat in a war in which it had been billed internationally as a regional moral degenerate; and, of course, with its military defeat came the collapse of its social, political, and economic institutions. (W.E.B. DuBois estimated in 1909[37] that the southern loss in freed slave property alone amounted to approximately two billion dollars, and that the southern war debt added the loss of approximately another one and a half billion.) Further humiliation came when southern institutions were, during the decade of Reconstruction following the war, rebuilt according to often alien plans, largely by intruding northerners and recently freed, and often belligerent, blacks.

During Reconstruction southern tempers simmered, and slowly but decisively the white reaction began. At first it took the form of vigilante harassment directed mostly against blacks who were asserting their new rights. With the popularity of such reaction, the Ku Klux Klan began to flourish with its regular nightriding sprees of terror, mutilation, and destruction. And when Reconstruction ended in the late 1870s and the "intruders" returned North, the South began to legalize the heretofore illegal forms of racial harassment. In addition, the Klan and other such organizations continued to expand their activities as a supplement to the new "Black Codes," the "Jim Crow" laws which still denied blacks the right to vote and the right to receive decent education. Further, the United States Supreme Court ruled in 1883 that the Civil Rights Act of 1875 was unconstitutional; and the Supreme Court ruled in 1896 in *Plessy* v. *Ferguson* that "separate but equal" public accommodations were "reasonable" provisions for blacks. In short, the position of black Americans had, by the turn of the century, once more grown dismal indeed.

Interestingly, from within this crucible of social turmoil came four writers who, in transcending the immediate turmoil surrounding them, can be described as among the first black writers dedicated to the perfection of the literary art forms in which they wrote. Paul Dunbar was probably America's first accomplished black poet; Charles Chesnutt and James W. Johnson were the best writers of fiction their race had yet produced; and W.E.B. DuBois was one of the most gifted and perceptive essayists yet to appear of any color.

Paul Laurence Dunbar

Paul Laurence Dunbar (1872-1906), the son of two former slaves, was born and reared in Dayton, Ohio. After a successful public school education Dunbar, too poor for college and too black for most other jobs, worked as an elevator operator for several years and wrote poetry during his free hours. His first two volumes of verse, *Oak and Ivy* (1893) and *Majors and Minors* (1895), were read by William Dean Howells, who encouraged Dunbar to write dialect verse, and who sponsored some of the poet's subsequent volumes, thereby almost assuring his national reputation. In 1898 Dunbar married Alice Ruth Moore, also a writer, who published two collections of short stories, *Violet and Other Tales* (1895) and *The Goodness of St. Rocque and Other Stories* (1899), as well as a play in 1918, *Mine Eyes Have Seen* (under her new name, Alice Dunbar Nelson). Eight years later, after an unsuccessful marriage, Dunbar died of tuberculosis at the age of thirty-four.

At the suggestion of Howells, Dunbar willingly placed limits on the subject matter treated in his work. He seldom deals with themes of protest, and he rarely mentions racial injustice. (His novel, *The Sport of the Gods* (1902), and his short story, "The Lynching of Jube Benson," are exceptions.) Dunbar, like Chesnutt, realized, as probably Howells did not, that his new national reputation as a writer depended for its survival upon the approval of an overwhelmingly white audience of rising middle-class readers who were weary of discussions of racial injustice. (Had they not already "freed the blacks"?)

There was, in addition, something of a problem for both Dunbar and Chesnutt in the fact that the small but growing urban black middle class of professionals and white-collar workers no doubt took little comfort from the observation that the two finest authors of their race consistently used characters that they could seldom identify with. And it was true that Dunbar all but ignored the black middle class, choosing instead to use exclusively white protagonists in three of his four novels and, for the most part, "plantation" stereotypes in his three collections of short stories as well as in most of his poems (all of which were published in 1913 as *The Complete Poems of Paul Laurence Dunbar*). Much of Dunbar's strength as

an artist comes from his precise use of meter and, especially, of
dialect, the spelling of which renders with pinpoint accuracy the
slave vernacular, as well as from his capturing of the wit of the
expressions themselves. His precision is clearly seen in his poem
"Protest":

Who say my hea't ain't true to
       you?
   Dey bettah heish dey mouf.
I knows I loves you thoo an' thoo
   In watah time er drouf.

I wush dese people'd stop dey
       talkin'.
   Don't mean no mo' dan chicken's
       squawkin':
I guess I knows which way I's
       walkin',
   I knows de norf f'om souf.

I does not love Elizy Brown.
   I guess I knows my min'.
You allus try to tek me down
   Wid evaht'ing you fin'.
Ef dese hyeah folks will keep on
       fillin'
Yo' haid wid nonsense, an' you's
       willin'
I bet some day dey'll be a killin'
   Somewhaih along de line.

O' cose I buys de gal ice-cream,
   Whut else I gwine to do?

I knows jes' how de t'ing 'u'd
    seem
    Ef I'd be sho't wid you.
On Sunday, you's at chu'ch
    a-shoutin',
Den all de week you go 'roun'
    poutin'—
I's mighty tiahed o' all dis
    doubtin',
    I tell you cause I's true.[38]

Dunbar's "accommodationist" racial sentiments, found in both his fiction and his poetry, are plain in those numerous poems in which he appears to assume the role of the narrator, and, as such, delivers advice on how one should be patient with his misfortunes, how he should continue to dream of a better time, how he must, in short, persevere. The best example in all of Dunbar's work, and one which well expresses Dunbar's personal sentiments, is the much quoted "Keep A-Pluggin' Away," taken from the poet's Howells-sponsored third volume, *Lyrics of Lowly Life* (1895):

I've a humble little motto
That is homely, though it's
    true,—
    Keep a-pluggin' away.
It's a thing when I've an object
That I always try to do,—
    Keep a-pluggin' away.
When you've rising storms to
    quell,
When opposing waters swell,
It will never fail to tell,—
    Keep a-pluggin' away.

If the hills are high before
And the paths are hard to climb,
  Keep a-pluggin' away.
And remember that successes
Come to him who bides his
        time,—
  Keep a-pluggin' away.
From the greatest to the least,
None are from the rule released.
Be thou toiler, poet, priest,
  Keep a-pluggin' away.

Delve away beneath the surface,
There is treasure farther down,—
  Keep a-pluggin' away.
Let the rain come down in tor-
        rents,
Let the threat'ning heavens frown,
  Keep a-pluggin' away.
When the clouds have rolled
        away,
There will come a brighter day
All your labor to repay,—
  Keep a-pluggin' away.

There'll be lots of sneers to swal-
        low,
There'll be lots of pain to bear,—
  Keep a-pluggin' away.
If you've got your eye on heaven,
Some bright day you'll wake up
        there,—

> *Keep a-pluggin' away.*
> *Perseverance still is king;*
> *Time its sure reward will bring;*
> *Work and wait unwearying,—*
>   *Keep a-pluggin' away.*[39]

In this poem Dunbar unwittingly reinforces the prejudice-concealing notion of many whites around the turn of the century (and now), that social and economic opportunities are available to all who work hard, are thrifty, and "wait"—in short, the Horatio Alger thesis, the "bootstrap theory." This particular theme, incidentally, was picked up by several black novelists after the turn of the century. About three of these novelists—Oscar Micheaux (*The Conquest*, 1913), Henry F. Downing (*The American Cavalryman*, 1917), and Mary Etta Spencer (*The Resentment*, 1921)—Robert Bone, in his critical study, *The Negro Novel in America* (1965), says: "They 'play white' in their novels in much the same sense as children 'play house.' . . . Their antagonists are not prejudiced whites but rather those 'lazy' or 'indifferent' members of the race who, in their view, willfully refuse to succeed." Such a sweeping judgment, while no doubt currently popular, is particularly unfair to Micheaux, later the first black motion picture producer, who, in *The Conquest*, does indeed take some blacks to task:

Before I had any colored people to discourage me with their ignorance of business or what is required for success, I was stimulated to effort by the example of my white neighbors and friends who were doing what I admired, building an empire.

In fairness to Micheaux, however, it must be pointed out that *The Conquest* is more appropriately called an autobiography than a novel and that it reflects the author's actual experiences as a

successful South Dakota pioneer and the obstacles which he faced
—obstacles which, as he describes them, were erected, interestingly enough, more often by fellow blacks than by whites.

Charles Waddell Chesnutt

The second gifted writer of the period, Charles Waddell
Chesnutt (1858-1932), also avoided open conflict with the values
of his readers. Chesnutt was also born in Ohio, in Cleveland, though
early in his life he moved to North Carolina, his parents' former
home, and there he grew up. He published his first short story in a
local newspaper when he was fourteen. He studied the classics,
became a teacher when he was sixteen, and became principal
of the State Normal School at Fayetteville at age twenty-three.
A few years later he moved back to Cleveland, married, studied
law, and soon became a successful attorney.

In the mid-1880s Chesnutt took up writing. In 1887 he began
publishing his stories in the *Atlantic Monthly*, soon thereafter gaining, like Dunbar, a national reputation. His reputation did not
include, incidentally, a public knowledge of his racial identity,
which he kept secret, even from the editors at *Atlantic*, for almost
a decade. It is an interesting comment on the fickle American attitude toward race at the time to note that the eventual publication of
Chesnutt's identity as black brought restrictions upon the subjects
that he was able thenceforth to treat. On this point, critic Robert
M. Farnsworth, in his introduction to the 1969 reprint of Chesnutt's
first collection of stories, *The Conjure Woman*, says:

The Conjure Woman, *Charles Chesnutt's first book (1899),
illustrates the terms under which the white American reading
public at the end of the nineteenth century was willing to let
an Afro-American put his foot on the ladder of literary success.
The plantation story had emerged as a popular form in the late
Reconstruction period. In some hands it was used as Southern*

white propaganda to establish a nostalgically sentimental picture of slave-master relations prior to the Civil War. Typically, the master was paternalistically benevolent and the good slave was appreciatively humble and loyal. Implicitly, such stories attacked the social rationale behind the Reconstruction effort, but they were applauded and promoted not just by Southern whites but by Northern whites as well. The hunger for such fantasy indicates the retreat of the American white public from the demands the Reconstruction effort made after the exhausting and enervating Civil War.

Indeed, a reading of the stories of this dialect collection, such as "The Goophered Grapevine," "Po' Sandy," "Mars Jeems's Nightmare," and "Sis' Becky's Pickaninny," tends to confirm Farnsworth's observations. Especially pertinent is the account given by the white narrator of "The Goophered Grapevine" of his first meeting with "Uncle" Julius McAdoo, a head-shaking but sly former slave:

> *We alighted from the buggy, walked about the yard for a while, and then wandered off into the adjoining vineyard. Upon Annie's complaining of weariness I led the way back to the yard, where a pine log, lying under a spreading elm, afforded a shady though somewhat hard seat. One end of the log was already occupied by a venerable-looking colored man. He held on his knees a hat full of grapes, over which he was smacking his lips with great gusto, and a pile of grapeskins near him indicated that the performance was no new thing. We approached him at an angle from the rear, and were close to him before he perceived us. He respectfully rose as we drew near, and was moving away, when I begged him to keep his seat.*
> *"Don't let us disturb you," I said. "There is plenty of room for us all."*
> *He resumed his seat with somewhat of embarrassment.*

While he had been standing, I had observed that he was a tall man, and, though slightly bowed by the weight of years, apparently quite vigorous. He was not entirely black, and this fact, together with the quality of his hair, which was about six inches long and very bushy, except on the top of his head, where he was quite bald, suggested a slight strain of other than negro blood. There was a shrewdness in his eyes, too, which was not altogether African, and which, as we afterwards learned from experience, was indicative of a corresponding shrewdness in his character. He went on eating the grapes, but did not seem to enjoy himself quite so well as he had apparently done before he became aware of our presence.

"Do you live around here?" I asked, anxious to put him at his ease.

"Yas, suh. I lives des ober yander, behine de nex' san'-hill, on de Lumberton plank-road."

"Do you know anything about the time when this vineyard was cultivated?"

"Lawd bless you, suh, I knows all about it. Dey ain' na'er a man in dis settlement w'at won' tell you ole Julius McAdoo 'uz bawn en raise' on dis yer same plantation. Is you de Norv'n gemman w'at's gwine ter buy de ole vimya'd?"

Like Dunbar, Chesnutt displays an excellent grasp of dialect, but what makes his stories especially sound artistically is his ability to create something larger than the accumulated events of a narrative. The insights of his characters, black and white, lift the stories (and he is a much better short story writer than novelist) to a plane on which universal observations can be made and conclusions drawn. The wily Uncle Julius McAdoo, for example, who is found in all seven of the stories in *The Conjure Woman*, is not simply a recast of Old John, the slave who occasionally outwits his white antagonist. In fact, Uncle

Julius and the white narrator are not presented as antagonists but rather as complementing elements of the southern Reconstruction culture. Chesnutt creates the "artist's reality" which allows him to transcend the direct reflection of black-white cultural conditions that had, until this period, been the hallmark of black American authors.

In 1899 Chesnutt also published a biography of Frederick Douglass and his second and last collection of short stories, *The Wife of His Youth and Other Stories of the Color Line.* In two of the stories, "The Sheriff's Children" and "The Web of Circumstance," Chesnutt mildly takes to task southern mistreatment of blacks; but, for the most part, the stories deal with that newly formed northern urban minority of sophisticated middle-class blacks, called by DuBois the "talented tenth." Chesnutt explores the values, symbols, and prejudices of this caste of black Americans, a caste which was, in fiction and in fact, set completely apart from the larger body of black citizens, as the title story reveals. It opens:

Mr. Ryder was going to give a ball. There were several reasons why this was an opportune time for such an event.

Mr. Ryder might aptly be called the dean of the Blue Veins. The original Blue Veins were a little society of colored persons organized in a certain Northern city shortly after the war. Its purpose was to establish and maintain correct social standards among a people whose social condition presented almost unlimited room for improvement. By accident, combined perhaps with some natural affinity, the society consisted of individuals who were, generally speaking, more white than black. Some envious outsider made the suggestion that no one was eligible for membership who was not white enough to show blue veins. The suggestion was readily adopted by those who were not of the favored few, and since that time the society, though possessing a longer and more pretentious name, had been known far and wide as the "Blue Vein Society," and its members as the "Blue Veins."

The Blue Veins did not allow that any such requirement existed for admission to their circle, but, on the contrary, declared that character and culture were the only things considered; and that if most of their members were light-colored, it was because such persons, as a rule, had had better opportunities to qualify themselves for membership. Opinions differed, too, as to the usefulness of the society. There were those who had been known to assail it violently as a glaring example of the very prejudice from which the colored race had suffered most; and later, when such critics had succeeded in getting on the inside, they had been heard to maintain with zeal and earnestness that the society was a lifeboat, an anchor, a bulwark and a shield,—a pillar of cloud by day and of fire by night, to guide their people through the social wilderness. Another alleged prerequisite for Blue Vein membership was that of free birth; and while there was really no such requirement, it is doubtless true that very few of the members would have been unable to meet it if there had been. If there were one or two of the older members who had come up from the South and from slavery, their history presented enough romantic circumstances to rob their servile origin of its grosser aspects.

Much of this same rich prose is found in Chesnutt's lesser work, his three novels, *The House Behind the Cedars* (1900), *The Marrow of Tradition* (1901), and *The Colonel's Dream* (1905)—works which, for all of their nineteenth-century conventions, two-dimensional characters, coincidence in abundance, melodramatically mistreated heroines, and so on, nonetheless make for worthwhile reading. For some reason, still not fully understood, Chesnutt stopped writing in 1905. He turned again to his successful law practice in Cleveland until his death in 1932.

James Weldon Johnson

While other fiction deserving mention was published around the turn of the century—Sutton Griggs' *Imperium in Imperio* (1899), Pauline Hopkins' *Contending Forces* (1900), and G. Langhorne Pryor's *Neither Bond nor Free* (1902)—only one writer of fiction, James Weldon Johnson (1871-1938), was to approach the stature of Charles Chesnutt prior to the Harlem Renaissance of the 1920s. Johnson was born in Jacksonville, Florida, a city which he says in his autobiography, *Along This Way* (1933), was, during his childhood, "known far and wide as a good town for Negroes." At that time Jacksonville had many black policemen and firemen, several black city council members, and a few black judges. In short, Johnson did not experience the effects of discrimination until he was nearly grown. In fact, as an infant, he was nursed by a white neighbor while his mother recovered from an illness. He notes, however, in his autobiography that by 1933, when he returned to Jacksonville, the cultured white aristocracy was gone and "Jacksonville is today a one hundred per cent Cracker town."

As a boy, Johnson read Bunyan, Dickens, Scott, and the Brothers Grimm. He graduated from Atlanta University in 1894, studied law in Jacksonville, and went to New York in 1901 to take up music (he and his brother wrote "Lift Every Voice and Sing," considered by many the "Negro National Anthem"). He later became American consul first in Venezuela, then in Nicaragua, and was for many years Secretary of the NAACP.

It was while in Nicaragua that he wrote his most outstanding literary work, his only novel, *The Autobiography of an Ex-Colored Man* (1912), a work which deals openly with the theme of "passing." The protagonist finds himself torn between his obligation to the black race and his desire for success for himself and for his family. Even though he appears white and is, because of his New England upbringing, more familiar with white

American culture than with black, and even though he has hopes of a brilliant future in music as a "white" and significantly less hope as a black, is he nonetheless obligated to live black?

In *Autobiography* Johnson has taken the usually over-simplified "tragic mulatto" theme that had been present in black literature for almost a century and has added a depth of psychological complexity that had not existed before. The protagonist and narrator, whose identity dilemma is reinforced by his never revealing his name, is an outstanding musician who wishes to contribute to the progress of the black race by being the first internationally known black composer, but who is fearful of the personal cost. After much mental turmoil he "passes" permanently into white society, marries a white, and becomes a comfortable, successful businessman—but not without significant moral cost, as the final two paragraphs of the novel reveal:

> *Several years ago I attended a great meeting in the interest of Hampton Institute at Carnegie Hall. The Hampton students sang the old songs and awoke memories that left me sad. Among the speakers were R. C. Ogden, ex-Ambassador Choate, and Mark Twain; but the greatest interest of the audience was centered in Booker T. Washington, and not because he so much surpassed the others in eloquence, but because of what he represented with so much earnestness and faith. And it is this that all of that small but gallant band of coloured men who are publicly fighting the cause of their race have behind them. Even those who oppose them know that these men have the eternal principles of right on their side, and they will be victors even though they should go down in defeat. Beside them I feel small and selfish. I am an ordinarily successful white man who has made a little money. They are men who are making history and a race. I, too, might have taken part in a work so glorious.*

My love for my children makes me glad that I am what I am and keeps me from desiring to be otherwise; and yet, when I sometimes open a little box in which I still keep my fast yellowing manuscripts, the only tangible remnants of a vanished dream, a dead ambition, a sacrificed talent, I cannot repress the thought that, after all, I have chosen the lesser part, that I have sold my birthright for a mess of pottage.

Unfortunately, Johnson never wrote another novel. He turned mostly to poetry, and over the next two decades published three volumes of verse (none of it matching the quality of *Autobiography*), *Fifty Years and Other Poems* (1917), *God's Trombones: Seven Negro Sermons in Verse* (1927), and *St. Peter Relates an Incident* (1935). In addition, he wrote an excellent nonfiction study of black culture in New York, *Black Manhattan* (1930), as well as his autobiography, *Along This Way*, written largely to disclaim the widespread feeling that his novel was, in fact, his autobiography.

W. E. B. DuBois

The last major figure of the period is William Edward Burghardt DuBois (1868-1963), who was born in Great Barrington, Massachusetts. DuBois attained academic credentials as impressive as those of any modern American intellectual: B.A., Fisk; B.A., Harvard; M.A., Harvard; Ph.D., Harvard (the first black to achieve this distinction); and post-graduate study, University of Berlin. He became, during the century of his life, America's most knowledgeable scholar on race relations. He tirelessly researched the facets of black culture, interpreted and evaluated what he discovered, and tried to explain his findings to an unresponsive nation. DuBois taught sociology at Atlanta University, where he established one of the first black-studies programs and where he later founded the black culture periodical *Phylon*. He became a vocal opponent of Booker T. Washington's "accommodationist" racial policies[40] and wrote his finest book, *The Souls of Black Folk* (1903), partly at least, as an alternative to Washington's cautious approach to black betterment. In 1905 he formed the Niagara Movement for the improvement of the status of black intellectuals, and in 1909 he helped found the NAACP and became the first editor of the organization's publication, *Crisis*. In 1919 he convened the Pan-African Congress in Paris for the purpose of bringing together black leaders from Africa, the West Indies, and the United States to discuss their common problems.

By the 1930s DuBois was becoming embarrassingly militant, as viewed by the leadership of the mostly moderate American civil-rights organizations, and in 1934 he was asked to resign from NAACP. He then returned to the faculty of Atlanta University, but in 1944 he was asked to resign there also. By 1950, with his founding of the Peace Information Service, he began expanding his activities to an international scale, though he took a brief time out that year to run, unsuccessfully, for the United States Senate from New York on the American Labor Party ticket. By the mid-1950s DuBois had concluded that racial injustices could be adequately dealt with only through international socialist politics and not through the many often weak and patronizing national civil rights organizations. In 1957 he joined the Communist Party and shortly thereafter renounced his American citizenship; and in 1960 he moved to Ghana where, disillusioned, he died in 1963.

While DuBois wrote several pieces of mediocre fiction— the novels, *The Quest of the Silver Fleece* (1911) and *Dark Princess* (1928), and the trilogy, *The Black Flame* (1957, 1959,

1961)—it is clearly his nonfiction prose for which he must be remembered, chiefly his answer to Washington, *The Souls of Black Folk*, and his penetrating *Autobiography of W.E.B. DuBois* (1968). Washington's guiding principles as a black leader were to offer blacks an industrial education (supported mostly by whites) which would produce an "efficient, respectable" labor force of blacks. Washington did not address himself to the major concerns of DuBois and other activists, social and political rights, but instead felt that blacks should first develop economically and trust that this new economic strength would somehow lead to the rights that DuBois stressed. Implicit in this approach, to the dismay of the black intellectuals around the turn of the century, was the tacit willingness for blacks to have to "prove" their stability and responsibility to their white benefactors, in return for whatever social and political advantages which *might* follow.

Blacks like DuBois and Kelly Miller,[41] however, made three fundamental demands of American society—demands revealed in *The Souls of Black Folk:* the right to vote, the right to social equality, and the right to appropriate and quality education. Of DuBois' classic work, historian John Hope Franklin says, "It was several things at once: a deeply moving statement on the consciousness of color, a searching criticism of the philosophy of Washington, a quite scholarly examination of certain phases of the history of the Negro, and an evaluation of some of the mainsprings of the culture of the Negro American."[42] DuBois opens his work with an expression of his conviction that, not simply the problem of his book or the problem of his people, the issue of race is the problem of the very century itself:

> *Herein lie buried many things which if read with patience may show the strange meaning of being black here at the dawning of the Twentieth Century. This meaning is not without*

interest to you, Gentle Reader; for the problem of the Twentieth Century is the problem of the color line.

Setting out, then, with a singularly disciplined scholarly detachment, DuBois carefully moves through discussions of the cultural impact of recently acquired freedom; of the evolution of black leadership (for the most part, the wrong black leadership); and, most important, of the effects of being forced to live a culturally dual existence. Of the last he says:

After the Egyptian and Indian, the Greek and Roman, the Teuton and Mongolian, the Negro is a sort of seventh son, born with a veil, and gifted with second-sight in this American world,—a world which yields him no true self-consciousness, but only lets him see himself through the revelation of the other world. It is a peculiar sensation, this double-consciousness, this sense of always looking at one's self through the eyes of others, of measuring one's soul by the tape of a world that looks on in amused contempt and pity. One ever feels his twoness,— an American, a Negro; two souls, two thoughts, two unreconciled strivings; two warring ideals in one dark body, whose dogged strength alone keeps it from being torn asunder.

Though DuBois could not know it in 1903, the resolution of the problem of black "twoness" would, with the dawn of the Harlem Renaissance, become the most pressing literary theme during that brief period which saw the rise of a greater number of gifted black writers than any period of comparable length in the history of black American literature.

V. 1920-1940: The Harlem Renaissance and Its Influence

There has been some controversy about exactly when the cultural movement called the Harlem Renaissance (or, as it was also known, the Negro Renaissance) began. Some claim that the publication of Claude McKay's poem, "The Harlem Dancer" (1917), signaled the opening of this dynamic black-arts period. Some point to McKay's "If We Must Die" (1919). Others suggest a variety of other publications and other cultural events as responsible for starting it all. It seems rather safe to say, though, that the Harlem Renaissance opened in 1919. For the Renaissance, like the national climate of which it was a part, the "Jazz Age" or the "Roaring Twenties," appears to have depended for its initial momentum upon the social energy released at the close of the First World War.

This energy produced a tumultuous year which seethed with national frustration and bitterness caused by new awareness of how ugly and inglorious the war "to make the world safe for democracy" had, in fact, been. It was also the year of the May Day Riots in New York; and of more than twenty major race riots in such cities as Washington, Chicago, and New York, and in such unlikely places as Omaha; Millen, Georgia; and Knoxville, Tennessee.[43] It was the year in which more than one hundred black Americans were reported lynched and probably far more than that number not reported.

Much of the race tension in the United States around 1920 was caused by the great migration of blacks to the northern urban centers which had begun about 1890 and had reached near flood proportions by the end of the war. It has been estimated that between 1890 and 1920 the cities of New York, Washington, Boston, Philadelphia, Chicago, Detroit, and Los Angeles increased their black population by nearly two million inhabitants—at a time when the total American black population was only slightly more than ten million.

Part of the result of the mass movement was a reaction among northern urban whites who feared the economic consequences of the influx of such masses—and the growth in these areas of the Ku Klux Klan and other terrorist organizations to keep the blacks "in their place." On the positive side was the development, in nearly all of the northern cities, of black culture organizations like the Writers' Guild in New York, the Black Opals in Philadelphia, and the Saturday Evening Quill Club in Boston.[44] Harlem, however, as James Weldon Johnson points out in *Black Manhattan*, became the capital of black American culture during this period and served as the training ground for most of the major writers who began their work during the Twenties.

It should be noted that the enormous success of the Renaissance came both because there was great artistic energy expended by blacks and because there was a new interest in black life styles among the reading public of the generation of restless whites who helped to give birth to the Jazz Age, which Scott Fitzgerald called "the most expensive orgy in history."[45] The curiosity about black culture was generated partly, too, by white writers who treated black themes: the drama of Eugene O'Neill (*The Emperor Jones*, 1920, and *All God's Chillun Got Wings*, 1923) and Paul Green (*In Abraham's Bosom*, 1926), as well as the fiction of Sherwood Anderson (*Dark Laughter*, 1925), DuBose Heyward (*Porgy*, 1925, and *Mamba's Daughters*, 1929), and, especially important, Carl Van Vechten (*Nigger Heaven*, 1926).

Given these influences, then—a restless, cynically hedonistic national climate; newly formed urban black culture organizations; and writers, white and black, interpreting black America—it is little wonder that suddenly publishers were eager to receive manuscripts from black authors and to publish them. The market was demanding, and the black reading public, too, was interested in what writers had to say about the way that they lived and the things that they enjoyed and the things that made them sad and angry.

Alain L. Locke: Explanation of the "New Negro"

While the first half of the decade saw, in the work of Claude McKay and Jean Toomer, some of the finest writing yet offered by black authors, it was not until 1925 that an attempt was made to intellectualize what was happening to black America. In that year a philosophy professor at Howard University, Alain LeRoy Locke (1886-1954) published *The New Negro*, an anthology of black essays, fiction, poetry, and drama, now considered a classic work.

Locke, born in Philadelphia, attained academic credentials comparable to those of DuBois, including a B.A. from Harvard, a B. Litt. from Oxford (as a Rhodes scholar), graduate study in philosophy at the University of Berlin, and a Ph.D. from Harvard in 1918. Shortly after this, he became chief spokesman and interpreter for the Renaissance. During his forty-year career in the Philosophy Department at Howard, Locke wrote and edited dozens of reviews, articles, and books on black art, literature, music, and cultural movements generally. Chief among them, in addition to his most important *The New Negro*, are *Four Negro Poets* (1927), *The Negro in America* (1933), *The Negro and His Music* (1936), and *The Negro in Art* (1941).

One of the most important documents of the Renaissance is Locke's essay, "The New Negro," which serves as the introduction to his anthology of the same title. In the essay he explains, with more perception than anyone before him, what had happened in the black American's relationship with himself and with American culture. The essay begins:

In the last decade something beyond the watch and guard of statistics has happened in the life of the American Negro and the three norns who have traditionally presided over the Negro problem have a changeling in their laps. The Sociologist, the Philanthropist, the Race-leader are not unaware of the New Negro, but they are at a loss to account for him. He simply cannot be swathed in their formulae. For the younger generation is vibrant with a new psychology. . . .

Could such a metamorphosis have taken place as suddenly as it has appeared to? The answer is no; not because the New Negro is not here, but because the Old Negro had long become more of a myth than a man. The Old Negro, we must remember, was a creature of moral debate and historical controversy. His has been a stock figure perpetuated as an historical fiction partly in innocent sentimentalism, partly in deliberate reactionism. The Negro himself has contributed his share to this through a sort of protective social mimicry forced upon him by the adverse circumstances of dependence. So for generations in the mind of America, the Negro has been more of a formula than a human being—a something to be argued about, condemned or defended, to be "kept down," or "in his place," or "helped up,"

to be worried with or worried over, harassed or patronized, a
social bogey or a social burden. . . .

But while the minds of most of us, black and white, have
thus burrowed in the trenches of the Civil War and Reconstruction,
the actual march of development has simply flanked these posi-
tions, necessitating a sudden reorientation of view. . . .

With this renewed self-respect and self-dependence, the life
of the Negro community is bound to enter a new dynamic phase,
the buoyancy from within compensating for whatever pressure
there may be of conditions from without. The migrant masses,
shifting from countryside to city, hurdle several generations of
experience at a leap, but more important, the same thing
happens spiritually in the life-attitudes and self-expression of the
Young Negro, in his poetry, his art, his education and his new
outlook, with the additional advantage, of course, of the poise
and greater certainty of knowing what it is all about. From this
comes the promise and warrant of a new leadership.

And there was new leadership. The "plantation" stereotypes
were irrevocably dead in black writing, as was the often melodramatic protest of the nineteenth century. Black American
literature had reached its maturity. There was pride in black
artistry as in blackness itself—for the first time on a broad
scale. With this pride and craftsmanship came an honest treatment
and open acknowledgement of blackness, a free expression of
black urban life, its "natural" music, dance, sex, even violence.
Unlike the next major period of "black pride," the 1960s, the
era of the Renaissance produced few stereotypes, or counter-
stereotypes (the black supermen who would appear four decades
later). Instead its major authors (and, as in the case of white
authors of the same period, there were many of them), Claude
McKay, Jean Toomer, Countee Cullen, Langston Hughes, Nella
Larsen, George Schuyler, Arna Bontemps, and Zora Neale Hurston,
were, to a writer, dedicated to the kind of artistic control and

emotional detachment which is critical to the production of enduring literature.

Claude McKay

The first important writer of the Renaissance was Claude McKay (1889-1948), who was born in Jamaica, where he began writing poems as a boy, and who came to the United States to attend college in 1912. That same year he published his first two small collections of poetry, *Constab Ballads* and *Songs of Jamaica*. After brief study at Tuskegee Institute and Kansas State College, McKay moved to New York where he continued writing poetry and where, in 1921, he became associate editor of Max Eastman's socialist periodical, *The Liberator*. Eastman later said of McKay: "His eyebrows arched high up and never came down, and his finely modelled features wore in consequence a fixed expression of ironical and rather mischievous scepticism. Claude *was* ironical and mischievous too, and acutely intelligent both about people and politics."[46]

McKay traveled to England, back to the United States, then to Russia in 1923, where at first he supported the Bolshevik cause. He later learned that the "special treatment" that he received as a "black and oppressed" American in Russia (the luxury hotel suites and the parades in his honor) was manufactured for propaganda purposes. Disillusioned with the Russian "liberators," McKay traveled to Spain, then to France, where he wrote *Home to Harlem* (1928), the best-seller for which he was chiefly known during his lifetime.

The protagonist of *Home to Harlem* is Jake, who is a black army deserter "stoking" his way "home to Harlem" when the novel opens. ("Roll on, Mister Ship, and stinks all the way as you rolls. Jest take me 'long to Harlem is all I pray. I'm crazy to see again the brown-skin chippies 'long Lenox Avenue.")

Jake meets Felice and pays her fifty dollars to sleep with him. Then, after she secretly returns the money and leaves before he wakes, he begins a search for her that carries him through the rest of the novel. His search brings him into contact with all of the elements of Harlem night life, cabarets, whorehouses, gambling dens (much to the dismay of DuBois and other intellectuals who chastised McKay for making public the "wrong image" of black life). Jake locates Felice, as the novel closes, and, lighthearted once more, they prepare to leave together for Chicago.

While McKay's contemporary popularity was based largely upon the success of *Home to Harlem*, his lasting reputation as a writer should not be; for, in both poetry and fiction, he produced better work. The memories of Jamaica and of Harlem provide the subjects for most of McKay's poems. Sometimes called "Jamaica's Robert Burns," McKay, even long after his departure from his homeland, was able to gain a peace of mind through his memories of "home." One of his most effective pastorals, in which he carefully contrasts the soft, gentle images of Jamaica with the "long years of pain" in the United States, is "I Shall Return":

I shall return again. I shall return
To laugh and love and watch with wonder-eyes
At golden noon the forest fires burn,
Wafting their blue-black smoke to sapphire skies.
I shall return to loiter by the streams
That bathe the brown blades of the bending grasses,
And realize once more my thousand dreams
Of waters rushing down the mountain passes.
I shall return to hear the fiddle and fife
Of village dances, dear delicious tunes
That stir the hidden depths of native life,

Stray melodies of dim-remembered runes.
I shall return. I shall return again
To ease my mind of long, long years of pain.[47]

Continuing the theme of the last line of the poem are most of McKay's Harlem poems, which express moods varying from contemplative melancholy to unconcealed anger. Among his most effective poems, and probably his best-remembered, is "Harlem Shadows":

I hear the halting footsteps of a lass
    In Negro Harlem when the night lets fall
Its veil. I see the shapes of girls who pass
    To bend and barter at desire's call.
Ah, little dark girls who in slippered feet
Go prowling through the night from street to street!

Through the long night until the silver break
    Of day the little gray feet know no rest;
Through the lone night until the last snow-flake
    Has dropped from heaven upon the earth's white breast,
The dusky, half-clad girls of tired feet
Are trudging, thinly shod, from street to street.

Ah, stern harsh world, that in the wretched way
    Of poverty, dishonor and disgrace,
Has pushed the timid little feet of clay,
    The sacred brown feet of my fallen race!
Ah, heart of me, the weary, weary feet
In Harlem wandering from street to street.[48]

A deep sense of sadness accompanies the progress of the "little dark girls," and the black race generally, from their attitude of reluctance to approach the inevitable ("*halting* footsteps"), through their attitudes first of determination ("*prowling* through the night") then of fatigue ("*trudging*, thinly shod, from street to street"), to their attitude of resignation and defeat ("*wandering* from street to street") [this author's italics].

McKay published other collections of poetry, *Spring in New Hampshire* (1920) and *Harlem Shadows* (1922); other novels, *Banjo* (1929) and *Banana Bottom* (1933); a collection of short stories, *Gingertown* (1932); and an autobiography, *A Long Way from Home* (1937).

It was his last book of verse, *Harlem Shadows*, and his last novel, *Banana Bottom*, for which McKay should be best remembered. Set in Jamaica, *Banana Bottom* expresses the theme—in contrast with that of Thomas Wolfe—"You *must* go home again." The subject of McKay's cultural conflict is the young black Jamaican girl, Bita Plant, who, when twelve years old, was raped by the village eccentric, Crazy Bow Adair, and who, after the incident, was taken in by a white missionary couple named Craig and later sent to Europe to school. The novel opens with the return of Bita to Jamaica as (or so the Craigs view her) "the transplanted African peasant girl that they had transformed from a brown wildling into a decorous cultivated young lady." The tension in the novel is generated by the conflict between the Craigs' restricted sense of social conduct, which they feel it their right to urge upon Bita, and Bita's devotion to complete participation in the life of her homeland, with its young peoples' parties, its adolescent flirting, its dancing.

The tension mounts when the Craigs impress upon Bita her obligation, to them and to herself, to marry Herald Newton, the young, hopelessly self-righteous missionary of whom they strongly approve. But, much to the distress of the Craigs, and, indeed, most of the community, except Bita, shortly before the marriage is to occur, Herald Newton is found—or so the rumor goes—defiling himself with a goat. At this point Bita, no longer under the influence of the embarrassed Craigs, turns her affection to the farmer Jubban, whom, shortly afterward, she marries. Bita, more at home in the village of Banana Bottom than in either the parsonage of the Craigs or the private schools of Europe, finds in her relationship with Jubban a peace that she could not know in any other way—a peace which her creator, McKay, who died destitute and bitter, would never know:

> *Thinking of Jubban and how her admiration for him had slowly developed into respect and love, Bita marvelled at the fact that they had never said "I love you" to each other. The thing had become a fact without the declaration.*
>
> *They lived their life upon a level entirely different from her early romantic conception of love. Once she had thought of love as a kind of mystical force, incomprehensible and uncontrollable. But gradually she had lost all that feeling of the quality of love, for it was a borrowed thing, an exotic imposition, not a real intrinsic thing that had flowered out of the mind of her race.*
>
> *She had no craving for Jubban to be other than what he was, experienced no hankering for that grace and refinement in him that the local soothsayers said was necessary to an educated person. She liked to play for him for he had a natural feeling for music and showed appreciation of even the most difficult things. But he was in no way a hindrance to the intellectual side of her life. He accepted with natural grace the fact that she should excel in the things to which she had been educated as he should in the work to which he had been trained.*

Jean Toomer

The second important writer of the Renaissance (in fact, the most gifted author of the period and one of the most gifted in modern American letters) was Jean Toomer (1894-1967). Toomer was born in Washington, D.C., the grandson of the influential P.B.S. Pinchback, former Lieutenant Governor of Louisiana. After attending the University of Wisconsin and City College of New York, he published a few poems in newspapers, traveled about the United States, and in 1921 visited Georgia, the home of his ancestors, about which he said:

A visit to Georgia last fall was the starting point of almost every-thing of worth that I have done. I heard folk-songs come from the lips of Negro peasants. I saw the rich dusk beauty that I had heard many false accents about, and of which till then, I was somewhat skeptical. And a deep part of my nature, a part that I had repressed, sprang suddenly to life and responded to them. Now, I cannot conceive of myself as aloof and separated. My point of view has not changed; it has deepened, it has widened.[49]

Toomer's response to his Georgia experience was the writing of his masterful work, *Cane* (1923), a highly experimental and successful collection of prose sketches and poems woven together thematically into contrasting portraits of rural black peasant life and northern black urban life. While Robert Bone includes *Cane* in his *Negro Novel in America*, the work is much more nearly poetry than fiction, even its ostensibly prose sketches. One of the best examples of the poetic rhythm and imagery found throughout *Cane* is the opening of what is probably the most beautiful of the sketches, "Fern":

Face flowed into her eyes. Flowed in soft cream foam and plaintive ripples, in such a way that wherever your glance may momentarily have rested, it immediately thereafter wavered in the direction of her eyes. The soft suggestion of down slightly darkened, like the shadow of a bird's wing might, the creamy

*brown color of her upper lip. Why, after noticing it, you sought
her eyes, I cannot tell you. Her nose was aquiline, Semitic. If
you have heard a Jewish cantor sing, if he has touched you and
made your own sorrow seem trivial when compared with his,
you will know my feeling when I follow the curves of her
profile, like mobile rivers, to their common delta. They were
strange eyes. In this, that they sought nothing—that is, nothing
that was obvious and tangible and that one could see, and they
gave the impression that nothing was to be denied. When a
woman seeks, you will have observed, her eyes deny. Fern's
eyes desired nothing that you could give her; there was no
reason why they should withhold. Men saw her eyes and fooled
themselves. Fern's eyes said to them that she was easy. When
she was young, a few men took her, but got no joy from it. And
then, once done, they felt bound to her (quite unlike their hit
and run with other girls), felt as though it would take them a
lifetime to fulfill an obligation which they could find no name
for. They became attached to her, and hungered after finding
the barest trace of what she might desire. As she grew up, new
men who came to town felt as almost everyone did who ever
saw her: that they would not be denied. Men were everlastingly
bringing her their bodies. Something inside of her got tired of
them, I guess, for I am certain that for the life of her she could
not tell why or how she began to turn them off. A man in fever
is no trifling thing to send away. They began to leave her,
baffled and ashamed, yet vowing to themselves that some day
they would do some fine thing for her.*

There is something indefinably spiritual about *Cane*; there
is human anguish in the work, but it is not brutal; and there
is unnecessary death, but it does not seem so bad somehow.
Most important, there is a lyrical quality in some of the sketches
of Part I of *Cane* which is unsurpassed in American writing

of the twentieth century. And now that *Cane* has been discovered and returned to print once more, no bibliography of American literary masterpieces can be complete without it.

Contrary to a notion held by many for several decades, Jean Toomer did not simply flash onto the literary stage with *Cane*, then voluntarily retire to some mysterious spiritual retreat. Nor did he simply "pass" into white society and disappear, as some have claimed. After the publication of *Cane*, Toomer spent several months at the Gurdjieff Institute in France studying with the Russian mystic Georges Ivanovitch Gurdjieff. During the next ten years he married twice, and in 1934 he joined a Quaker community in Pennsylvania. The idea that Toomer wrote very little after *Cane* is erroneous. Hundreds of pages of Toomer's unpublished manuscripts are available for study in the Fisk University Library. Included are five plays, many essays, and an enormously meandering autobiography, in which Toomer appears endlessly to pursue that spiritual peace which he revealed so poetically in *Cane*, but which appears to have eluded him personally throughout his life.

Countee Cullen

The last two major poets of the Harlem Renaissance were Countee Cullen and Langston Hughes. Cullen (1903-1946) was born in New York City. After spending the first twelve years of his life with his grandmother, he was adopted by the Reverend Frederick Cullen, minister of the Salem African Methodist Church of Harlem. No doubt the influence of the Rev. Mr. Cullen, his religious conservatism coupled with a fierce social and political activism, produced in his stepson the conflicting sentiments about religion and race that dominate his work.

Cullen published his first poem, "Shroud of Color," in 1924 while a student at New York University, from which he graduated Phi Beta Kappa the next year. This first poem, in effect, asks the question which, in one way or another, appears repeatedly in Cullen's work: Where is the evidence that there is a God who displays concern for blacks? Cullen's distress about this matter is found in one of the most famous poems of his first collection, *Color* (1925), titled "Yet Do I Marvel":

I doubt not God is good, well-meaning, kind,
And did He stoop to quibble could tell why
The little buried mole continues blind,
Why flesh that mirrors Him must someday die,
Make plain the reason tortured Tantalus
Is baited by the fickle fruit, declare
If merely brute caprice dooms Sisyphus
To struggle up a never-ending stair.
Inscrutable His ways are, and immune
To catechism by a mind too strewn
With petty cares to slightly understand
What awful brain compels His awful hand.
Yet do I marvel at this curious thing:
To make a poet black, and bid him sing![50]

Having, in the first line, acknowledged tongue-in-cheek that God is "good, well-meaning, kind," Cullen then moves with gentle effectiveness through a series of examples of mythic anguish which quietly contradict the original assertion, until he arrives at the climax of his poem. Here he reaches the, again understated, "curious thing" (meaning, of course, the incredible thing), that there is a divine force which consciously imposes the limitations of blackness, and which expects, nonetheless, the black individual, the poet, to "sing."

Cullen seemed unable to resolve the problems of Christianity (as it relates to blackness) and blackness (as it relates to art). While there is consistent religious skepticism, there is not a definitive rejection of Christianity.

In Cullen's only novel, *One Way to Heaven* (1932), for example, the protagonist, though an unbelieving professional "convert," nonetheless, through his final faked act of faith, strengthens the genuine faith of his wife. And while there are Cullen's frequent proclamations that the black poet's only obligation is to his craft, he, at times, laments as loudly as other Renaissance poets about racial injustice, and he became active enough politically to join the Foster and Ford Committee of noted American authors who supported the Communist Party ticket in the election of 1932. Cullen's best-remembered answer to those of his generation who claimed that, as a poet, he had an obligation to serve as race spokesman, however, is the poem "To Certain Critics," which was collected in his fourth volume, *The Black Christ and Other Poems* (1929):

Then call me traitor if you must,
Shout treason and default!
Say I betray a sacred trust
Aching beyond this vault.
I'll bear your censure as your praise,
For never shall the clan
Confine my singing to its ways
Beyond the ways of man.

No racial option narrows grief,
Pain is no patriot,
And sorrow plaits her dismal leaf
For all as lief as not.
With blind sheep groping every hill,

Searching an oriflamme,
How shall the shepherd heart then thrill
To only the darker lamb?[51]

The firmness of this position was eroded, however, by
Cullen's general inconsistency on issues of race and art; and,
though Cullen published two more volumes of verse during his
lifetime, *The Medea and Other Poems* (1935) and *The Lost
Zoo* (1940), he withdrew from active engagement in literary
debates and became, during his last years, a high school French
teacher. A posthumous volume of Cullen's best poems, *On These
I Stand*—selected by the poet himself before his death—was
published in 1947. This is the collection to be studied for an
understanding of Cullen's range of subjects and careful poetic
craftsmanship.

Langston Hughes

A fellow Renaissance poet and fellow member of the Foster
and Ford Committee was Langston Hughes (1902-1967). Hughes,
rightfully called the "dean of black American letters," was born
in Joplin, Missouri, and reared in Lawrence and Topeka, Kansas.
He attended Columbia University for one year, went to sea
and worked in Paris for some two years, worked in New York
and Washington, D.C. for a short time, and returned to college
at Lincoln University in Pennsylvania, where he graduated in
1929. His early poems were published in *Crisis* and reflected
the intense black pride which was the hallmark of the time.
One of his earliest poems, and still one of his most memorable,
is "The Negro Speaks of Rivers" (1921), a free-verse expression
of the length and depth of black heritage:

I've known rivers:

I've known rivers ancient as the world and older than the flow of
human blood in human veins.

My soul has grown deep like the rivers.

I bathed in the Euphrates when dawns were young.
I built my hut near the Congo and it lulled me to sleep.
I looked upon the Nile and raised the pyramids above it.
I heard the singing of the Mississippi when Abe Lincoln went
down to New Orleans, and I've seen its muddy bosom turn
all golden in the sunset.

I've known rivers:
    Ancient, dusky rivers.

My soul has grown deep like the rivers.[52]

During the Twenties Hughes published two volumes of
poetry, *The Weary Blues* (1926) and *Fine Clothes to the Jew*
(1927). In 1930 he published his first novel, *Not Without
Laughter*, for which he received the Harmon Award for Literature.
It is a mediocre, partly autobiographical work about a young
boy's early years in a segregated Kansas town. While Hughes
wrote one more novel, a better one, called *Tambourines to
Glory* (1958) (about two Harlem women who parlay a street-
corner revival gimmick into a fortune), his reputation will rest
upon his poetry, his five volumes of "Simple" sketches, and
his Broadway play, *Mulatto* (1935).

Of more than a dozen books of poetry that Hughes published, the two most worthwhile are *Selected Poems* (1965),
the collection of his most successful work, and *Montage of a
Dream Deferred* (1951), in which he asks the question that
he had been moving toward for two decades—a question that

Lorraine Hansberry would borrow for her Broadway hit of 1959:

What happens to a dream deferred?
Does it dry up
Like a raisin in the sun?
Or fester like a sore—
And then run?
Does it stink like rotten meat?
Or crust and sugar over—
Like a syrupy sweet?

Maybe it just sags
Like a heavy load.

Or does it explode?[53]

In addition to his two autobiographies, *The Big Sea* (1940) and *I Wonder As I Wander* (1956); his history of the NAACP, *Fight for Freedom* (1962); his edited collections of African writing, black American folklore, black poetry, black short stories, and "Negro humor," Hughes wrote some ten plays. His best play is *Mulatto*, which has been translated into five languages,[54] and which ran longer on Broadway (373 consecutive performances) than any play written by a black American until Lorraine Hansberry's *A Raisin in the Sun* (1959).

Mulatto was hailed as a major contribution to the canon of black letters, for black drama had been very slow maturing. Virtually the only plays written by a black author in the nineteenth century were William Wells Brown's three propaganda pieces, *Miralda* (1855), *Experience* (1856), and *The Escape* (1858), all designed for abolitionist platform reading. It was not until the climactic years of the Harlem Renaissance that two full-length black plays reached Broadway.[55] Garland Anderson's *Appearances* (1925), certainly not of the same strong and worthwhile stuff of *Mulatto*, features a black protagonist whose naive faith in the "American dream" and the inevitable victory of "right" is put to the test when he is charged with raping a white woman. Anderson, while determined that his protagonist, Carl, should have his faith confirmed, apparently was not as sure that his Broadway audience would share his view. Consequently, as the play draws to a close, its author pulls his final punches by granting Carl his exoneration not because he is, in fact, innocent of the alleged crime, but because the "victim" of the rape is proven a disreputable woman—and, far worse, a woman with black ancestry.

The second full-length black play to reach Broadway was *Harlem* (1929), by William J. Rapp and Wallace Thurman—author of the novels, *The Blacker the Berry* (1929) and *Infants of the Spring* (1932). The play, more characteristic of the thinking of the Renaissance than Anderson's melodrama, is set in Harlem with all of the accoutrements of Harlem in the late Twenties—rent parties, numbers running, black gangsters, and white gangsters. *Harlem* openly explores the experiences of the new black urban life and is a significant contribution to the period which it reflects quite well.

Hughes' very successful Broadway production of *Mulatto*[56] in 1935 marks the first major artistic accomplishment by a black playwright. The two-act play is set on a Georgia plantation in the early Thirties and features a somewhat stereotyped land owner, Colonel Norwood, his black housekeeper-mistress, Cora, and their eighteen-year-old mulatto son, Robert, who has been "ruined" by the five years of private education that Colonel Norwood has condescended to allow him. The conflict comes because of the incompatibility of the plantation owner's nineteenth-century vision of race and his son's obviously "new Negro" perception of his relationship to the Colonel. The Colonel's pronouncements are, for the most part, stock: "Cora, if you want that hardheaded yellow son of yours to get along around here, he'd better listen to me"; and "There's no nigger-child of mine, yours, ours—no darkie—going to disobey me." Robert's lines, however, are not stock, certainly not for white-upper-middle-class Broadway of 1935. Note the climactic scene which brings about the Colonel's death:

Robert   (Still standing) *What do you mean, "talk right?"*
Norwood   *I mean talk like a nigger should to a white man.*
Robert   *Oh! But I'm not a nigger, Colonel Tom, I'm your son.*
Norwood   (Testily) *You're Cora's boy.*
Robert   *Women don't have children by themselves.*
Norwood   *Nigger women don't know the fathers. You're a bastard.*
            (*Robert* clenches his fist. *Norwood* turns toward the
            drawer where the pistol is, takes it out, and lays it
            on the table. The wind blows the lace curtains at the
            windows, and sweeps the shadows of falling leaves
            across the paths of sunlight on the floor.)
Robert   *I've heard that before. I've heard it from Negroes,
            and I've heard it from white folks. Now I hear it
            from you.* (Slowly) *You're talking about my mother.*
Norwood   *I'm talking about Cora, yes. Her children are bastards.*

. . . .

Robert   *. . . But my mother sleeps with you.*
Norwood   *You don't like it?*
Robert   *No, I don't like it.*
Norwood   *What can you do about it?*

Robert   (After a pause) *I'd like to kill all the white men in the world.*

Norwood   (Starting) *Niggers like you are hung to trees.*

Robert   *I'm not a nigger.*

Norwood   *You don't like your own race? (Robert is silent.) Yet you don't like white folks either?*

Robert   (Defiantly) *You think I ought to?*

Norwood   *You evidently don't like me.*

Robert   (Boyishly) *I used to like you, when I first knew you were my father, when I was a little kid, before that time you beat me under the feet of your horses.* (Slowly) *I liked you until then.*

Norwood   (A little pleased) *So you did, heh?* (Fingering his pistol) *A pickaninny calling me "papa." I should've broken your young neck for that first time. I should've broken your head for you today, too—since I didn't then.*

A few moments later the Colonel leaps in front of Robert in an effort to prevent his son's leaving the house through the "front door"; the men struggle, and Robert strangles the Colonel to death. The expected sequence of events follows: Robert runs off to the swamp to hide; a mob forms for pursuit; Cora confronts the Colonel's corpse ("Damn you, Colonel Norwood! Damn you, Thomas Norwood! God damn you!"); and Robert, cut off in his escape, returns to the house, where, in the room of his mother and the Colonel, he shoots himself shortly before the return of the lynch mob.

Much of the strength of Hughes' play comes from the sensitivity that one can feel in the relationships of the characters. The thirty years that the Colonel and Cora have spent as mistress and lover have been, for the most part, years of affection. And the relationship between the Colonel and Robert is as stormy as it is precisely because, as the Colonel himself recognizes, Robert is temperamentally exactly like his father—a fact which, while at moments producing a subtle pride of fatherhood, the Colonel is culturally too old to accept. But Hughes has made his point: "There is a new world a'comin'," because there are individuals like Robert, like Hughes himself, willing to make the sacrifices necessary to see that it arrives in time.

The last four writers of note from the Twenties, the decade of the Renaissance, and the Thirties, the decade during which the influence of the Renaissance continued to be felt, were Nella Larsen, George Schuyler, Arna Bontemps, and Zora Neale Hurston.

Nella Larsen

Nella Larsen (1893-1963) was born in Chicago; later attended Fisk University and the University of Copenhagen (her mother was Danish); then became, in turn, a nurse, a librarian, a writer, and once again a nurse, in Brooklyn, where she died. She was married to, and divorced from, Dr. Elmer Imes, a physicist. As a writer, she published two novels, *Quicksand* (1928) and *Passing* (1929), and she was the recipient of a Harmon Foundation award and a Guggenheim Fellowship. Her better novel, *Quicksand*, treats very indirectly the familiar subject of the mulatto in American society. The protagonist, Helga Crane, twenty-three years old, restless, dissatisfied with the worship of the mediocre which has surrounded her most of her life, has, in fact, already concluded in her quiet way that the world and the people who inhabit it are wanting. In the richly metaphoric and detailed style for which Miss Larsen is known, the novel opens:

> *Helga Crane sat alone in her room, which at that hour, eight in the evening, was in soft gloom. Only a single reading*

lamp, dimmed by a great black and red shade, made a pool of light on the blue Chinese carpet, on the bright covers of the books which she had taken down from their long shelves, on the white pages of the opened one selected, on the shining brass bowl crowded with many-colored nasturtiums beside her on the low table, and on the oriental silk which covered the stool at her slim feet. It was a comfortable room, furnished with rare and intensely personal taste, flooded with Southern sun in the day, but shadowy just then with the drawn curtains and single shaded light. Large, too. So large that the spot where Helga sat was a small oasis in a desert of darkness. And eerily quiet. But that was what she liked after her taxing day's work, after the hard classes, in which she gave willingly and unsparingly of herself with no apparent return. She loved this tranquillity, this quiet, following the fret and strain of the long hours spent among fellow members of a carelessly unkind and gossiping faculty, following the strenuous rigidity of conduct required in this huge educational community of which she was an insignificant part. This was her rest, this intentional isolation for a short while in the evening, this little time in her own attractive room with her own books. To the rapping of other teachers, bearing fresh scandals, or seeking information, or other more concrete favors, or merely talk, at that hour Helga Crane never opened her door.

Helga abandons Naxos, the black southern school where she is teaching, and, as the novel progresses, moves into and away from a series of situations and roles, each of which she soon finds unsatisfying, and each of which, unknown to her, is drawing her closer to the inescapable "quicksand" of the title. First, she serves as secretary and traveling companion to a lecturer on racial injustice, Mrs. Hayes-Rore, "a plump lemon-colored woman with badly straightened hair and dirty finger-nails," the wealthy widow of a once highly prominent black South Side Chicago politician. Next she works at a New York insurance company while living with Mrs. Hayes-Rore's niece, Anne Grey, and exploring with glee the experiences offered by New York—until, as at Naxos, the sights begin to grow monotonous and her acquaintances stale.

Helga then spends several years in Copenhagen with her aunt (her mother was Danish, her father black American) where, unlike her experience in the United States, her dark skin attracts compliments and young men as well. Having grown weary of the life of continuous parties and sitting room chatter arranged by her aunt and having refused the proposal of one of Denmark's most promising young artists, she returns to New York. There, on a cold, rainy night, she takes temporary refuge from the storm in a storefront church, where she meets the Reverend Mr. Pleasant Green, a visiting black Alabama preacher, and where she is "converted."

This is the point at which the otherwise fine novel weakens. Helga, cultured, middle-class, has done or said nothing throughout the course of the novel which prepares the reader for her "conversion," much less for her subsequent marriage to the uncouth Mr. Green or for her willingness to travel to his southern backwoods parish as the preacher's wife. Miss Larsen has, it is true, pictured Helga as growing increasingly desperate in her attempt to find a satisfying social niche; but the transition from the settings of Chicago, Copenhagen, and New York to that of Mr. Green's "vineyard of the Lord" in rural Alabama is simply not workable.

Once this awkward transition is complete, however, the intensity of the novel, as reflected in Helga's determined efforts to be happy, resumes. Now at the edge of the "quicksand," Helga tries to endure conversations with Sary Jones and Clementine Richards (who had herself expected to capture the Reverend Mr. Green) and tries to endure her four children, by the last of whom she was nearly maimed at childbirth. Even more difficult, she must try to endure her husband, whose "We must accept what God sends" has long since worn thin. She begins to think of escape, of abandoning everything connected with Mr. Green, the children, Alabama:

> *It was so easy and so pleasant to think about freedom and cities, about clothes and books, about the sweet mingled smell of Houbigant and cigarettes in softly lighted rooms filled with inconsequential chatter and laughter and sophisticated tuneless music. It was so hard to think out a feasible way of retrieving all these agreeable, desired things. Just then. Later. When she got up. By and by. She must rest. Get strong. Sleep. Then, afterwards, she could work out some arrangement. So she dozed and dreamed in snatches of sleeping and waking, letting time run on. Away.*

But Helga's dream is not to be fulfilled. She is mired down too far. And, in spite of Helga's hopes and the reader's hopes for her, Miss Larsen, in a conclusion of powerful understatement, closes her novel with Helga, just recovered from childbirth, sinking slowly from sight:

> *And hardly had she left her bed and become able to walk again without pain, hardly had the children returned from the homes of the neighbors, when she began to have her fifth child.*

Nella Larsen's novel is not in the mainstream of Renaissance writing. In avoiding the exotic, or "primitive," quality of black life which was exalted by most black artists of the Twenties, she joins the ranks of such early middle-class authors as Charles W. Chesnutt (*The Wife of His Youth*, 1899); such contemporaries as Jessie R. Fauset (*There Is Confusion*, 1924, and *Plum Bun*, 1928); and such later writers as Dorothy West (*The Living*

Is Easy, 1948). Chronologically, though, her two novels were published in the closing months of the dynamic period of the Renaissance.

End of the Harlem Renaissance

But the end was in sight, and within a few months after the Crash of 1929, it was over. In a tone reminiscent of that of Scott Fitzgerald's essay "Echoes of the Jazz Age," Langston Hughes said of the spring of 1930, "That spring for me (and, I guess, all of us) was the end of the Harlem Renaissance. We were no longer in vogue, anyway, we Negroes. Sophisticated New Yorkers turned to Noel Coward. Colored actors began to go hungry, publishers politely rejected new manuscripts, and patrons found other uses for their money. . . . The generous 1920's were over."[57]

The running pace of black writing slowed during the Thirties. Writers were not so prolific, publishers were not so eager, and the reading public was not so demanding; but, nonetheless, the serious artists continued, and a few new ones began. James Weldon Johnson and Countee Cullen each published one book of poems, and Langston Hughes published four. And two new black poets came onto the scene: Sterling A. Brown with *Southern Road* (1932), and Frank Marshall Davis with *Black Man's Verse* (1935) and *I Am the American Negro* (1937). More important, however, was the output of fiction by new writers.

George S. Schuyler

One of the most important of these writers was George Samuel Schuyler (b. 1895), born in Providence, Rhode Island, and reared in Syracuse, New York. After serving eight years in the Army, Schuyler joined the staff of the Pittsburgh *Courier*, where, for several decades, he wrote articles—many of them satiric in the vein of Mencken, a significant influence on Schuyler's work—on such contemporary topics as black art, interracial marriage, prohibition, and the social status of women.

In 1931, Schuyler published the first successful satire yet written by a black American, a novel, *Black No More*, which directs its attack toward black social codes as well as white in its reflection of the author's own attitude toward race and toward the Harlem Renaissance which had drawn to a close shortly before the publication of this, his first novel. Schuyler could be considered an anti-Renaissance writer. He wrote, during the Twenties, numerous articles in which he consistently denied that such a phenomenon as the Renaissance existed at all except as the product of the imagination of a handful of black artists trying to publicize themselves. His most famous attack came in his essay, "The Negro-Art Hokum," published in *The Nation* in 1926, in which he asserts:

Negro art "made in America" is as non-existent as the widely advertised profundity of Cal Coolidge, the "seven years of progress" of Mayor Hylan, or the reported sophistication of New Yorkers. Negro art there has been, is, and will be among the numerous black nations of Africa; but to suggest the possibility of any such development among the ten million colored people in this republic is self-evident foolishness. . . .

As for the literature, painting, and sculpture of Aframericans —such as there is—it is identical in kind with the literature, painting, and sculpture of white Americans: that is, it shows more or less evidence of European influence. . . .

. . . Aside from his color, which ranges from very dark brown to pink, your American Negro is just plain American. Negroes and whites from the same localities in this country talk, think, and act about the same. Because a few writers with a paucity

*of themes have seized upon imbecilities of the Negro rustics
and clowns and palmed them off as authentic and characteristic
Aframerican behavior, the common notion that the black American
is so "different" from his white neighbor has gained wide currency.*

Of course, Schuyler's blind spot about the clearly existing
cultural differences between white American culture and its
black counterpart, differences which were in hundreds of ways
a matter of record, and which served as subjects for most of
the Renaissance authors, was shared by other middle-class blacks.
Indeed, Nella Larsen rather gently hints at much the same idea
when she uses the "rustic" setting of Alabama as the "quicksand"
in which her heroine is sinking to oblivion—a setting very
similar to that in Georgia in which Jean Toomer's characters
in the opening sketches of *Cane* find an enduring spiritual peace.

Schuyler's novel *Black No More* is the story of the impact
on American society of an electronic treatment which converts
blacks into whites. The black doctor who discovers the treatment
establishes a chain of "Black-No-More" clinics throughout the
United States, and there ensues one of the most bizzare social-
political-economic upheavals which one can imagine. Dr. Junius
Crookman, aided in promoting his enterprise by a former numbers
racketeer, Hank Johnson, makes his "Black-No-More" treatment
a national institution, and, in the process, turns the entire
country into an asylum of paranoiacs.

As the black population begins rapidly to disappear, the
slums suddenly cease to be profitable business investments;
enforcement of the Black Codes becomes unnecessary; poor white
southerners suddenly realize that they represent the lowest rung
on the socio-economic ladder; and, most amusing of all, confirmed racists go mad trying to determine who among them are,
in fact, former blacks. As the months and years pass and the
black population becomes almost extinct, ostensibly white couples

begin, with greater and greater frequency, to have black babies—who can, of course, themselves be transformed into white, though the period of time immediately following the births proves to be rather embarrassing for many new parents.

The climax of Schuyler's satire comes when Dr. Crookman publishes the findings of his study of the comparison of the original Caucasians and the converted Caucasians, with the startling revelation that it is still possible to distinguish the difference, that those who were formerly black are now slightly whiter than the original whites. The result is amusingly predictable:

To a society that had been taught to venerate whiteness for over three hundred years, this announcement was rather staggering. What was the world coming to, if the blacks were whiter than the whites? Many people in the upper class began to look askance at their very pale complexions. If it were true that extreme whiteness was evidence of the possession of Negro blood, of having once been a member of a pariah class, then surely it were well not to be so white! . . .

. . . A Dr. Cutten Prodd wrote a book proving that all enduring gifts to society came from those races whose skin color was not exceedingly pale, pointing out that the Norwegians and other Nordic peoples had been in savagery when Egypt and Crete were at the height of their development. Prof. Handen Moutthe, the eminent anthropologist (who was well known for his popular work on The Sex Life of Left-Handed Morons among the Ainus) *announced that as a result of his long research among the palest citizens, he was convinced they were mentally inferior and that their children should be segregated from the others in school. Professor Moutthe's findings were considered authoritative because he had spent three entire weeks of hard work assembling his data. Four state legislatures immediately began to consider bills calling for separate schools for pale children.*

Those of the upper class began to look around for ways to get darker. It became the fashion for them to spend hours at the seashore basking naked in the sunshine and then to dash back, heavily bronzed, to their homes, and, preening themselves in their dusky skins, lord it over their paler, and thus less fortunate, associates. Beauty shops began to sell face powders named Poudre Negre, Poudre le Egyptienne *and* L'Afrique.

And so, with the return of color discrimination, so vital to America's well-being, the novel closes with the nation's mental equilibrium restored once more.

Unlike George Schuyler, both Arna Bontemps and Zora Neale Hurston were products of and contributors to the Harlem Renaissance. Both were college students coming to maturity during the Twenties; both were publishing their early work in periodicals during the last half of the decade; and both continued to reflect the Renaissance spirit in the work that they published during the Thirties.

Arna Bontemps

Arna Bontemps (b. 1902) was born (the same year as Langston Hughes) in Alexandria, Louisiana, and was reared in California, where he attended the public schools. He graduated from Pacific Union College in 1923, the year that Toomer's *Cane* was published, and set out shortly afterward for Harlem, where he remained throughout the Renaissance. His early poems appeared in *Crisis* and *Opportunity* (several of them winning literary awards), and with the coming of the Thirties he earned an M.A. in library science at the University of Chicago. After teaching in New York City for several years, Bontemps, in 1943, became librarian at Fisk University, a position that he held until 1966. He then joined the staff of the Chicago Circle Campus of the University of Illinois for three years, and he is currently on the library staff at Yale.

Bontemps has published one volume of poetry, *Personals* (1963), but his prose works and his edited collections are more highly respected by most critics. He has written three novels, *God Sends Sunday* (1931), clearly in the Renaissance mold of fast living, fighting, gambling, and drinking; *Black Thunder* (1936), based on the slave insurrection of Gabriel Prosser in 1800; and *Drums at Dusk* (1939), another slave-rebellion work, this time set in Haiti. In addition, Bontemps has written such non-fiction prose works as *One Hundred Years of Negro Freedom* (1961) and *Anyplace But Here* (1966); and he has edited such volumes as *Golden Slippers* (1941), a children's collection, *American Negro Poetry* (1963), and—with Langston Hughes—*The Poetry of the Negro* (1949; rev. 1970) and *The Book of Negro Folklore* (1958).

Bontemps' finest novel, *Black Thunder*, opens with a statement, detached and journalistic, yet descriptive of a seething social unrest:

> *Virginia Court records for September 15, 1800, mention a certain Mr. Moseley Sheppard who came quietly to the witness stand in Richmond and produced testimony that caused half the States to shudder. The disclosures, disturbing as they were, preceded rumors that would positively let no Virginian sleep. A troop of United States cavalry was urgently dispatched, and Governor James Monroe, himself an old soldier, paced the halls of Ash Lawn with quaking knees and appointed for his estate three special aides-de-camp.*

What Mr. Sheppard quietly reveals is that two weeks earlier, on the night of August 30, 1800, more than one thousand armed slaves had joined together outside Richmond, Virginia, for the

purpose of entering the city, capturing the arsenals, and putting
to death every white encountered except Frenchmen, Methodists,
and Quakers.

Bontemps then moves back in time to establish the conditions
that spawned the plans for the revolt, which was not carried out
because flood waters from a recent torrential rainstorm blocked
the path of the rebels as they made their way from the countryside
toward Richmond and because many of the slaves, who had
never seen a storm of such proportions, viewed it as an evil
omen and lost much of their enthusiasm for the confrontation
which lay ahead. The slave conditions described by Bontemps
are well known to those familiar with nineteenth-century American
history or with the slave narratives of that period: wanton
beating and killing of slaves; sexual abuse of black women, and
sometimes black men; general social emasculation of slave men;
and so on.

What gives Bontemps' novel its exceptional strength is the
author's sound understanding of the black mentality of the period,
his avoidance of black stereotypes (though some white stereotypes, especially plantation masters and overseers, are present),
and his careful use of the history surrounding the insurrection
itself. The characterization is very good: Gabriel and his "woman,"
Juba, "with the slim hips and the savage mop of hair," are
carefully drawn, not as superhuman individuals bent on turning the events of history, but as believably *human* beings convinced that, as human beings, they deserve more from life
than has been forthcoming, or than *will be* forthcoming unless
they undertake to change the events· of their lives themselves.
And so, they try, and they fail; yet even in failing they cast a
cloud of fear across the white South that has still not altogether
lifted. Gabriel and Juba would not know, however, the extent
of their influence. As the novel closes, Juba is sold at auction,
looking "downcast, bitter, almost threatening," and Gabriel, just

before his execution, reflects stoically upon what was, unknown to him, one of the most historic ventures of his century:

Well, suh, I done sung my song, I reckon. It wasn't much, though. Nothing like Toussaint. The rain was against us. That Pharoah and his mouth wa'n't no mo'n I looked for. Something told me we was done when we turned back the first time. It was a bad night for such doings as we was counting on.

Zora Neale Hurston

The last major figure of the period was Zora Neale Hurston (1901-1960), who was born in the first all-black independent community in the United States, Eatonville, Florida, to a father who was a farmer and part-time preacher and a mother who died while Miss Hurston was still a child. After her mother's death, Miss Hurston was sent to live with relatives, first with one family then with another. The result, as noted in her auto-biography, *Dust Tracks on a Road* (1942), was a chaotic childhood, from which, at about age fourteen, she escaped. She worked her way through public school in Baltimore, attended Howard University for two years, then enrolled at Barnard College, where, under the influence of the anthropologist Franz Boas,[58] she began the study of black folklore. After her graduation from Barnard in 1928, Miss Hurston, with the aid of several grants, began graduate study in anthropology at Columbia University. Her study took her on folklore-hunting expeditions through most of the Deep South states as well as to the West Indies.

The two major influences in her intellectual life, the "new Negro" pride in black heritage and her intense interest in black folklore, dominate both the subject choice and style of virtually everything that she wrote. Two of her books are travel narratives/folklore collections, in which she describes her travel experiences while collecting the tales which are included in the volumes. The first, *Mules and Men* (1935), recounts her folklore expedition in rural Florida and the stories found there. The second, *Tell My Horse* (1939), details her visit to the West Indies on a similar venture.

In addition to her satire on American race relations, *Moses, Man of the Mountain* (1939), Miss Hurston wrote three novels, the first two, *Jonah's Gourd Vine* (1934) and *Their Eyes Were Watching God* (1937), deeply rooted in the folk tradition, and the third, *Seraph on the Suwanee* (1948), exploring a new theme popular in the 1940s and afterward, the relationship between sex and racism. She published nothing of significance after 1948, and, never a financially "practical" person, she died destitute in Fort Pierce, Florida, in 1960.

Their Eyes Were Watching God, often compared with George W. Henderson's "raceless" novel *Ollie Miss* (1935), is possibly the finest dialect novel yet written by an American author. Miss Hurston's superb knowledge of the social codes, emotional reactions, language, and spirit of "the folk"—in addition to her excellent facility for poetic expression—combine to make this a most memorable work. All of these features, the poetry, the dialect, the social pettiness, and, most important, the capacity to love, are immediately observable on the first page of the novel:

> *Ships at a distance have every man's wish on board. For some they come in with the tide. For others they sail forever on the horizon, never out of sight, never landing until the Watcher turns his eyes away in resignation, his dreams mocked to death by Time. That is the life of men.*
>
> *Now, women forget all those things they don't want to remember, and remember everything they don't want to forget. The dream is the truth. Then they act and do things accordingly.*
>
> *So the beginning of this was a woman and she had come*

back from burying the dead. Not the dead of sick and ailing with friends at the pillow and the feet. She had come back from the sodden and the bloated; the sudden dead, their eyes flung wide open in judgment.

The people all saw her come because it was sundown. The sun was gone, but he had left his footprints in the sky. It was the time for sitting on porches beside the road. It was the time to hear things and talk: These sitters had been tongueless, earless, eyeless conveniences all day long. Mules and other brutes had occupied their skins. But now, the sun and the bossman were gone, so the skins felt powerful and human. They became lords of sounds and lesser things. They passed nations through their mouths. They sat in judgment.

Seeing the woman as she was made them remember the envy they had stored up from other times. So they chewed up the back parts of their minds and swallowed with relish. They made burning statements with questions, and killing tools out of laughs. It was mass cruelty. A mood come alive. Words walking without masters; walking altogether like harmony in a song.

"What she doin' coming back here in dem overhalls? Can't she find no dress to put on?—Where's dat blue satin dress she left here in?—Where all dat money her husband took and died and left her?—What dat ole forty year ole 'oman doin' wid her hair swingin' down her back lak some young gal?—Where she left dat young lad of a boy she went off here wid?—Thought she was going to marry?—Where he left her?—What he done wid all her money?—Betcha he off wid some gal so young she ain't even got no hairs—why she don't stay in her class?—"

When she got to where they were she turned her face on the bander log and spoke. They scrambled a noisy "good evenin'" and left their mouths setting open and their ears full of hope. Her speech was pleasant enough, but she kept walking straight on to her gate. The porch couldn't talk for looking.

Janie has come home, her husband now buried, but she has come home with a serenity (a spiritual peace much like that of Toomer's women in *Cane*) that those of the "porch" do not know, a serenity that grows out of the experience of love as perfect as the human being can know it. And here Miss Hurston, in one of the fine works of American literature of this century, reveals her affirmation of universal human existence, not glibly nor naively, for there is much pain to be endured—but with an almost mystical finality that comes from knowing that love is possible, and that it can be, in the truest human sense, complete. This kind of deep, warm, and honest affirmation of the worth of human life and love did not appear again in black fiction (or, with one or two exceptions, in black poetry) for nearly two decades, until the publication of Gwendolyn Brooks' novel, *Maud Martha*, in 1953.

VI.   1940-1960: Urban Realism and Beyond

Richard Wright

In 1940 Richard Wright published his second full-length work, a novel, *Native Son*, which served as the culmination of the last twenty years of black American experience. The novel, probably as influential in guiding the direction and style of the author's contemporaries as any other work by an American writer, became an immediate best-seller and was chosen as a Book-of-the-Month selection. Especially important now, the novel serves as an excellent sequel to Wright's autobiographical *Black Boy*, which was published five years later.

In *Black Boy* Wright reveals his own migration North and, at the same time, that of several millions of other blacks who were born in the South and who had visions—however inaccurate they later proved to be—of northern prosperity and equality. Wright (1908-1960) was born near Natchez, Mississippi, and, because of the instability of his family, he was reared in half a dozen Mississippi towns. *Black Boy* begins when Wright is four years old. The author discusses the series of relatives that he lived with after his father deserted the family; he describes Granny, Aunt Maggie, and Aunt Addie. He writes of his experience in the orphanage in which he was placed when his mother could no longer care for him. And of his general refusal and inability to take his grandmother's religion seriously, he says:

> *Daily I went into my room upstairs, locked the door, knelt, and tried to pray, but everything I could think of saying seemed silly. Once it all seemed so absurd that I laughed out loud while on my knees. It was no use. I could not pray. I could never pray. But I kept my failure a secret. I was convinced that if I ever succeeded in praying, my words would bound noiselessly against the ceiling and rain back down upon me like feathers.*
>
> *My attempts at praying became a nuisance, spoiling my days; and I regretted the promise I had given Granny.*

Wright goes on to discuss the publication, in a black newspaper, of his first short story, "The Voodoo of Hell's Half-Acre," written when he was in eighth grade; the vigilante murder of a classmate's brother; Wright's being named valedictorian of his high school class, and his being told by his school principal that his valedictory speech must be "appropriate," that is, humble enough to please the whites who would be present at commencement. He describes his move to Memphis, Tennessee, in 1925, and, as the book closes, his preparation for moving to Chicago, his vision of the legendary North still intact.

Wright arrived in Chicago in 1927 and soon began to experience the conditions faced by other blacks still pouring North in search of something better than the Jim Crow restrictions of the South. This led to the collapse of the long-held vision. The charade of "separate but equal" public facilities was deceiving no one except those who worked very hard to deceive themselves.

(In 1935, for example, in ten southern states an average of $17.04 was spent to educate each black student in the public schools, as contrasted with $49.30 spent for each white student.[59])

As Wright and others found, however, conditions in the North—and nationwide, for that matter—were little better. While sociological data cannot tell all, it can reveal, in part, what caused *Native Son*, indeed the "urban realism" movement, to be born. For instance, in 1936 the average American dwelling unit for black families had three rooms, while the average for, generally smaller, white families had five to six rooms; and the median income of black families ranged from fifty to seventy per cent lower than that of white families.[60] In addition, four years later, in 1940, the year that *Native Son* was published, the average life expectancy of white males was 62 years, and for white females, 66 years—as contrasted with a life expectancy for nonwhite males of 51 years, and for nonwhite females, 54 years. And, worst of all, the infant mortality rate among whites was 4.3 per cent, as contrasted with 7.3 per cent among blacks.[61]

Becoming acutely aware of conditions such as these, Wright, in revolt, joined the Communist Party in the Thirties and began writing articles for the Communist newspaper, *The Daily Worker*. Also, he participated in the Federal Writers' Project in the Thirties; wrote his two best-known books, *Native Son* and *Black Boy*, in the early Forties; and, after he left the Party, migrated once more—this time to Paris in 1946, where he lived and wrote until his death in 1960.

Native Son presents a new approach to the treatment of urban black living. It shows a stunning portrait of urban ghetto conditions as never revealed before by a black author, conditions which irreparably twist the social and spiritual development of their victims. And here Wright breaks with all previous approaches to the black urban character. By dealing with neither the sophisticated middle-class black of Chesnutt and Larsen, nor with the carefree and relatively harmless "sporting" black of McKay, he focuses his attention on a protagonist, Bigger Thomas, who is (much to the alarm of many black critics) that very "bad nigger" stereotype that for generations has haunted white America.

Bigger's dreams are childlike and often vicious: He wants to be tough, to drive a large car, to fly a plane. Wright points out that Bigger Thomas, and thousands like him, are not allowed the cultural substance out of which useful and mature dreams grow. In unfolding the ugliness which traps the slum dweller, Wright opens the novel with the Thomas family beginning another dismal day in the almost uninhabitable room in which all of the members of the family sleep and in which other "inhabitants" reside as well:

> *"There he is!" the mother screamed again.*
>
> *A huge black rat squealed and leaped at Bigger's trouserleg and snagged it in his teeth, hanging on.*
>
> *"Goddamn!" Bigger whispered fiercely, whirling and kicking out his leg with all the strength of his body. The force of his movement shook the rat loose and it sailed through the air and struck a wall. Instantly, it rolled over and leaped again. Bigger dodged and the rat landed against a table leg. With clenched teeth, Bigger held the skillet; he was afraid to hurl it, fearing that he might miss. The rat squeaked and turned and ran in a narrow circle, looking for a place to hide; it leaped again past Bigger and scurried on dry rasping feet to one side of the box and then to the other, searching for the hole. Then it turned and reared upon its hind legs.*

As Bigger's warped life is revealed, the social and economic paradoxes which surround and embitter him become intolerably baffling. Mr. Dalton, the wealthy white for whom Bigger works as chauffeur, is a philanthropist, true; he gives jobs to blacks, and he donates ping-pong tables to the black youth association. Yet it is Mr. Dalton who owns the rat-infested tenements in which Bigger lives.

Dalton's daughter, Mary, and her friend, Jan, are young Communists who, in a single-minded and heavy-handed way, try to reveal their understanding of, and appreciation for, Bigger's "oppressed" condition by inviting Bigger to dine with them publicly and by riding in the front seat of the Dalton limousine with the embarrassed chauffeur. *Yet*, their very insensitivity to Bigger's feelings and wishes forces the protagonist into a most uncomfortable and dangerous social role, a role which indirectly leads to his destruction. For Mary's allowing herself the luxury of becoming drunk while alone with Bigger places the desperate chauffeur in the position of having either to leave her unconscious in the car, where she would certainly freeze to death, or to leave her unconscious in the living room where she would be found by her parents who would, no doubt, suspect the worst of what "may have happened." Or, he could, as he unfortunately chooses to do, take her upstairs to her bedroom, where, upon hearing Mrs. Dalton stirring, and trying to muffle Mary's unconscious groaning, Bigger accidentally smothers Mary to death with a pillow.

His doom virtually sealed, Bigger nonetheless takes the body to the basement, where, after hacking off the head to make it fit, he places it in the furnace and burns it. An investigation follows, and at first Jan is suspected. But soon Bigger is accused, is hunted and caught—but not until after he has senselessly murdered his girl friend—is "tried," and, despite the humanitarian eloquence of his Communist attorney, Max, is convicted and executed.

Wright makes clear his conclusion that individuals such as Bigger Thomas live by a strange and, by society's standards, a perverted code. They cannot hope to succeed by following acceptable social, economic, and legal channels; so they seek, instead, release from the frustration and anger generated by the cruel hoaxes perpetrated against them, socially and economically, by such people as the Daltons, and, legally, by such people as the racist prosecutor, Buckley. And that release, denied any other course, comes through the drive to destroy—themselves, others, it really does not matter. As Bigger himself explains shortly before his execution: " 'What I killed for must've been good!' Bigger's voice was full of frenzied anguish. 'It must have been good! When a man kills, it's for something. . . . I didn't know I was really alive in this world until I felt things hard enough to kill for 'em. . . . It's the truth, Mr. Max. I can say it now, 'cause I'm going to die. I know what I'm saying real good and I know how it sounds. But I'm all right. I feel all right when I look at it that way. . . .' "

Most of Wright's work echoes the themes of *Native Son:* A man must have enough control over his environment to feel that he can mold it, if only slightly, so that it can provide him with at least a part of the realization of his dreams. When he has no such control, he ceases to be a functioning member of that environment; and he thereby divorces himself from its mores and its legal restrictions. In his nonfiction work, *Twelve Million Black Voices* (1941), and *White Man, Listen!* (1957), Wright perceptively reveals, through pictures and language, the social and psychological effects on, and reactions of, human beings who find themselves expected to live under the most oppressive cultural conditions.

Even Wright's last novel, *Lawd Today* (1963), plays on the same theme. Its protagonist, Jake Jackson, a postal employee, is a man whose monotonous, poorly paying job, absurd living conditions, and nagging wife drain away all of his human sensitivity, leaving him another, though older, Bigger Thomas. Lil, his wife, ill and needing surgery that they cannot afford, is movingly described by Wright at the novel's end, after a fight in which only Jake's loss of consciousness prevents his killing her:

> *Lil dropped the piece of glass; its edges were stained from cuts in her hand. She stood over Jake a moment and watched his drunken sleep. Then she pulled down the shade, wrapped herself in a coat and sank to the floor. She pressed a wad of her gown hard into the cuts in her palm to stem the flow of blood and rested her head on her knees.*
>
> *"Lawd, I wish I was dead," she sobbed softly.*
>
> *Outside an icy wind swept around the corner of the building, whining and moaning like an idiot in a deep black pit.*

Richard Wright as Poet

It is interesting to note, incidentally, that Richard Wright, known to most exclusively as a writer of prose fiction and non-fiction, also occasionally wrote poetry and, in fact, in his poem "Between the World and Me" probably produced the finest piece of literary art of his career.[62] The imagery of the poem is superb as it recreates in the mind of the narrator the ugly events of a lynching—events so disgusting that even the usually disinterested elements of nature seem to protest. The experience is made especially vivid as the narrator surveys metaphorically the remains of the scene, and suddenly the event comes alive again, this time with the narrator himself serving as the victim:

And one morning while in the woods I stumbled suddenly
*   upon the thing,*
Stumbled upon it in a grassy clearing guarded by scaly oaks
*   and elms.*

And the sooty details of the scene rose, thrusting themselves
    between the world and me. . . .

There was a design of white bones slumbering forgottenly
    upon a cushion of ashes.
There was a charred stump of a sapling pointing a blunt
    finger accusingly at the sky.
There were torn tree limbs, tiny veins of burnt leaves,
    and a scorched coil of greasy hemp;
A vacant shoe, an empty tie, a ripped shirt, a lonely hat,
    and a pair of trousers stiff with black blood.
And upon the trampled grass were buttons, dead matches,
    butt-ends of cigars and cigarettes, peanut shells, a
    drained gin-flask, and a whore's lipstick;
Scattered traces of tar, restless arrays of feathers, and the
    lingering smell of gasoline.
And through the morning air the sun poured yellow surprise
    into the eye sockets of a stony skull. . . .
And while I stood my mind was frozen with a cold pity for
    the life that was gone.
The ground gripped my feet and my heart was circled by
    icy walls of fear—
The sun died in the sky; a night wind muttered in the grass
    and fumbled the leaves in the trees; the woods poured
    forth the hungry yelping of hounds; the darkness
    screamed with thirsty voices; and the witnesses rose
    and lived:
The dry bones stirred, rattled, lifted, melting themselves
    into my bones.
The grey ashes formed flesh firm and black, entering into my
    flesh.
The gin-flask passed from mouth to mouth; cigars and cigarettes

> glowed, the whore smeared the lipstick red upon her lips,
> And a thousand faces swirled around me, clamoring that
>   my life be burned. . . .
>
> And then they had me, stripped me, battering my teeth into
>   my throat till I swallowed my own blood.
> My voice was drowned in the roar of their voices, and my
>   black wet body slipped and rolled in their hands as
>   they bound me to the sapling.
> And my skin clung to the bubbling hot tar, falling from me
>   in limp patches.
> And the down and quills of the white feathers sank into my
>   raw flesh, and I moaned in my agony.
> Then my blood was cooled mercifully, cooled by a baptism
>   of gasoline.
> And in a blaze of red I leaped to the sky as pain rose like
>   water, boiling my limbs.
> Panting, begging I clutched childlike, clutched to the hot
>   sides of death.
> Now I am dry bones and my face a stony skull staring in
>   yellow surprise at the sun. . . .[63]

The Wright School

Influenced by Richard Wright, a movement described by Robert Bone as "urban realism," developed in the mid-1940s and was called the "Wright School." The writers usually included in this movement are Chester Himes (*If He Hollers Let Him Go*, 1945, and *Lonely Crusade*, 1947); Ann Petry (*The Street*, 1946); Curtis Lucas (*Third Ward Newark*, 1946); Willard Savoy (*Alien Land*, 1949); Philip B. Kaye (*Taffy*, 1950); and Lloyd Brown (*Iron City*, 1951). Three additional writers, who are not usually associated with the "urban realism" movement, but who should be, are William Attaway (*Blood on the Forge*, 1941); Willard Motley (*Knock on Any Door*, 1947); and, though producing his first novel almost two decades after the movement died out, Nathan Heard (*Howard Street*, 1968).

Attaway places his protagonists, the three Moss brothers, first in the rugged Kentucky countryside, then in a Pennsylvania steel town, and, as the novel ends, they are boarding a train for Pittsburgh, where they have been told of "a place where rent was nearly free and guys who knew how to make out would show them the ropes." Motley's protagonist, who, incidentally, is white, is Nick Romano, who is raised in a Denver slum and in South Side Chicago, who is educated in reform school and prison, and who, as the novel ends, is being executed for murder. And last, Heard's novel, late, though thematically much in the mainstream of the movement, deals with Newark's most notorious area of drug-pushing, prostitution, and murder and those people who try, almost always unsuccessfully, to make an existence amid the squalor.

Robert Bone says of the authors of the "Wright School":

For the Wright School, literature is an emotional catharsis—a means of dispelling the inner tensions of race. Their novels often amount to a prolonged cry of anguish and despair. Too close to their material, feeling it too intensely, these novelists lack a sense of form and of thematic line. With rare exceptions, their style consists of a brutal realism, devoid of any love, or even respect, for words. Their characterization is essentially sociological, but it may contain a greater attempt at psychological depth than is usually associated with the naturalistic novel. Their principal theme, reminiscent of Sherwood Anderson, is how the American caste system breeds "grotesques." The white audience, on perceiving its responsibility for the plight of the protagonist, is expected to alter its attitude toward race.[64]

In the main, Bone is right. Most of the writers of the movement are mediocre. The "rare exceptions," other than Richard Wright himself, are Willard Motley and Ann Petry, and the better artist of the two is Mrs. Petry.

Ann Petry

Ann Petry (b. 1911) was born and reared in Old Saybrook, Connecticut. She attended the University of Connecticut and Columbia University, and, after her marriage in 1938, she moved with her husband to Harlem, where she became a writer for the *Amsterdam News* and later *The People's Voice.* Her bibliography includes two "junior books," *Harriet Tubman: Conductor on the Underground Railway* (1955) and *Tituba of Salem Village* (1964); three novels, *The Street* (1946), *Country Place* (1947), and *The Narrows* (1953); and a collection of short fiction, *Miss Muriel and Other Stories* (1971).

Mrs. Petry's best works, her first two novels, are concerned with the effects of environment on the dreams of people, though the environments of the two are quite different. *The Street* is set on 116th Street in Harlem; *Country Place* is set in Lennox, Connecticut, "a quiet place, a country place, which sits at the mouth of the Connecticut River, at the exact spot where the river empties itself into Long Island Sound." Both settings are well drawn. Mrs. Petry obviously is intimate with the activities, the people, the dreams and nightmares of both; and, in many ways, she finds the moral white squalor of Lennox as debilitating as the physical and spiritual black squalor of the Harlem street.

It is *The Street*, though, which links Mrs. Petry with Richard

Wright and his other followers of the Wright School. The novel, the most outstanding of the "urban realism" works, opens with Lutie Johnson, who is young, black, beautiful, the mother of a young son, Bub, and the wife of a man who can find no work. In an effort to make her dream, and Jim's, come about, Lutie takes a job as a maid in the wealthy Chandler home in Connecticut and returns to New York once each month to see Jim and Bub— then once every two months, for the train fare, she decides, can be added to the money to "pay the interest on the mortgage."

As the months pass, the extent of the moral decay upon which the Chandlers' lives are built becomes more and more obvious. Following a Christmas morning suicide, as she prepares to leave the Chandler home, Lutie receives word from her father that Jim has taken a mistress into her own home, the home which she is supporting. Furious, she rushes back to New York, demands that Jim and the woman leave at once, then sets about trying to recast the dream for herself and Bub.

Able to afford only a top-floor tenement apartment on 116th Street, Lutie nonetheless aproaches her new life with a sense of determination and a sense of humor that, shortly afterward, begins quickly to fade:

> She leaned over to look at the names on the mail boxes. Henry Lincoln Johnson lived here, too, just as he did in all the other houses she'd looked at. Either he or his blood brother.
> The Johnsons and the Jacksons were mighty prolific. Then she grinned, thinking who am I to talk, for I, too, belong to that great tribe, that mighty mighty tribe of Johnsons.

From the time that she moves to "the street," Lutie's life begins its descent. Unable to get a good job; unable to tolerate the lecherous "super," who soon tries to rape her; and, worst of all, unable to shield Bub from the filthy and sinister influences of "the street," Lutie soon finds herself as boxed in as Bigger Thomas. Far worse in this case, her dreams are mature and worthwhile, and they should be realizable: to raise Bub in a building that does not smell of urine and lovemaking; to earn enough money to maintain her own dignity and self-respect; to get away from "the street."

However, like Bigger, Lutie is absolutely trapped. When Bub is tricked by the "super" into robbing mailboxes and is arrested, she grows as desperate as Bigger. She needs money for an attorney, but her only access to money is through her former employer, a band leader named Boots Smith, who has repeatedly tried to arrange a liaison between Lutie and "this nice white gentleman he knows," who "wants to know her better." The climax comes when Lutie refuses to "meet the gentleman" and is attacked by Smith. And, like Bigger Thomas, she reacts:

He was so close to her that she struck him on the side of the head before he saw the blow coming. The first blow stunned him. And she struck him again and again, using the candlestick as though it were a club. He tried to back away from her and stumbled over the sofa and sprawled there.

A lifetime of pent-up resentment went into the blows. Even after he lay motionless, she kept striking him, not thinking about him, not even seeing him. First she was venting her rage against the dirty, crowded street. She saw the rows of dilapidated old houses; the small dark rooms; the long steep flights of stairs; the narrow dingy hallways; the little lost girls in Mrs. Hedges' apartment; the smashed homes where the women did drudgery because their men had deserted them. She saw all of these things and struck at them.

With Smith dead, Lutie quickly decides that she must escape—she will go to Chicago—and, shortly afterward, in a deeply moving ending of contrast, Mrs. Petry closes her novel:

> *The train crept out of the tunnel, gathered speed as it left
> the city behind. Snow whispered against the windows. And as the
> train roared into the darkness, Lutie tried to figure out by what
> twists and turns of fate she had landed on this train. Her mind
> balked at the task. All she could think was, It was that street.
> It was that god-damned street.*
>
> *The snow fell softly on the street. It muffled sound. It
> sent people scurrying homeward, so that the street was soon
> deserted, empty, quiet. And it could have been any street in the
> city, for the snow laid a delicate film over the sidewalk, over the
> brick of the tired, old buildings; gently obscuring the grime
> and the garbage and the ugliness.*

As the Forties came to an end and the Fifties began, the Wright
School disappeared. Except for Ann Petry, Willard Motley, and,
occasionally, Richard Wright, all of whom had the ability to transcend the mere reporting of accumulated sociological observations, the writers of the movement, after almost a decade, simply
had no more to say. They had exposed virtually every form of the
filth, corruption, and depravity of urban slums, and there seemed
no place else for the "urban realism" movement to go—and so, it
died.

As the "urban realism" movement was dying, five novelists
were developing who, all with first novels, lifted black fiction, by
the mid-Fifties, to the highest level of artistic accomplishment that
it has yet reached. Indeed, between 1948, when Dorothy West
published her only novel, *The Living Is Easy*, and 1953, when
James Baldwin published *Go Tell It on the Mountain* and Gwendolyn Brooks produced her only novel, *Maud Martha*, black American literature reached its zenith. The last two authors of this gifted
group are William Demby (*Beetlecreek*, 1950) and Ralph Ellison
(*Invisible Man*, 1952).

Dorothy West

Dorothy West (b. 1910) was born in Boston and educated at Boston University and at the School of Journalism of Columbia University. She began writing during the Harlem Renaissance and published her early short stories in *Opportunity*. During the Thirties she edited the periodical *Challenge,* where she encouraged "new Negro" writing. In addition, she joined the Federal Writers' Project, met Richard Wright, and flirted briefly with Communism. During the Forties she continued to publish short stories and articles in magazines, and in 1948 she published a novel, *The Living Is Easy*. Reviving memories of the fiction of Charles Chesnutt, Jessie Fauset, and Nella Larsen, the novel treats the black aristocrats of Boston.

At once hated and pitied, the protagonist is Cleo Judson, wife of Bart Judson, who is the "Black Banana King," and mother of Judy, who is much darker than her mother and looks "just like Papa." Selfish from her youth, Cleo, above all—or anybody—else, wants "to get ahead." She lies to her husband about household expenses, and she steals money from him. Further, she tricks him into allowing her three sisters to move in with them, after which she virtually ruins the lives of her sisters, as well as their marriages. And she unmercifully badgers Judy not "to flatten" her nose, not to "show her gums" when she smiles—in short, to be "a little Boston lady" and to look as light as possible.

Cleo's obsession with money and with status drives her to be the first "colored lady" in a succession of stylish all-white neighborhoods ("We've taken a house in Brookline"). It drives her to do and say things to her husband, her daughter, her sisters, even herself which she regrets—but which she repeats. Miss West achieves an interesting balance in the character of Cleo. The character, on the surface a vicious, emasculating, totally self-serving woman deserving only scorn, is, one soon realizes, much more than this: Cleo is desperately afraid of being alone, of being unloved. And so, in the very acts of achieving the status which she feels will assure her of the respect, even love, of others, she alienates, one by one, everyone who does, in fact, already love her. Her sisters gradually develop their own independence and leave Cleo's fold. Judy gravitates more and more toward her father, whose simple and genuine love does not have social conditions attached to it. And Bart, upon learning that his business is ruined, confers quietly and tragically with Cleo, in the very sad ending of the novel, as he prepares, at almost sixty years of age, to leave for New York to look for work.

William Demby

Both William Demby and Ralph Ellison, in *Beetlecreek* (1950) and *Invisible Man* (1952), explore the "existential" problem of people trying to make individual moral choices about what the depth and nature of their lives will be. Demby (b. 1922) was born in Pittsburgh, though he grew up in Clarksburg, West Virginia, the mining town which provided the setting for *Beetlecreek*. He attended West Virginia State College, spent two years in the Army during World War II, where he wrote for *Stars and Stripes*, and returned to college at Fisk University, from which he graduated in 1947. That same year he returned to Italy, where he had been stationed during the war, to study art at the University of Rome. He has spent most of the years since 1947 in Italy with his Italian wife, and he has worked as a scriptwriter and translator for Italian films. Most important, he has written two novels, *Beetlecreek*, a fine work, and *The Catacombs* (1965), a strange one, also "existential," set in Rome.

In *Beetlecreek* Demby probes a society gone dead. His central characters, the old white recluse, Bill Trapp, and two blacks, fourteen-year-old Johnny Johnson and his uncle, David Diggs, make periodic efforts to free themselves from the corruption and decay of the black section of the small southern town of Beetlecreek. The town, like the stagnant creek which symbolically divides it into two parts, slowly pulls individuals out of the stream of active living and enmeshes them in the weeds of its own motionlessness. Demby says of the creek: "First there was a whirlpool to entice the floating object, then a slow-flowing pool, and, finally, the deadly mud backwater in the reeds. In the reeds would be other objects already trapped." Indeed the people of Beetlecreek are trapped by the inanity that they call living: the missionary club activities of Mary Diggs, David's wife; the incessant chatter about numbers, girls, and whites at the black barber shop; the sadistic rituals of the band of young black hoodlums who call themselves the Nightriders, and who have the kind of Ku-Klux-Klan mentality which makes their name appropriate.

Bill Trapp, Johnny, and David are the only ones in the swirl and mire of what is called life in Beetlecreek who have a chance to pull themselves out. The others have long since succumbed to the disease of decay. But Trapp, the old "carny," and his two new friends clearly see the options available to them. Trapp can give up his solitary exile and, through Johnny, can allow his trust in people and life to be restored. Johnny can accept the old man's friendship and thus repudiate the demands of the barber shop crowd and the Nightriders that he stay away from the "queer" hermit. And David, by abandoning his lifeless wife, Mary (whom he married because she was pregnant and he wanted to "do the right thing," and with whom he shares no love whatsoever), could return to the city for which both his education and his temperament make him better suited.

Demby sustains the drama of his plot with fine precision: Trapp moves closer to accepting people; Johnny moves closer to accepting the friendship of the recluse which will give them both life; and David seriously contemplates leaving Beetlecreek. But decay wins out. Johnny, unable finally to resist the demands of the Nightriders, not only agrees to abandon his friendship with Bill Trapp but also accepts the vigilante "assignment" of setting fire to his old friend's shack. With the completion of his assigned task and his confrontation with his betrayed friend, Johnny consigns them both to the "deadly mud backwater" which they nearly escaped:

> *"What have you done, Johnny?" was all he said. He put out his hand and touched Johnny's shoulder.*
>
> *When Johnny felt the old man's hand on him, he began to shake with terror and rage. The old man grabbed him and hugged him close.*
>
> *"What have you done, Johnny? What have you been up to?"*
>
> *There was a blinding light inside him, a blinding light that lit him up inside from his stomach to his head, a blinding green streak of lightning. Outside this inside light, he could feel the old man's hands on him. He felt as if his blood had been changed into hot steel. He must get away! He must get away!*
>
> *His fist closed tighter on the handle of the gasoline can and he felt his arm swinging out in a high swooping arc. And he heard a dull clang. And he felt Bill Trapp become limp. And he saw him fall to the ground.*

David, too, fails; for, while he does decide to abandon Beetle-creek, he chooses as his companion, Edith, a former sweetheart who has returned to town for a funeral—a girl who, from the city and familiar with its "good times," is simply an urban version of David's wife, and just as cold and lifeless. The novel closes with David and Edith aboard a bus leaving Beetlecreek: "The lights were turned off. David leaned over toward Edith and slipped his arms around her. She squirmed out of his grasp. 'Don't always be so goddamned lovey-dovey,' she said. Her voice was dry and scraping."

Demby's characters, like Ellison's protagonist in *Invisible Man*, are only incidentally black. While the black section of the town of Beetlecreek is the setting of Demby's novel, there is little significance in the author's focus on black life except, as Demby suggests, that the inanity of this black community simply reflects the corresponding inanity of the whole human community. It is this human community that Demby is probing, with its death-sustaining charade of organizations, rituals, and pettiness—a charade that an individual, given the capacity and courage to make personal moral choice, *can* repudiate, thereby redeeming himself for the *art* of living.

Ralph Ellison

Two years later Ralph Ellison, in what is probably the finest piece of fiction ever written by a black American, *Invisible Man*, takes up the same theme of the necessity of making individual moral choice. Ellison (b. 1914) was born in Oklahoma City, Oklahoma, spent three years at Tuskegee Institute in Alabama studying music, and, in 1936, made his way to New York, where he began writing. He met Richard Wright in the Federal Writers' Project in the late Thirties, and he contributed to *New Challenge* and *New Masses*.

Unlike many of the prominent black authors of the Thirties, Ellison did not join the Communist Party, though, like many others of the time, he came strongly under the influence of Wright. He later broke away from that influence as he moved, as an artist, substantially beyond Wright.

Invisible Man (1952), winner of the National Book Award for Fiction, treats the quest of institutional man for individual identity. The novel opens with the protagonist, young, black, and already the victim of Jim Crow laws and education, deciding to abandon the South and to seek some better destiny in Harlem, only to find that his problem is philosophical, not geographical. For the unnamed protagonist allows himself to be convinced that he must assume those identities that others feel best suited for him—such as the role of the grateful and humble black suggested by his college president, Dr. Bledsoe (Ellison's names are frequently symbolic), and the role of the bombastic class-warfare orator demanded by the Brotherhood (Communist Party) in Harlem.

It is only after he has divorced himself from all institutions (including the Liberty Paint Company, where his job is placing several drops of black additive in each bucket of "Optic White" paint, which will "cover anything" and which is used, symbolically enough, to paint government structures) and the role that each has demanded of him, and after he has locked himself in a secret basement room in Harlem, that the protagonist finally has the time and the courage to view himself as *he* wishes himself to be. And with his new awareness he plans to reenter the world, not as a stereotype, invisible even to himself, but as an individual who finally wishes to be visible, at least to himself. He now seems ready to make the moral decisions necessary for the state of visibility. With the conclusion of the novel, Ellison confirms his claim that the novel is not a "race" novel but is instead one concerned with contemporary human invisibility. Thus the protagonist ends his long tale:

> *In going underground, I whipped it all except the mind, the mind. And the mind that has conceived a plan of living must never lose sight of the chaos against which that pattern was conceived. That goes for societies as well as for individuals. Thus, having tried to give pattern to the chaos which lives within the pattern of your certainties, I must come out, I must emerge. . . . I'm shaking off the old skin and I'll leave it here in the hole. I'm coming out, no less invisible without it, but coming out nevertheless. And I suppose it's damn well time. Even hibernations can be overdone, come to think of it. Perhaps that's my greatest social crime, I've overstayed my hibernation, since there's a possibility that even an invisible man has a socially responsible role to play.*
>
> *"Ah," I can hear you say, "so it was all a build-up to bore us with his buggy jiving. He only wanted us to listen to him rave!" But only partially true: Being invisible and without substance, a dis-*

embodied voice, as it were, what else could I do? What else but try to tell you what was really happening when your eyes were looking through? And it is this which frightens me:

Who knows but that, on the lower frequencies, I speak for you?

James Baldwin

Probably one of the two or three most gifted contemporary American essayists, James Baldwin (b. 1924) was born in Harlem and educated in the New York City public schools. The influence of his family's intense sense of religion—his father was a part-time storefront preacher—can be found in much of Baldwin's work, especially in his best novel, *Go Tell It on the Mountain* (1953), in the title essay of his collection *Notes of a Native Son* (1955), and in his second, and last, play, *The Amen Corner* (1967).

Early in his life Baldwin planned to follow his father as a preacher, but, while still a teenager, he gave up that idea and the church as well. In "Notes of a Native Son," Baldwin describes his religious attitude as he assessed it on the day of his father's funeral—the day of a major race riot in Harlem through the debris and broken glass of which the Baldwin family made their way to the cemetery:

The day of my father's funeral had also been my nineteenth birthday. As we drove him to the graveyard, the spoils of injustice, anarchy, discontent, and hatred were all around us. It seemed to me that God himself had devised, to mark my father's end, the most sustained and brutally dissonant of codas. And it seemed to me, too, that the violence which rose all about us as my father left the world had been devised as a corrective for the pride of his eldest son. I had declined to believe in that apocalypse which had been central to my father's vision; very well, life seemed to be saying, here is some-

thing that will certainly pass for an apocalypse until the real thing comes along.

A short time later Baldwin went to Paris, where he stayed for nine years and where he wrote his first novel, *Go Tell It on the Mountain*. The novel is a portrait of the black ghetto church and its effect upon fourteen-year-old John Grimes and upon his family: his brutally righteous stepfather, Gabriel; his suffering mother, Elizabeth; and his bitter Aunt Florence. John's attraction to Elisha, a teen-age preacher, brings about the protagonist's conversion, but, in fact, little comes of it, as Baldwin makes clear that the urban church cannot possibly succeed in doing what it must attempt: that is, to give ghetto residents a hope that can sustain them as they continue to live amid squalor, disease, and persistent intimidation. As a temporary palliative, the church can help, but the sustaining hope must lie in social, economic, and legal reforms.

Baldwin has written four other novels: *Giovanni's Room* (1956), about the agony which seems naturally a part of homosexual love; *Another Country* (1962), about the love-hate syndrome which accompanies interracial sexual experience; *Tell Me How Long the Train's Been Gone* (1968), about the racial obligations attached to the success of black professionals, in this case, the accomplished actor, Leo Proudhammer; and his recent, especially bitter, *No Name in the Street* (1972).

Baldwin has also written a collection of short stories, *Going to Meet the Man*, the best of which, the title story, explores, better than any other piece of short fiction by a noted author to date, the intricate relationship between racial brutality and sexuality. The protagonist, a middle-aged southern deputy sheriff, can perform sexually only after his mind passes over a series of experiences of his life, the most important being his beating a young black civil rights worker until blood poured from his ears and nose, and his first observation of a lynching, where, with all of the other townspeople, he saw a black man burned alive and mutilated. The memories cause his manhood to return, and as the story closes, having assumed himself that hated-feared legendary black sexual prowess, he says to his wife: "Come on, sugar, I'm going to do you like a nigger, just like a nigger, come on, sugar, and love me just like you'd love a nigger."

In addition to two plays, the popular *Blues for Mister Charlie* (1964) and *The Amen Corner*, and to *Notes of a Native Son*, Baldwin has published two other essay collections, both excellent, *Nobody Knows My Name* (1961) and *The Fire Next Time* (1963). The last book closes with two lines of promise and threat from the slave song that serves as the source of the book's title: "God gave Noah the rainbow sign, No more water, the fire next time!" Baldwin's essays are not usually threatening, however. Indeed his purpose in writing the two lengthy essays which make up *The Fire Next Time* is to point out how obvious it should be that so little is gained and so much lost by the perpetuation of the institutionalized forms of injustice which have, virtually since the founding of this nation, been directed at black "native sons."

An appealing feature of Baldwin's nonfiction prose, one which distinguishes it from the sameness of the monotonously intense "militant" tracts which appeared in such profusion during the Sixties, is the deft touches of humor which are so gently woven into often serious essays and which go a long way toward illustrating that Baldwin, while serious of purpose and professionally successful, does not take himself and his ideas so dreadfully seriously as do so many contemporary essayists. Two examples will illustrate, both from the essay "Autobiographical Notes" in *Notes of a Native Son*:

I was born in Harlem thirty-one years ago. I began plotting novels at about the time I learned to read. The story of my childhood is the usual bleak fantasy, and we can dismiss it with the restrained observation that I certainly would not consider living it

*again. In those days my mother was given to the exasperating and
mysterious habit of having babies. As they were born, I took them
over with one hand and held a book with the other.*

And:

*Any writer, I suppose, feels that the world into which he was
born is nothing less than a conspiracy against the cultivation of his
talent—which attitude certainly has a great deal to support it. On
the other hand, it is only because the world looks on his talent with
such a frightening indifference that the artist is compelled to make
his talent important.*

Gwendolyn Brooks

In 1953, the same year that Baldwin published his first novel,
Gwendolyn Brooks also published her first—and her only one to
date. Miss Brooks (b. 1917) was born in Topeka, Kansas. While
she was still an infant, her parents moved to Chicago, where she
has spent most of her life. She began writing poetry as a child, and,
as a teenager, she regularly submitted poems to periodicals. She
graduated from Wilson Junior College in 1934.

One of America's most gifted contemporary poets, Miss
Brooks published her first volume of poetry, *A Street in Bronze-
ville*, in 1945, and the next year she was named a Fellow of the
American Academy of Arts and Letters. Also in 1946, and the next
year, she received a Guggenheim Fellowship. In 1949 she won
Poetry magazine's Eunice Tietjen Prize for Poetry. And in 1950
she was awarded the Pulitzer Prize for Poetry for her collection
Annie Allen (1949), the first black American to receive that award.
Miss Brooks has served as guest lecturer at universities throughout
the United States, and in 1962 she was invited to join Robert Frost
and other notable American poets at the Poetry Festival at the
Library of Congress. Miss Brooks is married to Henry Blakely, has
two children, and still lives in Chicago.

Miss Brooks' love of language, and of people and life, is apparent in her novel, *Maud Martha*, the story of the coming of age of a black Chicago girl, Maud Martha Brown, who is troubled by much that life offers her but who loves it anyway. There is in the novel the same determination found in Miss Brooks' poetry, a determination to make life work, though Maud Martha, even as a child, does not understand why her sister Helen, simply because her skin is lighter, is the recipient of greater respect, even love, than herself, despite the fact that she, Maud Martha, is brighter than her sister, and more feeling.

These peculiar ways of her world; various forms of discrimination that she experiences as she grows older; her only mildly happy married life with Paul, not quite what she had romantically envisioned; their "kitchenette" apartment, with the smelly hallways and shared bathroom, not at all what they had dreamed—none of these things defeat Maud Martha. And in her gentle way she makes her mark upon the world and upon the reader of her story. Her victories are small, but they are significant for they reveal that the hypocrisies and outright deceits of contemporary Wall-Street/Madison-Avenue society need not always win out. Perhaps the best example from the novel is the vignette "Millinery":

"Looks lovely on you," said the manager. "Makes you look —" What? Beautiful? Charming? Glamorous? Oh no, oh no, she could not stoop to the usual lies; not today; her coffee had been too strong, had not set right; and there had been another fight at home, for her daughter continued to insist on galivanting about with that Greek—a Greek!—not even a Jew, which, though revolting enough, was at least becoming fashionable, was "timely. . . . She started again—"Makes you look—" She stopped.

"How much is the hat?" Maud Martha asked.

"Seven ninety-nine."

Maud Martha rose, went to the door.

"*Wait, wait,*" *called the hat woman, hurrying after her.* . . . "*Now just how much, Madam, had you thought you would prefer to pay?*"

"*Not a cent over five.*"

"*Five? Five, dearie? You expect to buy a hat like this for five dollars? This, this straw that you can't even get any more and which I showed you only because you looked like a lady of taste who could appreciate a good value?*"

"*Well,*" *said Maud Martha,* "*thank you.*" *She opened the door.*

"*Wait, wait,*" *shrieked the hat woman. Good naturedly, the escaping customer hesitated again.* "*Just a moment,*" *ordered the hat woman coldly.* "*I'll speak to the—to the owner. He might be willing to make some slight reduction, since you're an old customer. I remember you. You've been in here several times, haven't you?*"

"*I've never been in the store before.*" *The woman rushed off as if she had heard nothing. She rushed off to consult with the owner. She rushed off to appeal to the boxes in the back room.*

Presently the hat woman returned.

"*Well. The owner says it'll be a crying shame, but seeing as how you're such an old customer he'll make a reduction. He'll let you have it for five. Plus tax, of course!*" *she added chummily; they had, always, more appreciation when, after one of these* "*reductions,*" *you added that.*

"*I've decided against the hat.*"

"*What? Why, you told—But, you said—*"

Maud Martha went out, tenderly closed the door.

Miss Brooks has published, in addition to those collections of poems already mentioned, *Bronzeville Boys and Girls* (1956), *The Bean Eaters* (1960), *Selected Poems* (1963), *In the Mecca* (1968), *Riot* (1969), and *Family Pictures* (1970). Her poetry reveals the same careful craftsmanship that is found in *Maud Martha*, the precise use of diction and syntax, the gently effective rhythm. She is, in fact, probably the most careful artist since Countee Cullen, whose view that his first obligation was to his craft she seems to share. While one seldom loses sight of the racial consciousness in her work, one virtually never observes racial themes taking control of the poems to the detriment of the poetic form.

Miss Brooks' thematic concerns are stretched on the universal frames of children's dreams, mothers' hopes, man's need for love and respect—for self and for others—and the human obligation that everyone has to promote justice in all its forms. The depth of her feeling and the exquisite precision of her poetic technique are observable in the poem "People Who Have No Children Can Be Hard," taken from her award-winning collection, *Annie Allen*:

People who have no children can be hard:
Attain a mail of ice and insolence:
Need not pause in the fire, and in no sense
Hesitate in the hurricane to guard.
And when wide world is bitten and bewarred
They perish purely, waving their spirits hence
Without a trace of grace or of offense
To laugh or fail, diffident, wonder-starred.
While through a throttling dark we others hear
The little lifting helplessness, the queer
Whimper-whine; whose unridiculous
Lost softness softly makes a trap for us.
And makes a curse. And makes a sugar of
The malocclusions, the inconditions of love.[65]

Robert Hayden

While other poets of note were writing during this period—Melvin B. Tolson, *Rendezvous with America* (1944); Owen Dodson, *Powerful Long Ladder* (1946); and Frank Marshall Davis, *47th Street* (1948) (Langston Hughes' *Montage of a Dream Deferred*, 1951, was mentioned earlier)—only two, Robert Hayden and Margaret Walker, approach the stature of Gwendolyn Brooks.

Hayden (b. 1913)) was born in Detroit, earned a B.A. at Wayne State University and an M.A. at the University of Michigan, where he taught for two years. Since 1944, he has been a member of the faculty at Fisk University. He has received many writing awards and fellowships, among them the Rosenwald Fellowship in 1947 and a Ford Foundation grant in 1954. His first collection of verse, *Heart Shape in the Dust*, was published in 1940. Since that time, he has edited an anthology of black verse, *Kaleidoscope* (1967), and co-edited another anthology, *Afro-American Literature: An Introduction* (1971). In addition, he has published five volumes of poems, the most important of which are *A Ballad of Remembrance* (1962), for which he received the Grand Prize for Poetry in 1965 at the First World African Festival of Arts, and *Selected Poems* (1966). His most recent collection is *Words in the Mourning Time* (1970).

Selected Poems contains what is probably Hayden's most memorable poem, "Middle Passage" a uniquely designed piece in which, through the weaving together of objective narration, passages from a slave ship's log, excerpts from a ship officer's diary, testimony at a court of inquiry, an old sailor's tale, and much more, Hayden presents a composite picture of the hideous "middle passage" of a slave vessel. The account is based partly on the historical slave insurrection aboard the *Amistad*, a Cuban slaver, in 1839, during which the slaves freed themselves and murdered nearly all of the ship's crew.[66] Hayden begins his poem with the ironically symbolic names of four slave ships, three apparently Cuban, one American. He then moves to an objectively narrated passage and then on to an excerpt from a captain's log:

Jesús, Estrella, Esperanza, Mercy:

Sails flashing to the wind like weapons,
sharks following the moans the fever and the dying;
horror the corposant and compass rose.

Middle Passage:
voyage through death
to life upon these shores.

"10 April 1800—
Blacks rebellious. Crew uneasy. Our linguist says
their moaning is a prayer for death,
ours and their own. Some try to starve themselves.
Lost three this morning leaped with crazy laughter
to the waiting sharks, sang as they went under."

Later in the account comes a poignant excerpt, probably from an officers diary:

"8 *bells, I cannot sleep, for I am sick*
with fear, but writing eases fear a little
since still my eyes can see these words take shape
upon the page & so I write, as one
would turn to exorcism. 4 days scudding,
but now the sea is calm again. Misfortune
follows in our wake like sharks (our grinning
tutelary gods). Which one of us
has killed an albatross? A plague among
our blacks—Ophthalmia: blindness—& we
have jettisoned the blind to no avail.
It spreads, the terrifying sickness spreads.
Its claws have scratched sight from the Capt.'s eyes
& there is blindness in the fo'c'sle
& we must sail 3 weeks before we come
to port."

And, last, the court of inquiry account, as it was given by a Cuban officer, with another touch of irony, of the slave rebellion aboard ship:

Exhausted by the rigors of the storm,
we were no match for them. Our men went down
before the murderous Africans. Our loyal
Celestino ran from below with gun
and lantern and I saw, before the cane-
knife's wounding flash, Cinquez,
that surly brute who calls himself a prince,
directing, urging on the ghastly work.
He hacked the poor mulatto down, and then
he turned on me. The decks were slippery
when daylight finally came. It sickens me
to think of what I saw, of how these apes
threw overboard the butchered bodies of
our men, true Christians all, like so much jetsam.[67]

Margaret Walker

Two years after Hayden published his first book of poetry, Margaret Walker published her first collection of verse, the famous *For My People* (1942). Her only other collection, *Prophets for a New Day*, was published in 1970. Miss Walker (b. 1915) was born in Birmingham, Alabama, where she learned early the high cost of blackness in the Deep South. She graduated from Gilbert Academy in New Orleans in 1930 and published her first poem in *Crisis* the next year. She earned a B.A. at Northwestern University in 1935, and for a short time was associated with the Federal Writers' Project. She earned an M.A. at the University of Iowa in 1940, offering a collection of poems as her thesis; and in 1965 she received a Ph.D. at the University of Iowa, offering as her dissertation her now-well-known novel, *Jubilee*, for which the next year she received a Houghton Mifflin Literary Fellowship. During her career she has taught at Livingstone College, North Carolina, West Virginia State College, and, for many years, at Jackson State College, Mississippi. She is married to F. J. Alexander, has four children, and continues to live in Jackson.

Miss Walker's best-known poem is "For My People," originally published in *Poetry* magazine in 1937, and later used as the title poem of her volume which was published in 1942 and won the Yale University Younger Poets Award. The poem, written in free verse, rhythmically catalogues the progress of black American experience, from the rural folkways, religious practices, and exhausting labor of the South, through the cramped and confusing conditions of the northern urban centers, to what she hopes will be a racial awakening, blacks militantly rising up to take control of their own destinies:

For my people everywhere singing their slave songs repeatedly:
   their dirges and their ditties and their blues and jubilees,
   praying their prayers nightly to an unknown god, bending
   their knees humbly to an unseen power;

For my people lending their strength to the years, to the gone
   years and the now years and the maybe years, washing ironing
   cooking scrubbing sewing mending hoeing plowing digging planting
   pruning patching dragging along never gaining never reaping
   never knowing and never understanding;

. . . .

For the boys and girls who grew in spite of these things to be
   man and woman, to laugh and dance and sing and play and drink
   their wine and religion and success, to marry their playmates
   and bear children and then die of consumption and anemia and
   lynching;

For my people thronging 47th Street in Chicago and Lenox Avenue
in New York and Rampart Street in New Orleans, lost disinherited
dispossessed and happy people filling the cabarets and taverns
and other people's pockets needing bread and shoes and milk
and land and money and something—something all our own;

For my people walking blindly spreading joy, losing time being
lazy, sleeping when hungry, shouting when burdened, drinking
when hopeless, tied and shackled and tangled among ourselves
by the unseen creatures who tower over us omnisciently and
laugh;

. . . .

Let a new earth rise. Let another world be born. Let a bloody
peace be written in the sky. Let a second generation full of
courage issue forth; let a people loving freedom come to growth.
Let a beauty full of healing and a strength of final clenching
be the pulsing in our spirits and our blood. Let the martial
songs be written, let the dirges disappear. Let a race of men
now rise and take control.[68]

Miss Walker's single novel, *Jubilee* (1966), also deserves
comment. Translated into several languages, it serves especially
well as a response to white "nostalgia" fiction about the ante-
bellum and Reconstruction South—especially Margaret Mitchell's poor but popular *Gone with the Wind*. One cannot read one
of these novels without repeatedly contrasting it with the other. On
dialect: Miss Walker's is thoroughly researched and linguistically
accurate; Miss Mitchell's ranges from rather accurate to absurd.
On the role of blacks: Miss Walker reveals the various levels of
black mentality, as well as the devotion of some slaves to, and the
intense hatred of others for, their masters; Miss Mitchell presents

blacks before the Civil War as happy darkies completely devoted to "missy" and "massa." On "social controls": Miss Walker portrays vividly the savagery of white vigilante repression; Miss Mitchell portrays the Ku Klux Klan as an organization of noble and dedicated men with the highest moral objectives. In short, the novels make for an interesting and enlightening companion study—a study of painful historical reality and romanticized self-deception.

Paule Marshall

The last important novel of the period is *Brown Girl, Brownstones*, published in 1959 by Paule Marshall. Mrs. Marshall (b. 1929) was born in Brooklyn and has spent much of her life in the New York City area. Her parents immigrated to the United States around 1920 from the small British island of Barbados, one of the Windward group of the West Indies. After graduating Phi Beta Kappa from Brooklyn College, Mrs. Marshall worked for a time as a librarian, then joined the staff of *Our World* magazine. In this position she traveled extensively, spending considerable time in the West Indies, where she became closely acquainted with the dialects, customs, and folkways of her ancestors—all of which she would later draw heavily upon in her fiction. Aided by a Guggenheim Fellowship and awards from the Ford Foundation and from the National Institute of Arts and Letters, Mrs. Marshall has published three books of fiction, her fine novel, *Brown Girl, Brownstones*; a collection of four novelettes, *Soul Clap Hands and Sing* (1961); and *The Chosen Place, The Timeless People* (1969).

Containing poetic imagery as effective as that in Toomer's *Cane*, dialect as precise as that of Miss Hurston's *Their Eyes Were Watching God*, and the kind of gentle warmth found in Miss Brooks' *Maud Martha, Brown Girl, Brownstones* is the story of the youth and maturation of Selina Boyce. Selina is a Barbadian-American Brooklyn girl, only a year or so out of childhood, only a

year or so from the dreaded but inevitable menstruation and its
accompanying conditions of developing breasts and hips. But, at
the opening of the novel, she is just Selina, living, talking with close
friends, observing. She observes that her father, Deighton, is a
beautiful man, a dreamer (called by some a ne'er-do-well), dreaming of returning to the lush and idyllic Barbados. She observes that
her mother, Silla, forced by her father's lack of initiative, yet driven
by something far more potent than that alone, is obsessed with the
notion of "owning the house," the once-picturesque old brownstone
which now, though clean and well-tended, serves as a dwelling for
several boarders as well. And she observes the boarders: Miss
Thompson, with the sore foot that will not heal; old Miss Mary,
whose only comfort is her memories; and Miss Suggie, whose room
seems always to contain boyfriends and whose bedsprings squeak
ceaselessly for hours at a time.

And, as she observes, Selina grows; for she is observing life in
most of the forms that she, as a young adult, will know it—even the
shocking "betrayal," her mother's reporting her father's long-
forgotten illegal immigration to the authorities in retribution for
his acting as an impediment to her "getting ahead." But even the
act of betrayal provides the positive influence on Selina, now in her
late teens, of compelling her to make the necessary break with her
mother's life, her mother's decaying aspirations ("Silla was saying
numbly, 'Here it tis just when I start making plans to buy a house
in Crown Heights!' "). And, in a final moving scene of nostalgic
detail, the novel ends:

> *She walked through Fulton Park. Before, on a spring night,*
> *the mothers would have been sitting there, their ample thighs*
> *spread easy under their housedresses, gossiping, while around them*
> *spring rose from the pyre of winter. Tonight the moon discovered a*
> *ruined park which belonged to the winos who sat red-eyed and*
> *bickering all day, to the dope addicts huddled in their safe worlds*

and to the young bops clashing under the trees and warming the cold ground with their blood. But despite the ruin, spring stirred and, undaunted, arrayed the trees, hung its mist curtain high and, despite the wine-stench, sweetened the air. Selina strolled, unafraid, through the mist and lamplight, pausing at the pavillion to listen, with a dull desolation—to the lovers murmuring in the shadows. . . .

On the far perimeter of the plain, the new city houses were already up and occupied. As Selina stared at those monolithic shapes they seemed to draw near, the lighted windows spangling the sky like a new constellation. She imagined she heard footsteps ringing hollow in the concrete halls, the garbled symphony of radios and televisions, children crying in those rooms: life moving in an oppressive round within those uniformly painted walls.

The project receded and she was again the sole survivor amid the wreckage. And suddenly she turned away, unable to look any longer. For it was like seeing the bodies of all the people she had ever known broken, all the familiar voices that had ever sounded in those high-ceilinged rooms shattered—and the pieces piled into this giant cairn of stone and silence.

Lorraine Hansberry

The last writer of the period to be treated is Lorraine Hansberry, whose successful Broadway production, *A Raisin in the Sun*, in 1959, marked the highest public and critical achievement in drama written by a black American. To be sure, there were other black plays on Broadway between 1935, the year of Langston Hughes' production of *Mulatto*, and 1959; but there were not many. Among those worthy of mention are two plays of the Forties, both written in 1941: Richard Wright and Paul Green's adaptation of Wright's novel *Native Son*, a play called *Native Son: A Biography of a Young American*;[69] and Theodore Ward's play, set in the Reconstruction era, *Our Lan'*.

In the Fifties there were several important plays, William Branch's *A Medal for Willie* (1951), about the hypocritical southern ceremony for awarding to the mother of a dead black soldier a military medal for heroism; Louis Peterson's Broadway play, *Take a Giant Step* (1954); and, the most significant historically, though not artistically outstanding, Loften Mitchell's *A Land Beyond the River*,[70] produced for the first time off-Broadway in 1957. Mitchell's play is based upon the experience of the Reverend Joseph DeLaine of Clarendon County, South Carolina, whose legal suit to integrate the local school resulted in the United States Supreme Court decision in May, 1954, outlawing segregation in public schools.

It was with Miss Hansberry's play, though, that the high point was reached. Miss Hansberry (1930-1965) was born and reared in Chicago, where, while still a child, she experienced much the same kind of white hostility that the Younger family in her play are faced with once they decide to move into an all-white neighborhood. Miss Hansberry's father, a realtor, Carl Hansberry, was a party in the historic Supreme Court case *Hansberry* v. *Lee*, which affirmed the Hansberrys' right to live in a previously all-white Chicago neighborhood. Miss Hansberry later attended the University of Wisconsin for two years, moved to New York in 1950, and married the publisher Robert Nemiroff three years later. In 1959 she produced *A Raisin in the Sun*, winner of the New York Drama Critics Circle Award.

Not, as Miss Hansberry insisted, a "Negro play," *A Raisin* explores, with considerable depth, the "human dream" which has for centuries been the topic of enduring literature. The Younger family (Lena; her son, Walter; Walter's wife, Ruth; Walter's son, Travis; and Walter's sister, Beneatha) suddenly have once-in-a-lifetime access to the fulfillment of their hopes—the ten thousand dollar life insurance check, the last contribution of Lena's dead husband.

Suddenly all of the Younger dreams, seldom voiced or even thought of, spring to life, nourished by the knowledge that within a few days the check will arrive. Lena (Mama) dreams of a house "in a nice neighborhood," Beneatha of medical school, and Walter of owning a liquor store which will make him rich. The immediate problem, of course, is that ten thousand dollars cannot buy that much—hence the surface conflict of the play:

WALTER   Who the hell told you you had to be a doctor? If you so crazy 'bout messing 'round with sick people—then go be a nurse like other women—or just get married and be quiet . . .

BENEATHA   Well—you finally got it said—It took you three years but you finally got it said. Walter, give up; leave me alone —it's Mama's money.

WALTER   He was my father, too!

BENEATHA   So what? He was mine, too—and Travis' grandfather—but the insurance money belongs to Mama. Picking on me is not going to make her give it to you to invest in any liquor stores—(Underbreath, dropping into a chair)—and I for one say, God bless Mama for that!

While there is far more awareness of the complex nature of human emotions in Miss Hansberry's play than in any of the work of Richard Wright, it is nonetheless somewhat astonishing to realize how little it would take for Walter Younger to become Bigger Thomas. His desperation virtually seethes out of himself ("Mama—Mama—I want so many things. . . . I want so many things that they are driving me kind of crazy . . . Mama—look at me"). Even Ruth, the faithful supporter of Walter's hopes, is too tired, tired of working for whites, tired of the pregnancy that she has not told Walter about, and, simply, tired of the "dream" ("Honey, you never say nothing new. I listen to you every day, every night and every morning, and you never say nothing new").

The check arrives: Lena deposits thirty-five hundred dollars toward a house in what she later learns is an all-white neighborhood; and she gives what remains of the ten thousand dollars to Walter to take to the bank, three thousand for Beneatha, and the rest for himself. And it appears that the ten thousand may yet buy a dream for everyone—until the family learns that the "friend" to whom Walter gave both his money and Beneatha's to "take care of" getting the liquor license has disappeared. From this low point the Younger family, through their united confrontation with the Clybourne Park "welcoming committee," struggle back to a sense of dignity by sharing what was originally Lena's dream, which has now come to belong to all of them:

RUTH   (Looking around and coming to life) *Well, for God's sake —if the moving men are here—LET'S GET THE HELL OUT OF HERE!*

MAMA   (Into action) *Ain't it the truth! Look at all this here mess. Ruth put Travis' good jacket on him . . . Walter Lee, fix your tie and tuck your shirt in, you look just like somebody's hoodlum. Lord have mercy, where is my plant?* (She flies to get it amid the general bustling of the family, who are deliberately trying to ignore the nobility of the past moment) *You all start on down . . . Travis child, don't go empty-handed . . . Ruth, where did I put that box with my skillets in it? I want to be in charge of it myself . . . I'm going to make us the biggest dinner we ever ate tonight . . . Beneatha, what's the matter with them stockings? Pull them things up, girl . . .*

It was through the dream of Miss Hansberry, shared by her friends, that her second, and last, play, *The Sign in Sidney Brus-*

tein's Window (1964) survived the damning assault of Broadway critics, some of whom claimed that its first performance was also its "final" one. It is difficult to separate the feeling for the play from the feeling for Miss Hansberry, who, during the tumultuous months that *Sidney Brustein* continued to live, was fighting against cancer for her own survival.

The simultaneous battles are described in Robert Nemiroff's fine essay, "The One Hundred and One 'Final' Performances of *Sidney Brustein*,"[71] in which Miss Hansberry's husband explains the efforts of friends and celebrities like James Baldwin, Sammy Davis, Shelley Winters, Sidney Kingsley, Ossie Davis, Ruby Dee, Lillian Hellman, Steve Allen, Kaye Ballard, Anne Bancroft, Marlon Brando, and many others, to keep *Sidney Brustein* (and, perhaps, even Lorraine Hansberry) alive. These people contributed money, and they pleaded with others to contribute and to see the play, because they believed in it and because they believed in its author. Both *Sidney Brustein* and Miss Hansberry, however, survived only a relatively short time:

At 8:50 on the morning of Tuesday, January 12, 1965, Lorraine Hansberry, aged thirty-four, died of cancer. That same night, in respect to her memory, Henry Miller's Theatre stayed dark. It did not reopen thereafter and "The Sign in Sidney Brustein's Window *went into the record books"—as the* Herald Tribune *reported it—"after an extraordinary run on Broadway of 101 performances."*

In many ways more dramatic than the play itself, Mr. Nemiroff's essay reveals a deeply human drama about people who still believe in the integrity of art, and, more important in this "existential" age of spiritual nihilism, about people who believe in the integrity and moral courage of other people.

VII.   1960 to the Present: Satire, the Past—and Themes of Armageddon

Black writing of the last decade reflects a widespread uncertainty about the direction and possibility for improvement of American race relations. On one hand, there were writers who were optimistic enough—if sometimes guardedly so—to produce more successful satire than had been produced before during a single decade. On the other hand, just as convincing, were those authors whose bleak assessment of the national social, economic, and political climate caused them to predict the outbreak of an inevitable race war. And between the two groups were several authors who chose not to treat the contemporary scene at all.

Satire in Drama and Fiction

The zeal of the Civil Rights movement of the early Sixties, coupled with the youthful "New Frontier" spirit of the Kennedy years, on which many whites and blacks placed their hopes for a "newer world," allowed several black authors the luxury of moving back slightly from their material (that is, from the events of the decade) and developing the objectivity from which can grow successful satire. The best satire of the period consists of one play, Ossie Davis's *Purlie Victorious* (1961), and three novels, Kristin Hunter's *The Landlord* (1966), Ishmael Reed's *The Free-Lance Pallbearers* (1967), and William Melvin Kelley's *Dem* (1967).

Ossie Davis

Ossie Davis (b. 1917), known to more people as an actor than as an author, was born in Cogdell, Georgia, and later attended both Howard University and Columbia. He first appeared on Broadway in 1946 in the production of *Jeb*, and, since that time, has starred in several other Broadway plays, notably *A Raisin in the Sun* and *Purlie Victorious*, his own play. In addition, Davis, the husband of actress Ruby Dee, has appeared frequently in television drama—one of his most memorable performances being in the award-winning "Teacher, Teacher"—and in movies, among them "The Joe Louis Story."

In *Purlie Victorious*,[72] Davis collects black and white stereotypes, old and new, stacks one atop the other, then rains them down upon his readers' or viewers' heads until everyone must confess the comic absurdity of racial prejudice in all of its forms. Davis even makes the characters' names absurd—for the blacks an amusing mixture of "down home" and symbolism: Purlie Victorious Judson, Lutiebelle Gussiemae Jenkins, Idella Landy, and Gitlow Judson; and, for the whites, the vaguely obscene Charlie and Ol' Cap'n (Stonewall Jackson) Cotchipee.

Ol' Cap'n is a South Georgia planter; Gitlow Judson is his self-effacing black sharecropper; and Purlie Victorious is a young black preacher who intends to trick Ol' Cap'n into giving him five hundred dollars which was the inheritance of "Aunt Henrietta," but which, because Henrietta is dead, Purlie feels is rightfully his. To carry out his plan, Purlie has brought to the plantation Lutiebelle Gussiemae to impersonate "Cousin Bee," Henrietta's daughter, and to request that Ol' Cap'n give her the inheritance.

In continuing the farce of black-white artifices, Davis includes the giving and receiving of racial "awards": Ol' Cap'n, as a reward for "good and faithful service," makes Gitlow "Deputy-For-The-Colored," which means, of course, absolutely nothing, except that Gitlow acts as living confirmation of the Cap'n's "race policies":

OL' CAP'N—*And he was telling me, the Senator was, how hard it was—impossible, he said, to find the old-fashioned, solid, hard-earned, Uncle Tom type Negra nowadays. I laughed in his face.*

GITLOW   *Yassuh. By the grace of God, there's still a few of us left.*

OL' CAP'N   *I told him how you and me growed up together. Had the same mammy—my mammy was your mother.*

GITLOW   *Yessir! Bosom buddies!*

OL' CAP'N   *And how you used to sing that favorite ol' speritual of mine:* (Sings.) *"I'm a-coming . . . I'm a-coming, For my head is bending low,"* (GITLOW *joins in on harmony.*) *"I hear the gentle voices calling, Ol' Black Joe . . . "* (This proves too much for *CHARLIE*; he starts out.) *Where you going?*

CHARLIE   *Maybe they need me in the front of the store.*

OL' CAP'N   *Come back here! (CHARLIE returns.) Turn around —show Gitlow that eye. (CHARLIE reluctantly exposes black* eye to view.)

GITLOW   Gret Gawdamighty, somebody done cold cocked this child! Who hit Mr. Charlie, tell Uncle Gitlow who hit you? (*CHARLIE* does not answer.)

OL' CAP'N   Would you believe it? All of a sudden he can't say a word. And just last night, the boys was telling me, this son of mine made hisself a full-fledged speech.

GITLOW   You don't say.

OL' CAP'N   All about Negras—NeGROES he called 'em—four years of college, and he still can't say the word right—seems he's quite a specialist on the subject.

GITLOW   Well, shut my hard-luck mouth!

OL' CAP'N   Yessireebob. Told the boys over at Ben's bar in town, that he was all for mixing the races together.

GITLOW   You go on 'way from hyeah!

OL' CAP'N   Said white children and dark children ought to go the same schoolhouse together!

GITLOW   Tell me the truth, Ol' Cap'n!

As part of the scheme for gaining the five hundred dollars, Purlie announces to the emotionally moved planter that he has just been named "Great White Father of the Year":

PURLIE   Therefore, as a humble token of their high esteem and their deep and abiding affection, especially for saving that five hundred dollar inheritance for Cousin Bee, they have asked me to present to you . . . this plaque! (PURLIE unveils a "sheepskin scroll" from his inside coat pocket. *OL'CAP'N* reaches for it, but *PURLIE* draws it away. *CHARLIE* appears in the doorway Upstage Center followed by *GITLOW.) Which bears the following citation to wit, and I quote: "Whereas Ol' Cap'n has kindly allowed us to remain on his land, and pick his cotton, and tend his cattle, and drive his mules, and whereas Ol' Cap'n still lets us have our hominy grits and fat back on credit and whereas Ol' Cap'n never resorts to bull whip except as a blessing and a bene-diction, therefore be it resolved, that Ol' Cap'n Cotchipee be cited as the best friend the Negro has ever had, and officially proclaimed Great White Father of the Year!"*

OL' CAP'N (Stunned.) *I can't believe it—I can't believe it!* (Sees *CHARLIE.) Charlie, boy—did you hear it? Did you hear it, Charlie, my boy—GREAT WHITE FATHER OF THE YEAR!*

Shortly afterward, as the play ends, Ol' Cap'n becomes rigid with shock when he learns that his own son, Charlie, has helped Purlie Victorious buy the building (to be used for a civil-rights church) for which use Purlie had intended the five hundred dollars. And Gitlow exclaims, "The first man I ever seen in all this world to drop dead standing up!"

Kristin Hunter

The second important satirist of the Sixties was Kristin Hunter (b. 1931), author of two novels, *God Bless the Child* (1964) and *The Landlord* (1966). Mrs. Hunter was born in Philadelphia, received a B.S. in Ed. from the University of Pennsylvania in 1951, and, like both of her parents, became a teacher. She later joined the staff of the Pittsburgh *Courier*. In 1956 she received the Fund for the Republic Award for her CBS television documentary,

"Minority of One"; and in 1959 she received a John Hay Whitney Fellowship.

The Landlord is the very funny account of Elgar Enders' "search for love." Elgar is thirty years old, has a father worth millions, and wants to be—does he *ever* want to be—loved. And so, with several thousands of his virtually unlimited dollars, he buys a piece of rental property in an all-black neighborhood, moves into one of the apartments himself, and settles back to wait for his tenants to begin loving him. Elgar soon learns, however, that he has what must be the most bizarre collection of tenants that any "landlord" ever had to deal with.

First, there is Copee, who, though black, thinks that he is an Indian. Copee spends most of his time haranguing the white man who stole his land and hurling his spear at passersby, and at Elgar. Then there is Copee's sensual wife, Fanny, whose means of livelihood is a never-ending series of lawsuits—against a hairdresser who "ruined" her hair (though Fanny ruined it herself); against a storeowner in whose store she fell (though, of course, she fell purposely), and so on. And there is Marge, a former blues singer, now a self-styled neighborhood philosopher; and DuBois, the homosexual "professor" who operates his own decidedly unaccredited "college" ("We're having a special on degrees this week. . . . Get your B.A. and your M.A. at the same time. Only forty-nine ninety-five for both").

Mrs. Hunter's satire gently touches most of the urban "race types," the black deluded by his sense of martyrdom (Copee), the devoted and suffering super-liberal (Elgar), the black who has risen above the "pettiness" of racial conflict (DuBois). And she moves on to other "types" as well, especially the urban bureaucrat, in the humorously drawn character of the urban-renewal expert, Phosdicker, who holds a public meeting to explain why all of the homes in the neighborhood are soon to be destroyed:

Striving considerately to keep his syllable count well down, Phosdicker launched into his Law of Irreversible Tendencies, a formula for determining whether a case of neighborhood blight was curable or terminal. His accents were grave, but the dear old man could not keep an eager twinkle out of his eye; it was his theory, his pet, and he loved it dearly. Elgar understood, and pardoned him.

There were, it seemed, certain symptoms which infallibly made for a grave diagnosis, including unlidded trashcans, broken windows, abandoned cars, and ailanthus trees. The latter were particularly crucial; the Authorities had found, Phosdicker declared sadly, that no neighborhood could be saved once it had exceeded the fatal ratio of one ailanthus tree per dwelling unit.

Poplar Street, it seemed, suffered from a plague of three ailanthus trees per each of its dwelling units. Elgar stared, aghast, as Phosdicker, with the kindly manner of a good gray doctor reluctantly showing his patient a hopeless X-ray, displayed a photograph of the ominous sproutings in Elgar's side alley. . . .

"In summary . . . " Phosdicker was hurrying to wind up his speech, as if he feared further interruptions. "To restore a sick neighborhood to health, we must give it an economic transfusion. And how do we propose to do this for Poplar Street, my friends?" Phosdicker, beaming (he really was a good man, you felt it; he really believed in the good he was doing), answered his own question. "By making it a place where prosperous people, successful people, self-respecting people, property-maintaining *people will want to live."*

Mrs. Hunter's book, later adapted into a motion picture, is beautifully written. Her respect for language and her keen ear for understated tongue-in-cheek humor make *The Landlord* an important work. As the novel ends, all is resolved: Copee is institutionalized; Marge is married; Fanny becomes a prosperous hair-

dresser; DuBois now administers a legitimate college; and Elgar—
well, Elgar is loved.

Ishmael Reed

Undoubtedly among the most ludicrously and humorously
bombastic pieces of satire written by an American author this century are Ishmael Reed's two novels, *The Free-Lance Pallbearers*
(1967) and *Yellow Back Radio Broke-Down* (1969). Ishmael Reed
(b. 1938) was born in Chattanooga, Tennessee, and later attended
the University of Buffalo. His poems have been anthologized in
Poets of Today, The Poetry of the Negro, and *Dices or Black Bones:*
Black Voices of the Seventies; and he has published one collection
of poetry, *Catechism of D Neo-American Hoodoo Church* (1970).
He has served as guest lecturer at the University of California at
Berkeley and at the University of Washington at Seattle.

Described as everything from brilliant to silly, Reed's satire,
for all of its chaos, *does* work. His satiric poetry, too, once one
understands Reed's bizarre style, has meaning. In his poem, "I Am
a Cowboy in the Boat of Ra," Reed smashes together many of the
same elements that are found throughout his second novel, *Yellow*
Back Radio Broke-Down, especially hoodoo worship and the
assault on the Old West's "man's man" heroism. The poem ends:

Be a good girl and
Bring me my Buffalo horn of black powder
Bring me my headdress of black feathers
Bring me my bones of Ju-Ju snake
Go get my eyelids of red paint.
Hand me my shadow

I'm going into town after Set

I am a cowboy in the boat of RA

look out Set   here i come Set
to get Set   to sunset Set
to unseat Set   to Set down Set

    usurper of the Royal couch
    imposter RAdio of Moses' bush
    party pooper O hater of dance
    vampire outlaw of the milky way[73]

In the novel, too, set in the western town of Yellow Back Radio and peopled with such characters as the black cowboy hero, the Loup Garou Kid, as well as with child-murdering parents and nineteenth-century Indians flying helicopters, Reed very cleverly makes his marks. He pummels the "frontier" myth, the capitalist ethic, and people who would rather see the death of their children than the death of their outworn values. It is fantastic, and at times a bit obscene, but it is effective satire.

It is with his first novel, *The Free-Lance Pallbearers*, however, that Reed scores his greatest writing triumph. In this work he takes on an entire nation, its foibles, its indiscretions, its stupidities —and all in slightly more than one hundred pages. The novel opens:

I live in HARRY SAM. HARRY SAM is something else. A big not-to-be-believed out-of-sight, sometimes referred to as O-BOP-SHE-BANG or KLANG-A-LANG-A-DING-DONG. SAM has not been seen since the day thirty years ago when he disappeared into the John with a weird ravaging illness.

The John is located within an immense motel which stands on Sam's Island just off HARRY SAM.

A self-made Pole and former used-car salesman, SAM's father was busted for injecting hypos into the underbellies of bantam roosters. The ol man rigged many an underground cockfight.

SAM's mother was a low-down, filthy hobo infected with hoof-and-mouth disease. A five-o'clock-shadowed junkie who died of diphtheria and an overdose of phenobarb. Laid out dead in an abandoned alley in thirty-degree-below snow. An evil lean snake with blue, blue lips and white tonsils. Dead as a doornail she died, mean and hard; cussing out her connection until the last yellow flame wisped from her wretched mouth.

But SAM's mother taught him everything he knows.

"Looka heah, SAM," his mother said before they lifted her into the basket and pulled the sheet over her empty pupils. "It's a cruel cruel world and you gots to be swift. Your father is a big fat stupid kabalsa who is doin' one to five in Sing Sing for foolin' around with them blasted chickens. That is definitely not what's happening. If it hadn't been for those little pills, I would have gone out of my rat mind a long time ago. I have paid a lot of dues, son, and now I'm gonna pop off. But before I croak, I want to give you a little advice.

"Always be at the top of the heap. If you can't whup um with your fists, keek um. If you can't keek um, butt um. If you can't butt um, bite um and if you can't bite um, then gum the mothafukas to death. And one more thing, son," this purple-tongued gypsy said, taking a last swig of sterno and wiping her lips with a ragged sleeve. "Think twice before you speak 'cause the graveyard is full of peoples what talks too much."

In this highly condensed collage of allusions, Reed creates the setting for a very funny exposé of the social madness which the author sees as contemporary American culture. The name of the kingdom, for example, is "HARRY SAM," common, "everyday," unpretentious, American (Uncle Sam), described in the nonsense "rock-and-roll" idiom ("O-BOP-SHE-BANG") which, during the Fifties, sent millions of young people mad and dozens of untalented musicians to Millionaire's Row. In these first few paragraphs, as throughout the novel, repeated references are made to institutions and expressions which are peculiarly American: institutions like the "immense motel," the "self-made Pole," the "used-car salesman," the neon signs proclaiming "EATS EATS EATS" and "SAVE GREEN STAMPS"; and expressions like "out-of-sight," "john," "busted," "low-down," "dead as a doornail," and "croak."

And the stock American characters are all here, too: the protagonist, Bukka Doopeyduk, the "Uncle Tom" black; U2 Polyglot, dean at Harry Sam College who is preparing a scholarly paper titled "The Egyptian Dung Beetle in Kafka's 'Metamorphosis' "; the black nationalist, Elijah Raven ("But Elijah!" I persisted. "It was only a few weeks ago that you were saying familiar things like 'Hello' or 'Hya doin' or 'What's happening, my man.' Sometimes even slapping the palm of your hand into mine."); Eclair Porkchop, the well-fed black preacher-leader; M/Neighbor and F/Neighbor, the anonymous inhabitants of the Harry Sam Housing Projects; and Fannie Mae, Bukka Doopeyduk's sweet and simple wife.

Reed's satire is well balanced; it assaults the follies of both the white and the black communities. Indeed, his purpose is to reveal that there are no heroes, not in the Old West, not in the kingdom's capital, not in the black ghetto. There are simply people who accept ridiculous myths more readily than they should; who, when put to the test of serving people or self, invariably choose the latter; who, in their grotesque beliefs, can be very, very funny (Bukka Doopeyduk's pride in his golden bedpan is not, in fact, so unusual). And it is here that Reed, in some ways, surpasses most other current "absurdist" writers (whether Theatre-of-the-Absurd playwrights like Ionesco, Albee, or Beckett; or contemporary comic novelists like Mailer, Salinger, or Heller). For once accepting the absurdity of human existence, especially *American* human existence, rather than continuing *ad infinitum* "to expose" that absurdity to those of lesser vision, he *uses* it (to teach? perhaps somewhat) but mainly to amuse, to entertain—and entertain he does.

William Melvin Kelley

The last important black satirist of the Sixties, William Melvin Kelley (b. 1937), was born in New York City and attended Harvard University, where he studied under Archibald MacLeish and John Hawkes. He has taught at the New School for Social Research and has been writer-in-residence at the State University of New York, College at Geneseo. He has received a John Hay Whitney Foundation award, as well as an award from the Rosenthal Foundation of the National Institute of Arts and Letters for his first novel, *A Different Drummer* (1962). In addition to publishing his stories and essays in *Negro Digest, Saturday Evening Post*, and *Esquire*, Kelley has published four more full-length works of fiction: a collection of short stories, *Dancers on the Shore* (1964), and three novels, *A Drop of Patience* (1965), his satire *Dem* (1967), and *Dunfords Travels Everywhere* (1970).

Kelley's best work is his captivating first novel, *A Different Drummer*. (The title comes from Thoreau: "If a man does not keep pace with his companions, perhaps it is because he hears a different drummer. Let him step to the music which he hears, however measured or far away.") The setting of the novel is a fictional Deep South state about which "The Thumb-Nail Almanac" says: "In June 1957, for reasons yet to be determined, all the state's Negro inhabitants departed. Today, it is unique in being the only state in the Union that cannot count even one member of the Negro race among its citizens."

The novel focuses on Tucker Caliban, a small, quiet black farmer, who, unknown to anyone, hears the "different drummer" of his regal African ancestry. One day Tucker orders a truckload of salt delivered to his farm. He spreads the salt over his fields, killing their fertility; burns down his home; shoots his farm animals; and with only his wife, their baby, and a large carpetbag, sets off on foot for the bus stop in the small town of Sutton, where he boards a bus and leaves the state forever. Kelley spends the remainder of the novel exploring the cultural reasons for the mass exodus; for within days, as if guided by the same "drummer" as Tucker, all of the black inhabitants of the state are gone. Only old Mister Harper, the white village patriarch, understands what the black migration means, the black hope for a better life and the white despair which follows with its residual cruelty:

"Boy! Look at this car!" The old man swiveled and shouted at him. "Study it!"

Dewey turned and watched the car. There was a fat Negro driving. His wife sat peacefully beside him, her eyes awake and bright. In her arms was a small child, a girl with many tiny parts in her hair; she was sleeping. The back seat was piled high with luggage.

"Yes, I feel sorry for my men. They ain't got what those colored folks have."

As the novel closes, Bradshaw, the prosperous northern black civil rights leader, who is as bewildered by the exodus as the southern whites, passes through the town in his limousine for one last look and is captured by the bewildered and offended whites lingering there. One of the throng, Bobby-Joe, reminds the others, "You fellows know this is our last nigger: Just think on that. Our last nigger, ever." And, with that, Bradshaw is humiliated, tortured, and finally murdered in a white folk rite as old as the American South itself. But, as Kelley makes clear, it is the *last time*.

Dem, a satire on "dem white folks," is artistically less successful than *A Different Drummer* largely because Kelley seems too close to his subject, too intense about it. It is, nonetheless, a worthwhile novel which represents a kind of satire different from that of either Kristin Hunter or Ishmael Reed. Set in New York City, *Dem* explores the improbable subject of superfecundation, "the fertilization of two ova within a short period of time by spermatozoa from separate copulations." One ovum of the white Mrs. Mitchell Pierce is fertilized by Mr. Pierce, the other by Mrs. Pierce's black lover— the result, twins, one white, one black.

Kelley's attack (and it is clearly more an attack than the other works of satire discussed) is aimed at upper-middle-class white America, which Kelley portrays as not simply in pursuit of sick values and status gimmicks, but, in addition, both stupid and mindlessly cruel. Early in the novel, Mitchell and Tam Pierce pay a Sunday afternoon social call on John Godwin, one of Mitchell's junior-executive colleagues. When they arrive, they find Godwin, in business suit and white work gloves, mowing the lawn, while next door there is a lawn party ("Several people sat in steel chairs, around a white steel table. There was a bottle, square and half-empty, and several bowls of potato chips in its center. The people drank and stared at each other"). Here, as throughout the novel, Kelley pictures this world as full of sterile whiteness (white gloves, white table and chairs, white appliances) and cold steel. And, a few minutes later, Mitchell, upstairs in Godwin's house, looking for the bathroom, finds Godwin's family:

All the doors on the second floor were closed. He had opened a closet, and a child's room, when he found Godwin's family—his wife, whose name, he remembered now, was Cindy, and two children—on the bed in what must have been the master bedroom. The room was neat, the bed under them made, the closet doors closed, the cushions on a small love seat rounded, dent-free. Cindy lay on her back, an attractive woman, short, blond, nicely built, her purple skirt bunched around plump thighs, flowered underpants looping one ankle, her eyes and mouth open. The children, a boy in a blue bathrobe and a little girl with pigtails, one tied with red, the other white ribbon, had been placed so that they seemed to be nestling, asleep, against their mother. Godwin had even wrapped Cindy's arms around them.

At first, Mitchell watched them from the door, but strangely excited and wanting to see more, he crept closer to the bed. Cindy's neck had been broken, he was sure. The children had probably been strangled; dark blue marks ringed their necks.

And here Kelley comes down hard on his target. Godwin's society, and Mitchell's, is viciously parasitic; it feeds both upon itself and upon other societies—hence Godwin's Marine training ("I know seventy different ways to kill with my bare hands"). But this same society, in addition to being sterile and cruel, is at the same time immature, almost childlike, as well. For, following Tam's amazing delivery, Mitchell sets off on a ludicrous search through Harlem for the father of the black twin, Tam's lover, and, unsuccessful, suffers his final humiliation at the close of the novel. Here, in spite of his efforts to conceal the fact that his wife has given birth to twins, he is asked by the black doorman of his apartment building about the condition of *both* babies. With this, Mitchell resigns himself to his own impotence in the face of the collective knowledge and virility of the black community which seems to be conspiring to ruin his empty life. And, in a final emasculating act, Kelley ends his novel by sending Mitchell Pierce to the fetal security of his bathtub, where "he sank down deep into the hot water, and, on his side, his eyes closed and his hands clamped between his thighs, he filled the darkness with fantasies."

Return to the Twenties and Thirties

The second important movement in black literature in the Sixties was a reassessment of the past of the American Twenties and Thirties. Using the advantage of several-decades' distance, four novelists interpreted the black cultural experiences of these turbulent decades, and three of them have made important new contributions to the understanding of that earlier time. Gordon Parks (*The Learning Tree*, 1963), while saying little that is new, has written a useful novel about rural Kansas. Hal Bennett's portrait of rural Virginia (*A Wilderness of Vines*, 1966), Sarah E. Wright's view of Maryland's Eastern shore (*This Child's Gonna Live*, 1969), and Robert Deane Pharr's study of southern urban black sporting life (*The Book of Numbers*, 1969) are very good novels, the last two of which are especially outstanding.

Sarah E. Wright

Born in Maryland in 1929, educated at Howard University and Cheyenne State Teachers College, Wyoming, Sarah E. Wright has written a beautifully painful novel. The beauty of *This Child's Gonna Live* is found in the careful use of diction and the deep understanding of a dialect humor which can sustain when there is little else available. In fact, Miss Wright's precise rendering of dialect approaches the quality of Zora Hurston's, and her treatment of folk humor equals Miss Hurston's. The pain is found in the unnecessarily brutal suffering of the children of Mariah Upshur, the protagonist. There is, of course, nothing new in the portrayal of human misery in a piece of literature written by a black author; indeed, much black writing is little else. What makes the agony of this novel so immediate to the reader is the fact that, like Lutie Johnson in *The Street*, absolutely everything that Mariah can do to prevent the suffering of her children is, quite simply, not nearly enough.

Mariah is a resident of rural Tangierneck in Maryland, the wife of the simple Jacob ("How come you always harping on death? You need to pray, Mariah. Have a good talk with God"), and the mother of three children—with another expected—nicknamed Skeeter, Rabbit, and Gezee. Mariah is confronted with successive rounds of pneumonia and worms in her children, the disrespect of Miss Bannie and the other whites who own "the neck," and, worst of all, the scorn of the destitute but viciously self-righteous blacks who can punish "sin" in ways to be envied even by southern whites. Mariah, in fact, even as an adult, has nightmares about the beatings which she received from her parents as a child:

Mariah heavy with a sleep that wouldn't let her go. Mariah groaning in her sleep from the beating. A switch can draw blood, but getting beat up with a stovelid lifter can make a person cry for her own death. Those things are made of iron. A beating on your back and legs with one will make a person's soul cave in.

Mariah's dream (similar to Lutie Johnson's) is to get her children off "this goddamn neck," and, to that end, she saves dimes, quarters, whatever, so that someday. . . . Miss Wright's blending of humorous dialect expressions, especially Mariah's, into day-to-day conversations, in addition to revealing the kind of affirmation that makes survival essential, provides the reader with a necessary periodic relief from the intensity of suffering. For Mariah's children, life *is* better than death, even the "Beetlecreek" kind of living-death which virtually the entire population of Tangierneck, black and white, views as living. And because Mariah senses that it is so, she is determined that her three children, as well as the one unborn, are "gonna live."

The combining of humor and seriousness is found repeatedly in the novel. One of the best examples comes shortly after the birth of the baby in a mock confrontation between Mariah and her sons:

And Mariah took herself a good look at those boys, trying to bully her about those icicles. Said to them, "If you all don't get your asses down that road and get my word to Pop Clem you ain't gonna get nothing in your stockings for Christmas but ashes! We ain't got no kinda money that'll pay Santa Claus to bring you nothing like you wants nohow. I was gonna try to bargain with him a little bit today. Don't think I'm gonna go neither step now, 'cause you all ain't been nothing but bad all year. Ain't going nowhere, you hear me?"

Rabbit let go of the icicle he was holding behind his back and tried to throw it in a quick curvy way so it would land out of her sight, but it landed right by her feet.

Mariah got such a hunch to laugh. Quick as she got it, she got another one to cry. Rabbit was just a-shivering and shaking so, and Skeeter's face was all screwed up worse than Chicken Little's when the sky was falling down. Her boys wasn't nothing but some kind of little no way. And she did think maybe Santa Claus ought to do something special for them though they had been right considerable bad. But good a whole lot of times, too! Jesus, Jesus, ain't nothing fitting enough I can do for them. I ain't even fitting for them! Such a sickness in my soul!

"Mamma, I ain't knowed icicles was bad for you," Skeeter squeaked.

"Me neither, Mamma." Rabbit like to have shook his own head off.

And, a few minutes later, when the boys are alone:

Skeeter saying, "Shit, man, you ain't had to throw away all of them icicles. You know Mamma ain't gonna chop off nobody's hands. She's too weak to even chop up that wood. ... ."

And Rabbit saying, "You better stop that cussing boy! Santa Claus can hear every word you say."

And Skeeter getting back at Rabbit, "You cusses all the time, bugger. Ain't no need of stopping now just 'cause you wants Santa Claus to bring you a train.

And Rabbit kicking up some sand, saying, "Yes, Santa Claus is gonna bring me a train, 'cause I stopped cussing last week. And I said my prayers. And he's gonna bring me that train so I can take Mamma out of this place and she won't even have to talk to that death man no more!"

Mariah's moments of personal affirmation, however, are few; and her lowest point, her greatest defeat, comes when she is summoned home from her work in the oyster house by the woman who looks after the children (" . . . your Rabbit, I really do think he got the TB bad, or the worms. Worm crawled right out of his behind this morning"). Rabbit dies, and Mariah once again reassesses her commitment to life and its endless succession of agonies. But finally, consistent with the completely believable courage upon which her life is based, she decides once again at the close of the novel that "this child"—Skeeter, Gezee, the baby, even Mariah herself—"this child's gonna live."

Robert Deane Pharr

Also exploring the South of the Thirties was Robert Deane Pharr (b. 1916), born in Richmond, Virginia, reared in New Haven, Connecticut, graduated from Virginia Union University, and currently a resident of New York City. Pharr has said about his fine first novel, *The Book of Numbers* (1969): "I resolved to write a novel where Negroes did not say the things white people expected them to say. They would not be having interracial affairs as expected. Nor would they all be downtrodden. They would live, laugh, and drink as they always do in real life."

With that mandate Pharr has written the best novel of black urban "sporting life" in black American literature—it surpasses even McKay's famous *Home to Harlem*. Several features make the novel distinctive in subject and design. In subject: Its setting is the black ward of an unnamed southern city; white characters are mentioned on only three pages of the more than four hundred of the novel; the central characters are blacks who own a "numbers bank" in the ward and who accumulate well over a million dollars.

In design: The entire work is built upon motifs having to do with "numbers." The novel begins and ends with Biblically ("Book of Numbers") prophetic statements. It opens, "In the beginning there was only Dave and Blueboy." And it closes, "The gods, in their mercy, refused to let Lila dream of what had already been decreed. . . . it was best for her not to know that most things do not last always, and that only the things of black granite—like Delilah's own spirit, like the Numbers, and like the Niggers—are forever."

The number motif is also found in the repeated references to the pads, or "numbers books," of the numbers runners in the story. And, last, one of the unifying devices of the plot structure is the regular insertion, in seemingly unrelated material, of brief references to the enterprise which is, in fact, the source of the hopes, the disappointments, even the lives of the characters. For example, Chapter 11 closes: "The sunlight made a pretty red glow in the whiskey bottle on the table. That was the day that 582 came out. . . ." And Chapter 16: "He stomped out of the kitchen, and a few moments later the three young people heard him go up the stairs, whistling a happy tune. The number that day had been 054. More than twenty people hit it." And Chapter 19: "Blueboy put his arm around Dave and said, 'Colonel says he wants to talk with you over the Lil Savoy as soon's you get a chance. He says he's gonna explain it to you.' The number that day was 505, and Dave and Blueboy had to pay out over two thousand dollars in hits."

Pharr has created a fascinating study of the effects upon people of the possession of vast wealth, the attainment of deep friendship, and the certainty of being loved. He goes much further, though, as he explores the effect of new hope in people who have forgotten that luxury. These are the many "little" people in the ward who, by placing their daily ten-cent or twenty-five-cent number wager with a chance to win more than a hundred dollars, become, briefly and in a small way, a part of the economic mainstream of a society which, both politically and financially, depends for its own health upon the "numbers."

Themes of Armageddon

Several black writers who, during the mid and late Sixties explored contemporary American culture to determine exactly what it offered, and what it might be offering, its black citizens, expressed the disillusionment felt by many others who saw that the slow wheels of government machinery and national conscience seemed to obscure what little gains had been forthcoming from the civil rights efforts early in the decade. The Watts race riot in August, 1965,[74] and the subsequent racial uprisings in Detroit and Newark, confirmed in the minds of many the notion that "the fire next time" was inevitable. Out of that notion there grew the "Armageddon" themes of such poets as Don L. Lee (*Don't Cry! Scream*, 1969), Sonia Sanchez (*We A Badddd People*, 1970), and, most important, Imamu Amiri Baraka (LeRoi Jones) and Nikki Giovanni; and of such writers of fiction as John A. Williams (*The Man Who Cried I Am*, 1967, and *Sons of Darkness, Sons of Light*, 1969) and Sam Greenlee (*The Spook Who Sat by the Door*, 1969).

Etheridge Knight

Not in the mainstream of the "Armageddon" movement, though clearly a spokesman for the dispossessed blacks who would have the most to gain from such an upheaval, is Etheridge Knight (b. 1931), born in Corinth, Mississippi. Knight was educated for two years in public high school and for eight years in public penitentiaries, six of those years in the Indiana State Prison, for robbery.

Before prison, Knight served in the U.S. Army in Korea and worked in a factory in Indianapolis. During and since prison, he has published poems and short stories in *Negro Digest, Jaguar,* and *Music Journal.* He has published two complete works, his collection of verse, *Poems from Prison* (1968), with a preface by Gwendolyn Brooks, and *Black Voices from Prison* (1970), which contains, in addition to his own essays and poems, essays and a one-act play written by fellow inmates at the Indiana State Prison. Knight was paroled in 1968, and he is now a member of the black studies faculty at the University of Pittsburgh, where he is writing an historical novel based upon the life of Denmark Vesey.

Knight says of his life: "I died in Korea from a shrapnel wound and narcotics resurrected me. I died in 1960 from a prison sentence and poetry brought me back to life." Much of Knight's concern, as revealed in his poetry, is about the injustice accorded black Americans, and most of his immediate concern is about the absolutely disastrous effects of prison confinement and brutality upon human beings. But underlying a great part of his work (and a quality that places him artistically above most contemporary black poets) is the broader exploration of a variety of human relationships—black and black, black and white—in an effort to understand the complexity of the effects that people have upon one another, socially, psychologically, philosophically.

By combining variations of internal rhyme with bits of prison and "street" diction and a genuine desire to *feel*, Knight writes some good poetry. An example is "A WASP Woman Visits a Black Junkie in Prison":

After explanations and regulations, he
Walked warily in.
Black hair covered his chin, subscribing to
Villainous ideal.
"This can not be real," he thought, "this is a
Classical mistake;

This is a cake baked with embarrassing icing;
Somebody's got,
Likely as not, a big fat tongue in cheek!
What have I to do
With a prim blue and proper-blooded lady?
Christ in deed has risen
When a Junkie in prison visits with a Wasp woman.

"Hold your stupid face, man,
Learn a little grace, man; drop a notch the sacred shield.
She might have good reason,
Like: 'I was in prison and ye visited me not,'—or
     some such.
So sweep clear
Anachronistic fear, fight the fog,
And use no hot words."
After the seating
And the greeting, they fished for a denominator,
Common or uncommon;
And could only summon up the fact that both were
     human.

"Be at ease, man!
Try to please, man!—the lady is as lost as you:
'You got children, Ma'am?' " he said aloud
The thrust broke the damn, and their lines wiggled in
     the water.
She offered no pills
To cure his many ills, no compact sermons, but small
And funny talk:
"My baby began to walk . . . simply cannot keep his
     room clean . . . "
Her chatter sparked no resurrection and truly
No shackles were shaken

But after she had taken her leave, he walked softly,
And for hours used no hot words.[75]

Imamu Amiri Baraka (LeRoi Jones)

There were other fine poets starting in the Sixties, of course: A. B. Spellman (*The Beautiful Days*, 1965), Dudley Randall (*Cities Burning*, 1968), Mari Evans (*Where Is All the Music?* 1968), and Sarah Webster Fabio (*A Mirror: A Soul*, 1969). But clearly the most gifted poet—and a fine dramatist and writer of fiction as well—was Imamu Amiri Baraka (LeRoi Jones).

Baraka was born in 1934 in Newark, New Jersey, and at age nineteen graduated from Howard University. After serving four years in the Air Force, he did graduate work and taught at the New School for Social Research and at Columbia University. Baraka has published in dozens of anthologies and magazines, including *Poetry, Saturday Review*, and *The Nation*; and he has been awarded both John Hay Whitney and Guggenheim fellowships. In 1958 he founded the short-lived magazine *Yugen*, and in 1964 he organized the Black Arts Theatre in Harlem. He adopted his Muslim name in 1968.

In addition to editing, with Larry Neal, an anthology of black writing, *Black Fire* (1968), Baraka has published more than a dozen major works, among them his well-known collections of poetry, *Preface to a Twenty Volume Suicide Note* (1961), *The Dead Lecturer* (1964), *Black Magic Poetry* (1969), and *It's Nation Time* (1970). Much of Baraka's poetry explores themes of lost hope, of empty dreams. Perhaps the most moving is the title poem to his first volume which treats the innocent faith of a child, a faith which the child herself will soon realize is supported only by the emptiness contained in "her own clasped hands":

Lately, I've become accustomed to the way
The ground opens up and envelops me

Each time I go out to walk the dog.
Or the broad-edged silly music the wind
Makes when I run for a bus . . .

Things have come to that.

And now, each night I count the stars,
And each night I get the same number,
And when they will not come to be counted,
I count the holes they leave.

Nobody sings anymore.

And then last night, I tiptoed up
To my daughter's room and heard her
Talking to someone, and when I opened
The door, there was no one there . . .
Only she on her knees, peeking into

Her own clasped hands.[76]

Couched in Baraka's often fragmented syntax and startling imagery are many of the questions which have always been posed by serious writers: questions of why man exists at all, why he must fail so abysmally in defining his own purpose in existing, and what difference it would make to anyone, including himself, if he did not continue to exist. Such questions, and their answers, make inappropriate the "strictly race diatribe" label with which some critics have sought to damn Baraka's work.

Baraka has published several collections of essays, notably *Blues People* (1963), "the first real attempt to place jazz and the blues within the context of American social history"; *Home* (1966), a collection of social and political ideas which Baraka developed between 1960 and 1965; and *Black Music* (1967), a study of outstanding contemporary musicians. He has also produced and published some twenty plays, among them a fine one, *Dutchman* (1964); a very good one, a television play, "The Death of Malcolm X" (1969); and the popular and shocking collection, *Four Black Revolutionary Plays* (1969).

Winner of the Obie Award for the best off-Broadway play of 1964, *Dutchman* treats the white American ritual of death reserved for blacks. Lula, white and seductive, boards the subway and sits next to Clay, black and middle-class. After a period of temptation, in which Lula sensuously brushes Clay's leg and promises sex at her apartment, Lula begins, through a series of progressively more insulting remarks, to strip away Clay's sophisticated veneer.

The first assault comes when, after a period of sexy word play, Lula startles Clay by suddenly saying, "I bet you never once thought you were a black nigger." As Clay pretends to be unaffected by the remark, Lula continues to goad him to the level of fury which will justify her climactic act: "Do the gritty grind, like your ol' rag-head mammy"; and "Clay, you liver-lipped white man"; and "Uncle Tom Big Lip." With that, Clay responds—as indeed, she has planned for him to respond:

And you tell this to your father, who's probably the kind of man who needs to know at once. So he can plan ahead. Tell him not to preach so much rationalism and cold logic to these niggers. Let them alone. Let them sing curses at you in code and see your filth as simple lack of style. Don't make the mistake, through some irresponsible surge of Christian charity, of talking too much about the advantages of Western rationalism, or the great intellectual legacy of the white man, or maybe they'll begin to listen. And then, maybe one day, you'll find they actually do understand exactly what you are talking about, all these fantasy people. All these blues people. And on that day, as sure as shit, when you really believe you can "accept" them into your fold, as half-white trusties late of the subject peoples. With no more blues, except the very old ones, and not a watermelon in sight, the great missionary heart will have triumphed, and all of those ex-coons will be stand-up Western men, with eyes for clean hard useful lives, sober, pious and sane, and they'll murder you. They'll murder you, and have very rational explanations. Very much like your own. They'll cut your throats, and drag you out to the edge of your cities so the flesh can fall away from your bones, in sanitary isolation.

And with Clay's exploding centuries of pent-up black wrath, with his becoming, for all on the subway to see, the wild, the dangerous, black man, Lula has confirmed her own diseased preconceptions, and, with the silent approval of the other passengers, she stabs Clay to death—as she has planned to do from the start.

In sharp contrast to the bitter but controlled quality of *Dutchman* is the senselessly shrill quality of Baraka's play—produced the same year—*The Slave*, one of the most hysterical of the "Armageddon" works of the Sixties. The protagonist, Walker Vessels, while leading the black revolution which has the city under siege, comes to the home of his white ex-wife and her white professor husband, whom Walker absurdly abuses and finally murders. Unknown to his ex-wife, he has already murdered his own two children in their bedrooms upstairs. Typical of the shrieking quality of the play is the following speech, delivered by Walker as explosions of the revolution rumble in the background: "Don't, goddamnit, don't tell me about any goddam killing of anything. If that's what's happening. I mean if this shitty town is being flattened . . . let it. It needs it."

In the drama of Imamu Baraka is seen the dilemma faced by most contemporary black writers who have been seriously a part of the converging radical ideologies of the 1960s: Is it better to risk losing control as a serious artist by seizing the current opportunity to use one's work as a medium for shouting ugly, and usually deserved, rhetoric at white America? Or is it better to maintain control of one's work, as an artist is compelled to do, and thereby receive approval at the hands of literary critics but scorn from the militants of one's race? Baraka, it seems, has done both.

It is interesting to observe, incidentally, that black drama, which received little support from white middle-class theatre-goers prior to 1959, became one of the most popular forms of black expression in the Sixties. This near-phenomenon can be explained, in part, by recognizing the impact on many white Americans of the civil rights movement of the early Sixties, with its side effects of growing "conscience" and guilt.

There seems to have developed a strain of "white liberal masochism," especially among the young white college and professional classes, a psychological exercise which has apparently grown out of a white caste guilt about the historic and current mistreatment of American blacks. This guilt has been satiated, in part at least, by exposure to the hatred found in contemporary black literary forms, especially the drama. What seems to have begun with the reading and viewing of black literature as an obligation owed the black race, gradually, as the 1960s progressed, evolved into part of the anti-middle-class-white ritual which has occupied the minds and actions of so many whites in the last five years. This ritual has become for many of its participants more than simply a rejection of their inherited value systems; it is often virtually a rejection of themselves.

And from the black community, reinforcing the new self-rejection of many whites, came the "Black Is Beautiful" cultural movement of the decade, with its submovement of the late Sixties, "*Only* Black Is Beautiful." Capitalizing on these moods, in addition to Imamu Baraka, were such dramatists as Ed Bullins (*Clara's Ole Man*, 1965, *Goin' a' Buffalo*, 1968, and *The Electronic Nigger*, 1968), Douglas Turner Ward (*Happy Ending*, 1965, and *Day of*

Absence, 1965), Jimmy Garrett (*We Own the Night*, 1967), Sonia Sanchez (*Sister Son/ji*, 1969), and Nettie McCray (*Growin' into Blackness*, 1969).

Imamu Baraka's last area of accomplishment, one too often overlooked, is his production of very good fiction, especially his novel, *The System of Dante's Hell* (1965), and his collection of stories and sketches, *Tales* (1967). Baraka's fiction is not easy to read, hence its lack of popularity; but it is worth the effort. *The System of Dante's Hell*, often dismissed as a chaotic, fragmented jumble, is, in fact, a carefully structured portrayal of a chaotic, fragmented mind at work. The reader is tempted to spend too much effort trying to match Baraka's "circles" of hell with Dante's— invariably without corresponding success, for Dante's hell is neatly categorized and distant, while Baraka's hell is immediate, because, as he says at the close of the novel, "Hell is actual, and people with hell in their heads." The novel is the account of a man's social and spiritual descent into the lowest "circle" of the hell of his own mind.

What many find confusing about the novel is the collage of sketchy memories with which the novel begins:

A house painter named Ellic, The Dog, "Flash." Eddie, from across the street. Black shiny face, round hooked nose, beads for hair. A thin light sister with droopy socks. Smiling, Athletic. Slowed by bow legs. Hustler. Could be made angry. Snotty mouth. Hopeless.

The mind fastens past landscapes. Invisible agents. The secret trusts. My own elliptical. The trees' shadows broaden. The sky draws together darkening. Shadows beneath my fingers. Gloom grown under my flesh.

Or fasten across the lots, the grey garages, roofs suspended over cherry trees. The playground fence. Bleakly with guns in the still thin night. Shadows of companions drawn out along the ground. Newark Street green wood, chipped newsstands. Dim stores in the winter. Thin brown owners of buicks.

Baraka has captured here the sketchy memories as the mind would indeed produce them from a distance of more than twenty years: a childhood pet or friend, a first girlfriend, a familiar street —and later, the smell of one particular alley, the sound of a neighbor's voice, a parent's command. As the novel progresses, the fragments become extended into episodes as the distance in time is shortened.

Simultaneously, the social and spiritual degeneration becomes more intense. And, just before the close of the novel, when the memories nearly reach the length of short stories, the protagonist reaches the lowest point in his mental hell, the obscene hallucination of drunkenness, anonymity, and greasy, purchased sex:

She had my pants in her fingers pulling them over my one shoe. I was going to pull them back up and they slipped from my hands and I tried to raise up and she pushed me back. "Look, Ol nigger, I ain't even gonna charge you. I like you." And my head was turning, flopping straight back on the chenille, and the white ladies on the wall did tricks and grinned and pissed on the floor.

The protagonist, having reached the lowest point, realizes that his only hope for survival lies in ascending out of the decay and depravity: "And a light rain came down. I walked away from the house. Up the road, to go out of Bottom." Then, in the final paragraph, the author's affirmation is expressed: "Once, as a child, I would weep for compassion and understanding. And Hell was the inferno of my frustration. But the world is clearer to me now, and many of its features, more easily definable."

Nikki Giovanni

Attempting to define the features of the "world" in more specifically social (black) terms is Nikki Giovanni, currently the most popular, though not the most gifted, of the "Armageddon" authors. Miss Giovanni was born in Knoxville, Tennessee, in 1943; was reared in Cincinnati; and later graduated from Fisk University and attended graduate school at the University of Pennsylvania. She organized the Cincinnati Black Arts Festival in 1967. In addition to having her poems published in many recent anthologies and in *Negro Digest* and *Black Dialogue*, she has published four volumes of poetry, *Black Feeling, Black Talk* (1968), *Black Judgement* (1968), *Re: Creation* (1970), and *Spin a Soft Black Song* (1971). (The first two volumes were combined into *Black Feeling, Black Talk/Black Judgement* in 1970.)

Miss Giovanni's subject is, to put it briefly, "blackness"— blackness as it relates to love, to manhood, to womanhood, to beauty, to unity, and to hatred. And many of her poems are dedicated to individuals, often other black poets, who appear to recall in her these feelings: "Our Detroit Conference (For Don L. Lee)"; "Poem (For Dudley Randall)"; "Personae Poem (For Sylvia Henderson)"; "A Historical Footnote to Consider Only When All Else Fails (For Barbara Crosby)"; and the most directly violent and one of the most frequently quoted of all her work, "The True Import of Present Dialogue, Black vs. Negro (For Peppe, Who Will Ultimately Judge Our Efforts)," which opens:

Nigger
Can you kill
Can you kill
Can a nigger kill
Can a nigger kill a honkie

Can a nigger kill the Man
Can you kill nigger
Huh?[77]

    The most controlled and moving of Miss Giovanni's poems, extremely different in tone from that sameness of the greatest part of her "revolution" verse, is her nostalgic poem entitled "Nikki-Rosa":

childhood remembrances are always a drag
if you're Black
you always remember things like living in Woodlawn
with no inside toilet
and if you become famous or something
they never talk about how happy you were to have
your mother
all to yourself and
how good the water felt when you got your bath
from one of those
big tubs that folk in chicago barbecue in

And though you're poor it isn't poverty that
concerns you
and though they fought a lot
it isn't your father's drinking that makes any difference
but only that everybody is together and you
and your sister have happy birthdays and very good
Christmasses
and I really hope no white person ever has cause
to write about me
because they never understand
Black love is Black wealth and they'll
probably talk about my hard childhood

and never understand that
all the while I was quite happy[78]

Warmth, however, is rare in Miss Giovanni's poetry; and even the love is restricted to those who are a part of "the cause" or who have become the symbols or the victims of it. And there is ever present, sometimes in the place of the artist, the young, angry, absolutely dedicated black woman, who is described in "My Poem" at the close of *Black Judgement*:

i am 25 years old
black female poet
wrote a poem asking
nigger can you kill
if they kill me
it won't stop
the revolution

. . . .

the revolution
is in the streets
and if i stay on
the 5th floor
it will go on
if i never do
anything
it will go on[79]

John A. Williams

The most convincing and controlled of the "Armageddon" writers is John A. Williams (b. 1925), who was born near Jackson,

Mississippi, reared in Syracuse, New York, and later attended
Syracuse University. Williams now lives in New York City. He
has served as lecturer at City College of New York and has published short stories and essays in *Negro Digest, Holiday, Saturday
Review*, and *Ebony*.

Williams was commissioned by *Holiday* magazine in 1963 to
take an extended automobile trip throughout the United States—a
kind of black "Travels with Charley"—to "test America," especially America's racial attitudes. The results, as explained in
his nonfiction account of the trip *This Is My Country Too* (1964),
were dismal. He was refused the services of ostensibly public accommodations; he was harassed repeatedly by state and city
policemen; he was assaulted by southern racists—and the list of
insults and humiliations goes on.

Between 1960 and 1969, Williams published five novels,
and it is significant to note the sharp contrast between the vision
of America found in his early fiction and that found in the
novels that he wrote after his trip for *Holiday*. In *The Angry
Ones* (1960), for example, the protagonist is Steve Hill, well-
educated, qualified for work in publishing or advertising, but
black and, therefore, unemployed much of the time. After a
lengthy succession of rejections and an uncomfortable period
of employment with an unethical "vanity" publisher, Steve Hill,
as a reflection of Williams' own guarded optimism of the early
Sixties, receives "his chance." The novel closes with Hill saying:
"I stood up as I sipped my coffee and peered out the window.
It seemed that spring was coming early."

By 1967, however, and the publication of his fourth novel,
The Man Who Cried I Am, Williams' faint optimism was gone.
Having seen many black hopes burned along with a dozen
urban ghettoes and having experienced repeated personal abuse
on his odyssey through "his country" as well as the kind of
professional injustice experienced by the black writers in the

novel, Williams presents in this powerful and bitter book his forecast of the destiny of American blacks.

The protagonist, Max Reddick, is a successful black writer who, over a period of months, as he slowly dies of cancer, tries to re-establish the few pleasant relationships of his past, including reconciliation with his estranged white wife. Max moves passively toward death until he suddenly finds himself in possession of the shocking details of a highly classified American government document (a document outlining a plan, incidentally, similar to one which John Williams believes actually exists) called "The United States of America—King Alfred." The plan begins: "In the event of widespread and continuing and coordinated racial disturbances in the United States, King Alfred, at the discretion of the President, is to be put into action immediately."

Max reads on through the list of participating federal, state, and local agencies which will carry out the Plan (the CIA, FBI, Department of Defense, National Guard, state and local police forces), through the list of "minority" organizations which will be its targets (CORE, SNCC, NAACP, SCLC, and others), and through the detailed hour-by-hour program for carrying out the Plan. He realizes that he has in his possession a blueprint for the mass incarceration and *extermination* of American blacks and their "sympathizers," a contingency plan which has existed for more than a decade. In one of the memoranda included in the plan, Max reads:

There are 12 major Minority organizations and all are familiar to the 22 million. Dossiers have been compiled on the leaders of the organizations, and can be studied in Washington. The material contained in many of the dossiers, and our threat to reveal that material, has considerably held in check the activities of some of their leaders. Leaders who do not have such usable material in their dossiers have been approached to take Govern-

ment posts, mostly as ambassadors and primarily in African countries. The promise of these positions also has materially contributed to a temporary slow-down of Minority activities. However, we do not expect these slow-downs to be of long duration, because there are always new and dissident elements joining these organizations, with the potential power to replace the old leaders. All organizations and their leaders are under constant, 24-hour surveillance.

The conclusion: Max telephones the black nationalist leader, Minister Q, tells him of King Alfred, and hangs up, never to know that the telephone was tapped and that minutes after the call "agents" are on their way to dispose of Minister Q. And Max, weakened by approaching death and trying to escape from two long-time friends who were "agents" all along, collapses and is searched and murdered:

Edwards did not find microfilm; he found the wad of blood and pus-filled cotton; he found the morphine. Now he understood the syringe and needle. Without hesitation, he attached the needle to the syringe, then withdrew the morphine. He pushed up Max's sleeve and hit the big vein in his arm. Like the old days with the Narcotics Department he thought, still moving swiftly. Jazz musicians in Europe dying of overdoses administered by agents tired of chasing them. Better than heart attacks. There were getting to be too many people found dead of "heart attacks."

In *Sons of Darkness, Sons of Light* (1969), his next-to-last novel (*Captain Blackman* was published in 1972), Williams reaches the culmination of the black "Armageddon" themes, the actual beginning of an American race war—not hysterically unbelievable as in Baraka's play *The Slave*, but methodical and distressingly convincing. Eugene Browning, the protagonist, is the middle-aged, black, and moderate employee of a federally funded black "self-help" organization. One day Browning feels compelled, for reasons which he never fully understands, to avenge the apparently unjustified killing of a black youth by a New York policeman, and he hires an assassin to kill the policeman. There unfolds an escalation of racial conflict, during which, in retaliation for the assassination, policemen make night-time invasions of black neighborhoods and assault all blacks encountered; in return, each day, throughout the United States, policemen are killed—more police invasions; more retaliation, and so on. At this point militant black groups organize plans for creating a state of national anarchy, to begin with the "closing down" of major cities by bombing important bridges, expressways, tunnels, and public facilities.

Unfortunately, Williams seems at a loss as to how to end the novel. Eugene Browning leaves New York just before a series of explosions paralyze the city, and he joins his family at their up-state country house, though the "war" that he un-knowingly started is rapidly extending in that direction as well. And with Browning and his wife making love, and with Browning saying, "It's going to be better," the novel closes, leaving the reader to conjecture that Williams assumes that disaster is inevitable and that one may as well fatalistically enjoy the short time remaining.

In any event, *Sons of Darkness, Sons of Light* is a troubling, yet powerfully exciting novel, and one which serves tragically but well as a reflection of its author's current vision of that truth which many millions of white Americans seem yet unwilling to concede—that it *is* "his country, too."

Conclusion

How does one answer those who ask, "But what is black American literature 'trying to do'?" or "What are the prospects for the future of black American literature?" One obviously cannot generalize about what hundreds of black writers have tried, and are trying, to do any more than one can draw a single conclusion about what literature itself is "trying to do." To realize the many purposes of black writers, one need only contrast the poetry of Jupiter Hammon with that of Jean Toomer or Gwendolyn Brooks or Imamu Baraka; or the fiction of William Wells Brown with that of George Schuyler or Ralph Ellison or John A. Williams; or the autobiographies of Frederick Douglass with those of James Weldon Johnson or Richard Wright; or the plays of Langston Hughes with those of Lorraine Hansberry or Ossie Davis.

To make such contrasts is to learn that these authors are doing the many things that literary artists have always tried to do: Some are exploring the agonies, the pleasures, the successes, the defeats of individual human beliefs and life itself; some

are attacking what they feel to be glaring social, economic, and
political injustices; some are lamenting the inadequacies of human
intelligence in dealing with unanswerable philosophical questions;
and some are exploring new methods for improving the quality
of the literary forms themselves. Perhaps the best comment on
the role of the black writer in relation to his art is made by
Ralph Ellison, who, in his collection of essays, *Shadow and Act*
(1964), says:

*If the Negro, or any other writer, is going to do what is
expected of him, he's lost the battle before he takes the field.
I suspect that all the agony that goes into writing is borne
precisely because the writer longs for acceptance—but it must
be acceptance on his own terms. Perhaps, though, this thing
cuts both ways: the Negro novelist draws his blackness too tightly
around him when he sits down to write—that's what the anti-
protest critics believe—but perhaps the white reader draws his
whiteness around himself when he sits down to read. He doesn't
want to identify himself with Negro characters in terms of our
immediate racial and social situation, though on the deeper human
level, identification can become compelling when the situation
is revealed artistically. The white reader doesn't want to get too
close, not even in an imaginary re-creation of society. Negro
writers have felt this and it has led to much of our failure.*

*Too many books by Negro writers are addressed to a
white audience. By doing this the authors run the risk of limiting
themselves to the audience's presumptions of what a Negro is
or should be; the tendency is to become involved in polemics,
to plead the Negro's humanity. You know, many white people
question that humanity but I don't think that Negroes can afford
to indulge in such a false issue. For us the question should
be, What are the specific forms of that humanity, and what in
our background is worth preserving or abandoning.*

To the question, "What are the prospects for the future of black American literature?" one must answer rather obliquely that the prospects will be determined largely by the course of social events in the United States during the next few years. Much black literature is social in content and is therefore affected directly by the social—particularly the racial—climate prevailing at the time that it is produced.

If, for example, many of the day-to-day humiliations experienced by black Americans are not eliminated, both by political act and by increased awareness on the part of white America, then the frustration and anger produced in black writers will make themselves felt in their literature, probably in the form of the shrill hatred found in some of the writing of the Sixties. And because many writers—especially the gifted ones like Imamu Baraka, William Melvin Kelley, and John A. Williams—either cannot avoid or do not wish to avoid the role of "race-war prophet," as the activities of blacks in general become more violent and uncontrolled, the literature of these writers could well become correspondingly violent and uncontrolled. Hence the "race war" may gain, but the literature will suffer.

If, on the other hand, after three and a half centuries of institutionalized injustice, racial enlightenment finally reaches the masses of white America, many outstanding black writers can free themselves from what they see as their obligation to be "race spokesmen." They can then turn their energies away from the exploration of the specifically black condition and toward the exploration of the universally human condition—an exploration which may help to explain what men and nations do to themselves when they perpetrate acts of cruel bigotry against other men and nations; an exploration which, on the positive side, may help to explain to men and nations what they, divorced from their absurd myths and prejudices, may yet have the capacity to become.

Notes

[1] See Part I, "Origins of American Negro Tales," of Dorson's lengthy Introduction to *American Negro Folktales* (Bloomington, Indiana, 1958).

[2] Peter M. Bergman's *The Chronological History of the Negro in America* (New York, 1969), in its year-by-year listing of major events in black history, reveals dozens of the anti-read-and-write state laws and city ordinances, many of which carried penalties of fines, imprisonment, and, sometimes, floggings for those individuals, black or white, who engaged in educating blacks.

[3] In addition to the Bontemps-Hughes and Dorson collections, two valuable sources of folk tales are Zora Neale Hurston's *Mules and Men: Negro Folktales and Voodoo Practices in the South* (Philadelphia, 1935), which was reprinted in 1970 with an Introduction by Darwin T. Turner, and J. Mason Brewer's *American Negro Folklore* (Chicago, 1968).

[4] Originally published in 1925, the Odum and Johnson book was reprinted in 1969 as a part of The New American Library, Inc. "Afro-American Studies" series.

[5] The diction, cadence, and imagery of the work songs are treated by Odum and Johnson in their chapter, "The Work Songs of the Negro."

[6] The Bontemps-Hughes collection and the Hurston collection contain several of the best-known "Old John" tales. Dorson includes in his collection a complete section called "Old Marster and John."

[7] Reprinted from Section I, "Animal and Bird Stories," of Dorson's *American Negro Folktales*.

[8] Reprinted from Hughes' *The Best of Simple* (New York, 1961).

[9] Examples of the monologue material of some of these entertainers are found in Part I, "Cool Comics—Contemporary Comedy," of Langston Hughes' collection, *The Book of Negro Humor* (New York, 1966).

[10] Reprinted from Hughes' *The Book of Negro Humor*.

[11] See, for example, Roger D. Abrahams' *Deep Down in the Jungle: Negro Narrative Folklore from the Streets of Philadelphia* (Hatboro, Pennsylvania, 1964); and Richard M. Dorson's *Negro Tales from Pine Bluff, Arkansas, and Calvin, Michigan* (Bloomington, Indiana, 1958).

[12] Reprinted from William H. Robinson's excellent anthology, *Early Black American Poets* (Dubuque, Iowa, 1969). Robinson includes poetry written by some thirty black poets of the eighteenth and nineteenth centuries, as well as a bibliography of the work of other poets who wrote during the same period but whose poems are not included in the collection.

[13] For further discussion of the conditions in which black Americans lived in the eighteenth century, see Carter G. Woodson, *The Negro in Our History* (Washington, D.C., 1922) and Benjamin Quarles, *The Negro in the Making of America* (New York, 1964).

[14] Reprinted from Oscar Wegelin's *Jupiter Hammon, American Negro Poet* (Miami, 1969).

[15] Reprinted from Wegelin's *Jupiter Hammon, American Negro Poet*.

[16] See Julian D. Mason, Jr., ed., *The Poems of Phillis Wheatley* (Chapel Hill, 1966).

[17] Reprinted from G. Herbert Renfro's *Life and Works of Phillis Wheatley* (Washington, D.C., 1916).

[18] Reprinted from Renfro's *Life and Works of Phillis Wheatley*.

[19] Vassa's autobiography has now been reprinted in Arna Bontemps' *Great Slave Narratives* (Boston, 1969).

[20] Reprinted from Bontemps' *Great Slave Narratives*.

[21] For a complete discussion of slave insurrections and the fears that thoughts of such uprisings inspired, see Joseph Cephas Carroll, *Slave Insurrections in the United States 1800-1865* (originally published in 1938; reprinted in 1969 by The New American Library).

[22] Gabriel's Revolt is the subject of Arna Bontemps' excellent novel, *Black Thunder* (New York, 1936).

[23] William Styron's best-selling novel, *The Confessions of Nat Turner* (New York, 1966), popularized the Virginia uprising and created a storm of controversy as well. Several black intellectuals, while, for the most part, acknowledging Styron's historical accuracy, claim that the novelist's understanding of black American social codes and mentality is deficient.

[24] In fairness to Horton, it should be noted that he intended to purchase his freedom with the income from *Hope of Liberty*— hence he chose to "plead" his protest. Unfortunately, the book did not sell well.

[25] Reprinted from Robinson's *Early Black American Poets*.

[26] Reprinted from Sterling Brown, Arthur P. Davis, and Ulysses Lee's *The Negro Caravan* (New York, 1941).

[27] Reprinted from Brown, Davis, and Lee's *The Negro Caravan*.

[28] Reprinted from Brown, Davis, and Lee's *The Negro Caravan*.

[29] Reprinted from Mrs. Harper's *Atlanta Offering: Poems* (Miami, 1969).

[30] Recent collections have brought back into print several slave narratives, some of which had been out of print for more than a century. Especially valuable collections are Gilbert Osofsky's *Puttin' on Ole Massa* (New York, 1969), which contains the narratives of Henry Bibb, William Wells Brown, and Solomon Northup; and Arna Bontemps' *Great Slave Narratives* (Boston, 1969), which contains the narratives of Gustavus Vassa, James W. C. Pennington, and William and Ellen Craft. In addition, Julius Lester's *To Be a Slave* (New York, 1970) contains brief documented recollections of former slaves, ranging from capture in Africa to life following the Civil War.

[31] Arthur Davis makes note of this rumor in his Introduction to the Macmillan reprint of *Clotel* (New York, 1970).

[32] As noted in Mark Twain's *Huckleberry Finn*, and in other fiction set in the early to mid-nineteenth century, the threat of being "sold South" to the legendary horrors of plantation life was one of the greatest deterrents to rebellious slave behavior in the border states.

[33] Brown used this same title some five years later for the second version of his novel *Clotel*.

[34] This play, seldom listed with Brown's other works, was credited to Brown in a review in William Lloyd Garrison's newspaper, *The Liberator*. See Doris E. Abramson's *Negro Playwrights in the American Theatre 1925-1959* (New York, 1969), p. 9.

[35] The original version of *Clotel*, out of print for more than a century, was reprinted by Macmillan in 1970.

[36] See Floyd J. Miller's Introduction to the recent printing

of *Blake* (Boston, 1970). This is the first time that the chapters of *Blake* have been assembled in book form.

[37] DuBois made this estimate in a paper which he presented to the American Historical Association in New York City, in December, 1909.

[38] Reprinted from Dunbar's *Complete Poems* (Dodd, Mead, 1913).

[39] Reprinted from Dunbar's *Complete Poems*.

[40] Washington's attitudes toward black improvement are found in his projection, *The Future of the American Negro* (Cambridge, Mass., 1899), and in his autobiography, *Up from Slavery* (New York, 1900).

[41] Miller, an early twentieth-century scholar, is best known for his collections of essays, *Race Adjustment* (New York, 1908) and *Out of the House of Bondage* (New York, 1914).

[42] Franklin introduces the collection *Three Negro Classics* (New York, 1965), which contains Washington's *Up from Slavery*, DuBois' *The Souls of Black Folk*, and Johnson's *The Autobiography of an Ex-colored Man*.

[43] See the section "1919" in Bergman's *Chronological History of the Negro in America*.

[44] See Bergman, "1920."

[45] See Fitzgerald's excellent essay "Echoes of the Jazz Age," in his collection *Crack-up* (New York, 1945).

[46] See Eastman's introduction to *The Selected Poems of Claude McKay* (New York, 1953).

[47] Reprinted from McKay's *Selected Poems*, by permission of Twayne Publishers.

[48] Reprinted from McKay's *Selected Poems*, by permission of Twayne Publishers.

[49] This observation was sent by Toomer to Max Eastman, editor of *Liberator*, as part of a biographical statement that

Eastman had requested. For the complete statement, see Arna
Bontemps' introduction to the Harper and Row reprint of *Cane*
(New York, 1969).

[50] Copyright, 1925 by Harper and Row, Publishers, Inc.;
renewed, 1953 by Ida M. Cullen. Reprinted by permission of
Harper and Row, Publishers, Inc.

[51] Copyright, 1929 by Harper and Row, Publishers, Inc.;
renewed, 1957 by Ida M. Cullen. Reprinted by permission of
Harper and Row, Publishers, Inc.

[52] Copyright, 1926 by Alfred A. Knopf, Inc., renewed 1954
by Langston Hughes. From *Selected Poems* by Langston Hughes.
Reprinted by permission of Alfred A. Knopf, Inc.

[53] Copyright, 1951 by Langston Hughes. From *The Panther
and the Lash*, by Langston Hughes. Reprinted by permission
of Alfred A. Knopf, Inc.

[54] See Doris E. Abramson's *Negro Playwrights in the American Theatre 1925-1959*, p. 67.

[55] See Abramson's chapter, "The Twenties: Black Renaissance."

[56] *Mulatto* has been anthologized in Webster Smalley's *Five
Plays by Langston Hughes* (Bloomington, Ind., 1963), and, more
recently, in William Brasmer and Dominick Consolo's *Black
Drama: An Anthology* (Columbus, Ohio, 1970).

[57] See Hughes' autobiography, *The Big Sea* (New York,
1963), p. 334.

[58] Professor Boas later wrote the Preface to Miss Hurston's
Mules and Men (Philadelphia, 1935).

[59] See Peter M. Bergman's *The Chronological History of
the Negro in America*, p. 470.

[60] See Bergman, p. 474.

[61] See Bergman, p. 486.

[62] David Littlejohn (*Black on White,* 1966) describes Wright's

"Between the World and Me" and Robert Hayden's "Middle Passage" as "the two finest poems by Negroes."

[63] From *White Man, Listen!* by Richard Wright. Copyright, 1957 by Richard Wright. Reprinted by permission of Doubleday and Company, Inc.

[64] See Robert A. Bone, *The Negro Novel in America* (New Haven, Connecticut, 1965), p. 158.

[65] Copyright, 1949 by Gwendolyn Brooks Blakely. Reprinted by permission of Harper and Row, Publishers, Inc.

[66] For a detailed account of the *Amistad* insurrection, see John Spears' *The American Slave-Trade* (New York, 1900).

[67] Reprinted from "Middle Passage" by Robert Hayden. From *Selected Poems*, Copyright, 1966 by Robert Hayden. Reprinted by permission of October House, Inc.

[68] Reprinted from Miss Walker's *For My People*. Copyright, 1942 by Yale University Press. Reprinted by permission of Yale University Press.

[69] Wright and Green's play has recently been anthologized in William Brasmer and Dominick Consolo's *Black Drama: An Anthology* (Columbus, Ohio, 1970), with an introduction, "The Black Playwright in the Professional Theatre of the United States of America, 1858-1959," by Darwin T. Turner.

[70] Mitchell's play has recently been anthologized in *Afro-American Literature: Drama* (Boston, 1970), edited by William Adams, Peter Conn, and Barry Slepian.

[71] Nemiroff's essay, the complete title of which is "The One Hundred and One 'Final' Performances of *Sidney Brustein: Portrait of a Play and Its Author*," is included in the Signet Book edition (New York, 1966) containing both *A Raisin in the Sun* and *The Sign in Sidney Brustein's Window*.

[72] *Purlie Victorious* is now anthologized in Brasmer and Consolo's *Black Drama: An Anthology*; Adams, Conn, and

Slepian's *Afro-American Literature: Drama*; and Lillian Faderman and Barbara Bradshaw's *Speaking for Ourselves* (Glenview, Ill., 1969).

[73] Reprinted from Adam David Miller's *Dices or Black Bones: Black Voices of the Seventies* (Boston, 1970), by permission of Ishmael Reed.

[74] The details of the causes and results of the Watts riot are recounted in the book *Burn, Baby, Burn! The Los Angeles Race Riot, August 1965* (New York, 1966), written by Jerry Cohen and William S. Murphy, journalists for the Los Angeles *Times*.

[75] Reprinted from Knight's *Black Voices from Prison* (New York, 1970), by permission of *Greater Works* Magazine.

[76] Reprinted by permission of Corinth Books/Totem Press.

[77] Reprinted from Miss Giovanni's *Black Feeling, Black Talk/Black Judgement* (New York, 1970), by permission of William Morrow and Company, Inc.

[78] Reprinted from *Black Feeling, Black Talk/Black Judgement* by permission of William Morrow and Company, Inc.

[79] Reprinted from *Black Feeling, Black Talk/Black Judgement* by permission of William Morrow and Company, Inc.

Black American Literature:
A Bibliography of Folklore, Poetry, Autobiography, Fiction, Drama, Anthologies, Literary Criticism and Bibliography, and Social and Historical Comment*

Folklore

Abrahams, Roger D. *Deep Down in the Jungle: Negro Narrative Folklore from the Streets of Philadelphia.* Hatboro, Pa.: Folklore Associates, 1964.

Adams, Edward C. L. *Congaree Sketches.* Chapel Hill: Univ. of North Carolina Press, 1927.

* In order that the literary works may be viewed in the order in which they were produced, four sections of the bibliography—Poetry, Autobiography, Fiction, and Drama—are arranged chronologically by each author's first work. The other four sections—Folklore, Anthologies, Literary Criticism and Bibliography, and Social and Historical Comment—are arranged alphabetically by each author's last name. The abbreviation *n.p.* in an entry indicates either that the work was never published (though some of the plays have been produced from manuscript) or that the city of publication and/or the name of the publisher can not be found.

Blackburn, Mary Johnson. *Folklore Mammy Days*. Boston: Baker and Company, 1924.

Bontemps, Arna, and Langston Hughes. *The Book of Negro Folklore*. New York: Dodd, Mead, 1958.

Brewer, J. Mason. *The Word on the Brazos*. Austin: Univ. of Texas Press, 1953.

————. *"Aunt Dicy" Tales*. Austin: The Author, 1957.

————. *"Dog Ghosts" and Other Texas Negro Folk Tales*. Austin: Univ. of Texas Press, 1958.

————. *Worser Days and Better Times: The Folklore of the North Carolina Negro*. Chicago: Quadrangle, 1965.

————. *American Negro Folklore*. Chicago: Quadrangle, 1968.

Brookes, Stella Brewer. *Joel Chandler Harris, Folklorist*. Athens: Univ. of Georgia Press, 1950.

Byrd, James W. *J. Mason Brewer: Negro Folklorist*. Austin: Steck-Vaughn, 1967.

Carmer, Carl Lamson. *Stars Fell on Alabama*. New York: Hill and Wang, 1934.

Christensen, A.M.H. *American Folk Lore Told on the Sea Islands of South Carolina*. Boston: J. G. Cupples, 1892.

Culbertson, A. V. *At the Big House Where Aunt Nancy and Aunt Phrony Held Forth on Animal Talk*. Indianapolis: Bobbs-Merrill, 1904.

Dobie, James Frank. *Follow De Drinkin' Gou'd*. Austin: Texas Folklore Society, 1928.

————. *Tone the Bell Easy*. Dallas: Southern Methodist Univ. Press, 1932.

————. *Texian Stomping Grounds*. Austin: Texas Folklore Society, 1941.

Dorson, Richard M. *Negro Folktales in Michigan*. Cambridge: Harvard Univ. Press, 1956.

————. *Negro Tales from Pine Bluff, Arkansas, and Calvin, Michigan*. Bloomington: Indiana Univ. Press, 1958.

————. *American Negro Folktales.* Bloomington: Indiana Univ. Press, 1958.

Fitz-James, J. *Bahamian Folk Lore.* Montreal: n.p., 1906.

Gonzales, A. E. *With Aesop Along the Black Border.* Columbia, S. C.: State College, 1920.

————. *Gullah Tales.* Columbia, S. C.: State College, 1922.

Harris, Joel C. *Uncle Remus, His Songs and His Sayings.* New York: Appleton, 1880.

————. *Nights with Uncle Remus: Myths and Legends of the Old Plantation.* Boston: Osgood, 1883.

————. *Daddy Jake the Runaway, and Short Stories Told After Dark.* New York: Century, 1889.

————. *Uncle Remus and His Friends: Old Plantation Stories, Songs, and Ballads, with Sketches of Negro Character.* Boston: Houghton Mifflin, 1892.

————. *Tar-Baby, and Other Rhymes of Uncle Remus.* New York: Appleton, 1904.

————. *Told by Uncle Remus: New Stories of the Old Plantation.* New York: McClure, Phillips, 1905.

————. *Uncle Remus and Brer Rabbit.* New York: Stokes, 1906.

————. *Uncle Remus and the Little Boy.* Boston: Small, Maynard, 1910.

————. *Uncle Remus Returns.* Boston: Houghton Mifflin, 1918.

Haywood, Charles. *A Bibliography of North American Folklore and Folksong.* New York: Dover, 1951.

Heyward, Dubose, and Hervey Allen. *Carolina Chansons: Legends of the Low Country.* New York: Macmillan, 1922.

Heyward, J. S. *Brown Jackets.* Columbia, S. C.: State College, 1923.

Hughes, Langston, ed. *The Book of Negro Humor.* New York: Dodd, Mead, 1966.

Hurston, Zora N. *Mules and Men.* Philadelphia: Lippincott, 1935.

————. *Tell My Horse.* Philadelphia: Lippincott, 1938.

Jackson, Bruce. *The Negro and His Folklore in Nineteenth Century Periodicals*. Austin: Univ. of Texas Press, 1967.

Johnson, Guy B. *John Henry: Tracking Down a Negro Legend*. Chapel Hill: Univ. of North Carolina Press, 1929.

————. *Folk Culture on St. Helena Island, South Carolina*. Chapel Hill: Univ. of North Carolina Press, 1930.

Jones, C. C., Jr. *Negro Myths from the Georgia Coast*. Boston: Houghton Mifflin, 1888.

Kennedy, R. Emmett. *Black Cameos*. New York: Boni and Liveright, 1924.

Milne, H. *Mama's Black Nurse Stories*. Edinburgh and London: n.p., 1890.

Odum, H. W., and Guy B. Johnson. *The Negro and His Songs*. Chapel Hill: Univ. of North Carolina Press, 1925.

————. *Negro Workaday Songs*. Chapel Hill: Univ. of North Carolina Press, 1926.

Parsons, Elsie C. *Folk Tales of the Sea Islands, South Carolina*. New York: n.p., 1902.

————. *Folk Lore of Andros Islands*. Cambridge, Mass.: American Folklore Society, 1918.

Puckett, N. N. *Folk Beliefs of the Southern Negro*. Chapel Hill: Univ. of North Carolina Press, 1926.

Scarborough, Dorothy. *From a Southern Porch*. New York: Putnam, 1919.

————. *On the Trail of Negro Folk Songs*. Cambridge: Harvard Univ. Press, 1925.

Sims, Mamie Hunt. *Negro Mystic Lore*. Chicago: To-morrow Publishing, 1907.

Spalding, Henry D. *Encyclopedia of Black Folklore and Humor*. Middle Village, N.Y.: Jonathan David, 1972.

Sterling, Philip. *Laughing on the Outside*. New York: Grosset and Dunlap, 1966.

Stoney, Samuel G., and Gertrude M. Shelby. *Black Genesis: A Chronicle*. New York: Macmillan, 1930.

Talley, T. W. *Negro Folk Rhymes, Wise and Otherwise*. New York: Macmillan, 1922.

Wiley, George E. *Southern Plantation Stories and Sketches*. New York: Broadway, 1905.

Young, M. *Plantation Bird Legends*. New York: Harper, 1902.

Poetry

Hammon, Jupiter. *An Evening Thought*. New York: n.p., 1760.

————. *An Address to Miss Phillis Wheatley*. New York: n.p., 1778.

Wheatley, Phillis. *Poems on Various Subjects*. London: Bell, Bookseller, Aldgate, 1773.

Falconar, Maria and Harriet. *Poems on Slavery*. London: n.p., 1788.

Bull, John. *The Slave and Other Poems*. London: n.p., 1824.

Horton, George Moses. *Hope of Liberty*. Raleigh, N.C.: Joseph Gales and Sons, 1829.

————. *Naked Genius*. Raleigh, N.C.: Fireside Book Publishing House, 1865.

Cannon, Noah C. *The Rock of Wisdom*. New York: Portrait, 1833.

Boyd, John. *The Vision and Other Poems*. London: Longman, 1834.

Brown, William Wells. *Anti-Slavery Harp*. Boston: Marsh, 1849.

Payne, Daniel A. *Pleasures and Other Miscellaneous Poems*. Baltimore: Sherwood and Co., 1850.

Whitfield, James M. *America and Other Poems*. Buffalo: Leavitt, 1853.

Harper, Frances E. W. *Poems on Miscellaneous Subjects*. Philadelphia: The Author, 1854.

————. *Moses: A Story of the Nile*. Philadelphia: Merrihew and Son, 1869.

————. *Poems*. Philadelphia: Merrihew and Son, 1871.

————. *Poems.* Philadelphia: The Author, 1900.

Rogers, Elymas Payson. *On the Fugitive Slave Law.* Newark: Holbrook, 1856.

————. *Repeal of the Missouri Compromise Considered.* Newark: Holbrook, 1856.

Clark, George W. *The Harp of Freedom.* New York: Miller, Orton, and Mulligan, 1856.

Thomas, Abel Charles. *The Gospel of Slavery: A Primer of Freedom.* New York: T. W. Strong, 1864.

Rhodes, Jacob. *The Nation's Loss.* Newark: Starbuck, 1866.

Bell, James Madison. *Triumph of Liberty.* Detroit: Tunis Steam Printing, 1870.

Boyd, Francis A. *Columbiana: Or the North Star.* Chicago: B. Hand, 1870.

Walden, Islay. *Miscellaneous Poems.* Washington, D.C.: The Author, 1873.

Whitman, Albery A. *Not a Man, and Yet a Man.* Springfield, Ohio: Republic, 1877.

————. *The Rape of Florida.* St. Louis: Nixon-Jones Printing, 1884.

————. *Twasinta's Seminoles: Or the Rape of Florida.* St. Louis: Nixon-Jones Printing, 1885.

————. *An Idyl of the South.* New York: Metaphysical, 1901.

Menard, J. Willis. *Lays in Summer Lands.* Washington, D.C.: Enterprise, 1879.

Lucas, Sam. *Careful Man Songster.* Chicago: n.p., 1881.

Turner, H. M. *The Conflict for Civil Rights.* Washington, D.C.: n.p., 1881.

Ray, Henrietta Cordelia. *Poems.* New York: J. J. Little, 1887.

————. *Sonnets.* New York: J. J. Little, 1893.

————. *Commemoration Ode: Or Lincoln.* New York: J. J. Little, 1893.

Rowe, George C. *Thoughts in Verse.* Charleston, S.C.: n.p., 1887.

————. *Our Heroes*. Charleston, S.C.: n.p., 1890.

Campbell, James E. *Driftings and Gleanings*. Chicago: The Author, 1888.

————. *Echoes from the Plantation and Elsewhere*. Chicago: The Author, 1895.

Vandyne, William J. *Revels of Fancy*. Boston: Grant, 1891.

Coffin, Frank B. *Coffin's Poems and Ajax's Ordeals*. Little Rock: The Colored Advocate Printers, 1892.

Dunbar, Paul Laurence. *Oak and Ivy*. Dayton, Ohio: United Brethren, 1893.

————. *Majors and Minors*. Toledo, Ohio: Hadley and Hadley, 1895.

————. *Lyrics of Lowly Life*. New York: Dodd, Mead, 1895.

————. *Lyrics of the Hearthside*. New York: Dodd, Mead, 1899.

————. *Lyrics of Love and Laughter*. New York: Dodd, Mead, 1903.

————. *Lyrics of Sunshine and Shadow*. New York: Dodd, Mead, 1905.

————. *Complete Poems*. New York: Dodd, Mead, 1913.

————. *Speakin' O' Christmas—and Other Christmas and Special Poems*. New York: Dodd, Mead, 1914.

Franklin, James T. *Mid-Day Gleanings*. Memphis: Tracy Printing, 1893.

————. *Jessamine: Poems*. Memphis: Tracy Printing, 1900.

Simpson, J. M. C. *The Emancipation Car*. Zanesville, Ohio: Sullivan and Brown, 1893.

Whitfield, Cupid A. *Poems of To-day*. Quincy, Florida: n.p., 1893.

Alwell, F. S. *The Open Door*. Winfield, Kansas: n.p., 1895.

Bibb, Eloise. *Poems*. Boston: The Monthly Review Press, 1895.

Cotter, Joseph Seamon. *A Rhyming*. Louisville: The New South Publishing Co., 1895.

————. *Links of Friendship*. Louisville: Bradley and Gilbert Co., 1898.

————. *A White Song and a Black One*. Louisville: Bradley and Gilbert Co., 1909.

————. *Collected Poems*. New York: Henry Harrison, 1938.

————. *Sequel to the 'Pied Piper of Hamelin'*. New York: Henry Harrison, 1939.

McClellan, George M. *Poems*. Nashville: A.M.E. Church, 1895.

————. *Songs of a Southerner*. Boston: Rockwell and Churchill, 1896.

————. *Path of Dreams*. Louisville: Morton, 1916.

Shoeman, Charles H. *A Dream and Other Poems*. Ann Arbor, Mich.: George Wahr, 1895.

Fordham, Mary Weston. *Magnolia Leaves*. Charleston, S. C.: Walker, Evans and Cogswell, 1898.

McGirt, James E. *Avenging the Maine*. Raleigh, N.C.: Edwards and Broughton, 1899.

Temple, George H. *The Epic of the Columbus Bell and Other Poems*. Reading, Pa.: The Author, 1900.

Thompson, Priscilla. *Ethiope Lays*. Rossmoyne, Ohio: The Author, 1900.

Braithwaite, W. S. *Lyrics of Life and Love*. Boston: Turner, 1904.

————. *The House of Falling Leaves*. Boston: Luce, 1908.

————. *Selected Poems*. New York: Coward-McCann, 1948.

Henderson, Elliott B. *Plantation Echoes*. Columbus, Ohio: Heer, 1904.

————. *Darky Meditations*. Springfield, Ohio: The Author, 1910.

————. *Uneddykated Folks*. Springfield, Ohio: The Author, 1911.

————. *Darky Ditties*. Columbus, Ohio: Heer, 1915.

Allen J. Mord. *Rhymes: Tales and Rhymed Tales*. Topeka: Crane, 1906.

McKay, Claude. *Constab Ballads*. London: Watts, 1912.

————. *Songs of Jamaica*. London: Augener, 1912.

————. *Spring in New Hampshire*. London: Richards, 1920.

————. *Harlem Shadows*. New York: Harcourt, Brace, 1922.

————. *Selected Poems*. New York: Bookman Associates, 1953.

Johnson, Fenton. *A Little Dreaming*. Chicago: Peterson, 1913.

————. *Visions of the Dusk*. New York: The Author, 1915.

————. *Songs of the Soil*. New York: The Author, 1916.

————. *The Daily Grind: 41 WPA Poems*. n.p., 1963.

Johnson, James Weldon. *Fifty Years, and Other Poems*. Boston: Cornhill, 1917.

————. *God's Trombones*. New York: Viking, 1927.

————. *St. Peter Relates an Incident of the Resurrection Day*. New York: Viking, 1930.

Cotter, Joseph Seamon, Jr. *The Band of Gideon and Other Lyrics*. Boston: Cornhill, 1918.

Johnson, Georgia Douglas. *The Heart of a Woman and Other Poems*. Boston: Cornhill, 1918.

————. *Bronze: A Book of Verse*. Boston: Brimmer Co., 1922.

————. *An Autumn Love Cycle*. New York: Neale, 1938.

Hill, Leslie P. *Wings of Oppression and Other Poems*. Boston: Stratford, 1921.

Cullen, Countee. *Color*. New York: Harper, 1925.

————. *Copper Sun*. New York: Harper, 1927.

————. *The Ballad of the Brown Girl*. New York: Harper, 1927.

————. *The Black Christ*. New York: Harper, 1929.

————. *The Medea and Other Poems*. New York: Harper, 1935.

————. *The Lost Zoo*. New York: Harper, 1940.

————. *On These I Stand*. New York: Harper, 1947.

Hughes, Langston. *The Weary Blues*. New York: Knopf, 1926.

————. *Fine Clothes to the Jew*. New York: Knopf, 1927.

————. *Dear Lovely Death*. New York: Troutbeck Press, 1931.

————. *The Dream Keeper*. New York: Knopf, 1932.

————. *Scottsboro Limited: Four Poems and a Play in Verse*. New York: Golden Stair, 1932.

————. *A New Song*. New York: International Workers Order, 1938.

————. *Shakespeare in Harlem*. New York: Knopf, 1942.

————. *In Freedom's Plow*. New York: Musette, 1943.

————. *Fields of Wonder*. New York: Knopf, 1947.

————. *One-way Ticket*. New York: Knopf, 1949.

————. *Montage of a Dream Deferred*. New York: Henry Holt, 1951.

————. *Ask Your Mama: Twelve Moods for Jazz*. New York: Knopf, 1961.

————. *Selected Poems*. New York: Knopf, 1965.

————. *The Panther and the Lash*. New York: Knopf, 1967.

Brown, Sterling A. *Southern Road*. New York: Harcourt, Brace, 1932.

Davis, Frank Marshall. *Black Man's Verse*. New York: Black Cat Press, 1935.

————. *I am the American Negro*. New York: Black Cat Press, 1937.

————. *47th Street*. New York: Decker Press, 1948.

Hayden, Robert E. *Heart Shape in the Dust*. Riverwood, Md.: Falcon Press, 1940.

————. *Figure of Time: Poems*. Austin, Texas: Hemphill Press, 1955.

————. *A Ballad of Remembrance*. London: Breman, 1962.

————. *Selected Poems*. New York: October House, 1966.

————. *Words in the Mourning Time*. New York: October House, 1970.

Madgett, Naomi Long. *Songs to a Phantom Nightingale*. New York: Fortuny's, 1941.

————. *One and the Many*. New York: Exposition, 1961.

————. *Star by Star*. Detroit: Harlo, 1965.

Walker, Margaret. *For My People*. New Haven: Yale Univ. Press, 1942.

————. *Prophets for a New Day*. Detroit: Broadside, 1970.

Dismond, H. Binga. *We Who Would Die*. New York: W. Malliet, 1943.

Tolson, Melvin B. *Rendezvous with America.* New York: Dodd, Mead, 1944.

———. *Libretto for the Republic of Liberia.* New York: Twayne, 1953.

———. *Harlem Gallery Book I.* New York: Twayne, 1965.

Wright, Bruce McM. *From the Shaken Tower.* n.p., 1944.

Brooks, Gwendolyn. *A Street in Bronzeville.* New York: Harper, 1945.

———. *Annie Allen.* New York: Harper, 1949.

———. *Bronzeville Boys and Girls.* New York: Harper, 1956.

———. *The Bean Eaters.* New York: Harper, 1960.

———. *Selected Poems.* New York: Harper, 1963.

———. *In the Mecca.* New York: Harper and Row, 1968.

———. *Riot.* Detroit: Broadside, 1969.

———. *Family Pictures.* Detroit: Broadside, 1970.

———. *The World of Gwendolyn Brooks.* New York: Harper and Row, 1971.

Dodson, Owen. *Powerful Long Ladder.* New York: Farrar, Straus, 1946.

———. *The Confession Stone.* London: Breman, 1960.

Hayden, Robert, and Myron O'Higgins. *The Lion and the Archer.* Austin, Texas: Hemphill Press, 1948.

Holloway, Ariel W. *Shape Them into Dreams.* New York: Exposition, 1955.

Morris, John C. *Cleopatra and Other Poems.* New York: Exposition, 1955.

Jarette, Alfred Q. *Black Man Speaks.* New York: Weinberg, 1956.

Wright, Beatrice. *Color Scheme.* New York: Pageant Press, 1957.

Miller, May. *Into the Clearing.* Washington, D.C.: Charioteer Press, 1959.

Johnston, Percy E. *Concerto for Girl and Convertible.* Elizabethtown, Pa.: Continental Press, 1960.

———. *Six Cylinder Olympus.* n.p.: Jupiter Hammon Press, 1964.

Pitcher, Oliver. *Dust of Silence*. San Francisco: Troubador, 1960.

Cuney, Waring. *Puzzles*. Utrecht, Holland: Breman, 1961.

Jones, LeRoi (Imamu Amiri Baraka). *Preface to a Twenty Volume Suicide Note*. New York: Corinth, 1961.

————. *The Dead Lecturer*. New York: Grove, 1964.

————. *Black Magic Poetry: 1961-1967*. Indianapolis: Bobbs-Merrill, 1969.

————. *It's Nation Time*. Chicago: Third World, 1970.

Adams, Doris B. *Longing and Other Poems*. Philadelphia: Dorrance, 1962.

Bontemps, Arna. *Personals*. London: Breman, 1963.

Horne, Frank. *Haverstraw*. London: Breman, 1963.

Miller, Clifford L. *Imperishable the Temple*. Mexico City: The Author, 1963.

Rivers, Conrad K. *The Black Bodies and This Sunburnt Face*. Cleveland: Free Lance Press, 1963.

————. *The Still Voice of Harlem*. London: Breman, 1968.

Lyle, K. L., M. Rubin, and May Miller. *Lyrics of Three Women*. Baltimore: Linden Press, 1964.

Major, Clarence. *Love Poems of a Black Man*. n.p., 1964.

————. *Swallow the Lake*. Middletown: Wesleyan Univ. Press, 1970.

————. *Private Line*. London: Breman, 1971.

Turner, Darwin T. *Katharsis*. Wellesley, Mass.: Wellesley Press, 1964.

Spellman, A. B. *The Beautiful Days*. New York: Poet's Press, 1965.

Black, Austin. *The Tornado in My Mouth*. New York: Exposition Press, 1966.

Henderson, David. *Felix of the Silent Forest*. New York: Poet's Press, 1967.

————. *De Mayor of Harlem*. New York: Dutton, 1970.

Lorde, Audre. *The First Cities*. New York: Poet's Press, 1967.

Stowers, J. Anthony. *The Aliens*. San Francisco: White Rabbit, 1967.

Cruz, Victor Hernandez. *Snaps*. New York: Vintage, 1968.

Emanuel, James A. *The Treehouse and Other Poems*. Detroit: Broadside, 1968.

———. *Pantherman*. Detroit: Broadside, 1970.

Evans, Mari. *Where Is All The Music?* London: Breman, 1968.

———. *I Am a Black Woman*. New York: Morrow, 1970.

Hill, Roy. *49 Poems*. Manhattan, Kansas: AG Press, 1968.

Knight, Etheridge. *Poems from Prison*. Detroit: Broadside, 1968.

Lee, Don. *Black Pride*. Detroit: Broadside, 1968.

———. *Think Black*. Detroit: Broadside, 1968.

———. *Don't Cry! Scream*. Detroit: Broadside, 1969.

———. *We Walk the Way of the New World*. Detroit: Broadside, 1970.

———. *Directionscore; Selected and New Poems*. Detroit: Broadside, 1971.

———. *Dynamite Voices I: Black Poets of the 1960's*. Detroit: Broadside, 1971.

Nelson, David. *Black Impulse*. New York: Drum, 1968.

Randall, Dudley. *Cities Burning*. Detroit: Broadside, 1968.

———. *Love You*. London: Breman, 1970.

Walker, Alice. *Once; Poems*. New York: Harcourt, Brace, 1968.

Clifton, Lucille. *Good Times*. New York: Random House, 1969.

Eckels, Jon. *Home is Where the Soul Is*. Detroit: Broadside, 1969.

Fabio, Sarah Webster. *A Mirror: A Soul*. San Francisco: Richardson, 1969.

Joans, Ted. *Black Pow-Wow*. New York: Hill and Wang, 1969.

———. *Afrodisia; New Poems*. New York: Hill and Wang, 1970.

Jordan, June. *Who Look at Me*. New York: Crowell, 1969.

———. *Some Changes*. New York: Dutton, 1971.

Marvin X. *Black Man Listen.* Detroit: Broadside, 1969.

Mungin, Horace. *Now See Here, Homes!* New York: Brothers Distributing Co., 1969.

Neal, Larry. *Black Boogaloo.* San Francisco: Journal of Black Poetry Press, 1969.

Patterson, Raymond R. *26 Ways of Looking at a Black Man and Other Poems.* New York: Award, 1969.

Plumpp, Sterling. *Portable Soul.* Chicago: Third World, 1969.

———. *Half Black, Half Blacker.* Chicago: Third World, 1970.

Reed, Clarence. *Not Forever Tears.* Newark: Jihad, 1969.

Sanchez, Sonia. *Homecoming.* Detroit: Broadside, 1969.

———. *We a Baddddd People.* Detroit: Broadside, 1970.

Washington, Raymond. *Vision from the Ghetto.* New Orleans: BlkArtSouth, 1969.

Young, Al. *Dancing.* New York: Corinth, 1969.

Addison, Lloyd. *The Aura and the Umbra.* London, Breman, 1970.

Barrax, Gerald W. *Another Kind of Rain; Poems.* Pittsburgh: Univ. of Pittsburgh Press, 1970.

Dumas, Henry. *Poetry for My People.* Carbondale: Southern Illinois Univ. Press, 1970.

Geary, Efton F. *Reflections of a Black Man.* San Antonio: Naylor, 1970.

Giovanni, Nikki. *Black Feeling, Black Talk/Black Judgement.* New York: Morrow, 1970.

———. *Re: Creation.* Detroit: Broadside, 1970.

———. *Spin a Soft Black Song.* New York: Hill and Wang, 1971.

Harper, Michael S. *Dear John, Dear Coltrane: Poems.* Pittsburgh: Univ. of Pittsburgh Press, 1970.

Missick, Rupert. *Naked Moon.* New York: Graham, 1970.

Murray, Pauli. *Dark Testament and Other Poems.* Norwalk, Conn: Silvermine, 1970.

Pritchard, N. H. *The Matrix: Poems 1960-1970.* New York: Doubleday, 1970.

Reed, Ishmael. *Catechism of D Neoamerican Hoodoo Church*. London: Breman, 1970.

Roberson, Ed. *When Thy King is a Boy: Poems*. Pittsburgh: Univ. Pittsburgh Press, 1970.

Scott-Heron, Gil. *Small Talk at 125th Street and Lenox*. New York: World, 1970.

Thompson, Julius Eric. *Hopes Tied Up in Promises*. Philadelphia: Dorrance, 1970.

Torregian, Sotere. *The Wounded Mattress*. Berkeley: Oyez, 1970.

Weatherly, Tom. *Maumau American Cantos*. New York: Corinth, 1970.

Wilson, Floria McCullough. *Not by Bread Alone*. New York: Carlton, 1970.

Zubena, Sister. *Calling All Sisters*. Chicago: Free Black Press, 1970.

————. *Om Black*. Chicago: The Author, 1971.

Brown, Patricia L., Don L. Lee, and Francis Ward. *To Gwen with Love: An Anthology Dedicated to Gwendolyn Brooks*. Chicago: Johnson, 1971.

Cortez, Jayne. *Festivals and Funerals*. New York: Phrase Text, 1971.

Davis, Joe, Jr. *The Sound of Thunder*. New York: Carlton, 1971.

Greenlee, Sam. *Blues for an African Princess*. Chicago: Third World, 1971.

Long, Doughtry. *Black Love Black Hope*. Detroit: Broadside, 1971.

Randolph, Jeremy. *Poems II*. New York: Rannick Playwrights, 1971.

Raven, John. *Blues for Momma and Other Low Down Stuff*. Detroit: Broadside, 1971.

Scott, Nathan A. *The Wild Prayer of Longing: Poetry and the Sacred*. New Haven: Yale Univ. Press, 1971.

Sterling X. *We Righteous Builders of Black Nations*. Chester, Pa.: Pyramid Publications, 1971.

Alhamis, Ahmed Akinwole. *Holy Ghosts: Poems*. Detroit: Broadside, 1972.

Aubert, Alvin. *Against the Blues: Poems*. Detroit: Broadside, 1972.

Cannon, C. E. *Saint Nigger*. Detroit: Broadside, 1972.

Carrington, Harold. *Drive Suite*. London: Breman, 1972.

Autobiography

Hammon, Briton. *A Narrative of the Uncommon Suffering and Surprising Deliverance of Briton Hammon*. Boston: Green and Russell, 1760.

Marrant, John. *A Narrative of the Lord's Wonderful Dealings with J. Marrant, a Black*. Halifax: J. Nicholson, 1812.

Vassa, Gustavus. *The Interesting Narrative of the Life of Olaudah Equiano*. Halifax: J. Nicholson, 1814.

Roper, Moses. *Narrative of the Adventures and Escapes of Moses Roper from American Slavery*. London: Harvey and Darton, 1837.

Grandy, Moses. *Narrative of the Life of Moses Grandy*. Boston: Oliver Johnson, 1844.

Clarke, Lewis Garrard. *Narrative of the Sufferings of Lewis Clarke*. Boston: D. H. Eli, 1845.

Douglass, Frederick. *Narrative of the Life of Frederick Douglass*. Boston: Anti-Slavery Office, 1845.

————. *My Bondage and My Freedom*. New York: Miller, Orton and Mulligan, 1855.

————. *Life and Times of Frederick Douglass*. Hartford: Park, 1881.

————. *Life and Times of Frederick Douglass*. Boston: DeWolfe, Fiske, 1892.

Lane, Lunsford. *Narrative of Lunsford Lane*. Boston: Hewes and Watson, 1845.

Clarke, Lewis Garrard and Milton Clarke. *Narratives of the Sufferings of Lewis and Milton Clarke.* Boston: B. Marsh, 1846.

Brown, William Wells. *Narrative of William Wells Brown.* Boston: Massachusetts Anti-Slavery Society, 1847.

————. *Three Years in Europe.* London: n.p., 1852.

Jefferson, Isaac (as dictated to Charles Campbell). *Memoirs of a Monticello Slave: The Life of Isaac Jefferson.* Unpublished manuscript, 1847.

Bibb, Henry. *Narrative of the Life and Adventures of Henry Bibb.* New York: The Author, 1849.

Brown, Henry Box. *Narrative of Henry Box Brown.* Boston: n.p., 1849.

Henson, Josiah. *The Life of Josiah Henson.* Boston, Phelps. 1849.

————. *Truth Stranger than Fiction.* Boston: Russell and Cleveland, 1858.

Truth, Sojourner. *Narrative of Sojourner Truth, Northern Slave.* Boston: n.p., 1850.

————. *Narrative of Sojourner Truth, a Bondswoman.* Boston: n.p., 1875.

Melbourn, Julius. *Life and Opinions of Julius Melbourn.* Syracuse: Hall and Dickson, 1851.

Paine, Lewis W. *Six Years in a Georgia Prison.* New York: B. Marsh, 1852.

Northup, Solomon. *Twelve Years a Slave: Narrative of Solomon Northup.* New York: Miller, Orton and Mulligan, 1853.

Ward, Samuel Ringgold. *The Autobiography of a Fugitive Slave.* London: J. Snow, 1855.

Steward, Austin. *22 Years a Slave and 40 Years a Freeman.* Rochester, N.Y.: William Alling, 1856.

Davis, Rev. Noah. *Narrative of Noah Davis.* Baltimore: John F. Weishampel, 1859.

Loguen, Jermain Wesley. *The Reverend J. W. Loguen as a*

Slave and as a Freeman. Syracuse: J. G. K. Truair, 1859.

Craft, William and Ellen. *Running a Thousand Miles for Freedom*. London: William Tweedie, 1860.

Brent, Linda. *Incidents in the Life of a Slave Girl*. London: Hodson, 1861.

Keckley, Elizabeth. *Behind the Scenes: Or Thirty Years a Slave and Four Years in the White House*. New York: G. W. Carleton, 1868.

Flipper, Henry. *The Colored Cadet at West Point*. New York: Homer, Lee, 1878.

Payne, Daniel. *Recollections of Seventy Years*. Nashville, Tenn.: A.M.E. Sunday School Union, 1888.

Smith, Amanda. *An Autobiography*. Chicago: Meyer, 1893.

Langston, John Mercer. *From the Virginia Plantation to the National Capitol*. Hartford, Conn.: American Publishing, 1894.

Washington, Booker T. *Up from Slavery*. New York: Doubleday, 1900.

Gibbs, Mifflin W. *Shadow and Light: An Autobiography*. Washington: The Author, 1902.

Miller, Kelly. *Out of the House of Bondage*. New York: Neale, 1914.

Corrothers, James D. *In Spite of the Handicap*. New York: Doran, 1916.

Walters, Alexander. *My Life and Work*. Chicago: Fleming H. Revell, 1917.

Moton, Robert Russa. *Finding a Way*. New York: Doubleday, 1920.

Gordon, Taylor. *Born to Be*. New York: Corici, 1929.

Johnson, James Weldon. *Along This Way*. New York: Viking, 1933.

Herndon, Angelo. *Let Me Live*. New York: Random House, 1937.

McKay, Claude. *A Long Way from Home*. New York: Furman, 1937.

DuBois, W. E. B. *Dusk of Dawn.* New York: Harcourt, Brace, 1940.

―――. *The Autobiography of W. E. B. DuBois.* New York: International Pubs., 1967.

Hughes, Langston. *The Big Sea.* New York: Knopf, 1940.

―――. *I Wonder as I Wander.* New York: Rinehart, 1956.

Terrell, Mary Church. *A Colored Woman in a White World.* Washington, D.C.: Randsdell, 1940.

Handy, W. C. *Father of the Blues.* New York: Macmillan, 1941.

Hurston, Zora Neale. *Dust Tracks on a Road.* Philadelphia: Lippincott, 1942.

Redding, J. Saunders. *No Day of Triumph.* New York: Harper, 1942.

―――. *On Being Negro in America.* Indianapolis: Bobbs-Merrill, 1951.

Wright, Richard. *Black Boy.* New York and London: Harper, 1945.

Thompson, Era Bell. *American Daughter.* Chicago: Univ. of Chicago Press, 1946.

Louis, Joe. *My Life and Story.* New York: Duell, 1947.

―――. *The Joe Louis Story.* New York: Grosset, 1955.

Robinson, Jackie. *My Own Story.* New York: Greenberg, 1948.

White, Walter. *A Man Called White.* New York: Viking, 1948.

Patterson, Haywood, and Earl Conrad. *Scottsboro Boy.* Garden City, N.Y.: Doubleday, 1950.

Horne, Lena (as told to Helen Arustein and Carlton Moss). *In Person: Lena Horne.* New York: Greenberg, 1951.

Waters, Ethel. *His Eye is on the Sparrow.* Garden City, N.Y.: Doubleday, 1951.

Goodwin, Ruby Berkeley. *It's Good to Be Black.* Garden City, N.Y.: Doubleday, 1953.

Armstrong, Louis. *Satchmo: My Life in New Orleans.* Englewood Cliffs, N.J.: Prentice-Hall, 1954.

Mays, Willie (as told to Charles Einstein). *Born to Play Ball.* New York: Putnam, 1955.

Anderson, Marian. *My Lord, What a Morning!* New York: Viking, 1956.

Holiday, Billie (with William Duffy). *Lady Sings the Blues.* Garden City, N.Y.: Doubleday, 1956.

Kitt, Eartha. *Thursday's Child.* New York: Duell, 1956.

Murray, Pauli. *Proud Shoes.* New York: Harper, 1956.

Gibson, Althea. *I Always Wanted to Be Somebody.* New York: Harper, 1958.

Campanella, Roy. *It's Good to Be Alive.* Boston: Little, Brown, 1959.

Dunham, Katherine. *A Touch of Innocence.* New York: Harcourt, Brace, 1959.

Bechet, Sidney. *Treat It Gentle.* New York: Hill and Wang, 1960.

Bates, Daisy. *The Long Shadow of Little Rock, a Memoir.* New York: McKay, 1962.

Patterson, Floyd (with Milton Gross). *Victory Over Myself.* New York: Random House, 1962.

Atkins, James A. *The Age of Jim Crow.* New York: Vantage, 1964.

Brown, Jimmy (with Myron Cape). *Off My Chest.* Garden City, N.Y.: Doubleday, 1964.

Gregory, Dick (with Robert Lipsyte). *Nigger: An Autobiography.* New York: Dutton, 1964.

Malcolm X (with Alex Haley). *The Autobiography of Malcolm X.* New York: Grove Press, 1964.

Brown, Claude. *Manchild in the Promised Land.* New York: Macmillan, 1965.

Cayton, Horace R. *Long Old Road.* New York: Simon and Schuster, 1965.

Davis, Sammy, Jr. *Yes I Can.* New York: Farrar, Straus, 1965.

Parks, Gordon. *A Choice of Weapons*. New York: Harper and Row, 1965.

Crumer, Cole, Sr. *My Life Is an Open Book*. New York: Carlton, 1966.

Green, Ely. *Ely*. New York: Seabury, 1966.

Russell, Bill (with Bill McSweeny). *Go Up for Glory*. New York: Coward-McCann, 1966.

Schuyler, George S. *Black and Conservative*. New Rochelle, N.Y.: Arlington House, 1966.

David, Jay, ed. *Growing Up Black*. New York: Morrow, 1968.

Bontemps, Arna, ed. *Great Slave Narratives*. Boston: Beacon, 1969.

Brown, H. Rap. *Die Nigger Die!* New York: Dial, 1969.

Osofsky, Gilbert, ed. *Puttin' On Ole Massa*. New York: Harper and Row, 1969.

Wormley, Stanton, and Lewis H. Fenderson, eds. *Many Shades of Black*. New York: Morrow, 1969.

Lester, Julius, ed. *To Be a Slave*. New York: Dell, 1970.

Fiction

Brown, William Wells. *Clotel; Or the President's Daughter*. London: Partridge and Oakey, 1853.

————. *Miralda; or the Beautiful Quadroon* (*Clotel* revised). New York: The Weekly Anglo-African Magazine, 1860-61.

————. *Clotelle; A Tale of the Southern States* (*Miralda* revised). Boston: James Redpath, 1864.

————. *Clotelle; or the Colored Heroine* (*Clotelle; A Tale* revised). Boston: Lee and Shepard, 1867.

Webb, Frank J. *The Garies and Their Friends*. London: Routledge, 1857.

Delany, Martin R. *Blake; or the Huts of America*. New York: Anglo-African Magazine, 1859.

Blackson, Lorenzo D. *The Rise and Progress of the Kingdoms of Light and Darkness*. Philadelphia: J. Nicholas, 1867.

Detter, Thomas. *Nellie Brown, or the Jealous Wife*. San Francisco: Cuddy and Hughes, 1871.

Purvis, T. T. *The Singing Maiden*. Philadelphia: Walton, 1881.

Howard, James H. W. *Bond and Free*. Harrisburg, Pa.: Edwin K. Myers, 1886.

Harper, Frances E. W. *Iola Leroy*. Boston: James H. Earle, 1892.

Kelly, E. D. *Megda*. Boston: James H. Earle, 1892.

Earle, Victoria. *Aunt Lindy: A Story Founded Upon Real Life*. New York: J. J. Little, 1893.

Johnson, Amelia E. *The Hazeley Family*. Rochester, N. Y.: American Baptist Publishing Society, 1894.

Stowers, Walter H., and William H. Anderson. *Appointed*. Detroit: Detroit Law Printing, 1894.

Burgess, M. L. *Ave Maria*. Boston: Press of the Monthly Review, 1895.

Nelson, Alice Dunbar. *Violet and Other Tales*. Boston: The Monthly Review, 1895.

————. *The Goodness of St. Rocque and Other Stories*. New York: Dodd, Mead, 1899.

Jones, J. McHenry, *Hearts of Gold*. Wheeling, W. Va.: Daily Intelligencer Steam Job Press, 1896.

Dunbar, Paul Laurence. *The Uncalled*. New York: Dodd, Mead, 1898.

————. *Folks from Dixie*. New York: Dodd, Mead, 1898.

————. *The Love of Landry*. New York: Dodd, Mead, 1900.

————. *The Strength of Gideon*. New York: Dodd, Mead, 1900.

————. *The Fanatics*. New York: Dodd, Mead, 1900.

————. *The Sport of the Gods*. New York: Dodd, Mead, 1902.

————. *In Old Plantation Days*. New York: Dodd, Mead, 1903.

————. *The Heart of Happy Hollow*. New York: Dodd, Mead, 1904.

————. *The Best Short Stories of Paul Laurence Dunbar* (Benjamin Brawley, ed.). New York: Dodd, Mead, 1938.

Chesnutt, Charles W. *The Conjure Woman*. Boston: Houghton Mifflin, 1899.

————. *The Wife of His Youth and Other Stories of the Color Line*. Boston: Houghton Mifflin, 1899.

————. *The House Behind the Cedars*. Boston and New York: Houghton Mifflin, 1900.

————. *The Marrow of Tradition*. Boston and New York: Houghton Mifflin, 1901.

————. *The Colonel's Dream*. New York: Doubleday, Page, 1905.

Griggs, Sutton E. *Imperium in Imperio*. Cincinnati: Editor Publishing, 1899.

————. *Overshadowed*. Nashville: Orion, 1901.

————. *Unfettered*. Nashville: Orion, 1902.

————. *The Hindered Hand*. Nashville: Orion, 1905.

————. *Pointing the Way*. Nashville: Orion, 1908.

Hopkins, Pauline. *Contending Forces*. Boston: Colored Cooperative Publishing, 1900.

Corrothers, James D. *The Black Cat Club*. New York: Funk and Wagnalls, 1902.

Durham, John S. *Diane, Priestess of Haiti*. *Lippincott's Monthly Magazine*, 1902.

Pryor, G. Langhorne. *Neither Bond Nor Free*. New York: J. S. Ogilvie, 1902.

Nash, T. E. D. *Love and Vengeance*. Portsmouth, Va.: The Author, 1903.

Brown, Handy N. *The Necromancer; or Voo-Doo Doctor*. Opelika, Ala.: n.p., 1904.

Johnson, Edward A. *Light Ahead for the Negro*. New York: Grafton Press, 1904.

McClellan, George M. *Old Greenbottom Inn and Other Stories*. Louisville: The Author, 1906.

McGirt, James E. *The Triumph of Ephraim*. Philadelphia: McGirt, 1907.

Grant, J. W. *Out of the Darkness*. Nashville: National Baptist Pub., 1909.

Walker, Thomas H. B. *Bebbly*. Gainesville, Fla.: Pepper, 1910.

Waring, Robert L. *As We See It*. Washington, D. C.: C. F. Sudwarth, 1910.

DuBois, W. E. B. *The Quest of the Silver Fleece*. Chicago: McClurg, 1911.

————. *The Dark Princess*. New York: Harcourt, Brace, 1928.

————. *The Ordeal of Mansart*. New York: Mainstream, 1957.

————. *Mansart Builds a School*. New York: Mainstream, 1959.

————. *Worlds of Color*. New York: Mainstream, 1961.

Cotter, Joseph Seamon. *Negro Tales*. New York: Cosmopolitan Press, 1912.

Johnson, James Weldon. *The Autobiography of an Ex-Colored Man*. Boston: Sherman, French, 1912.

Jones, York. *The Climbers, a Story of Sun-Kissed Sweethearts*. Chicago: Glad Tidings Publishing, 1912.

Micheaux, Oscar. *The Conquest*. Lincoln, Neb.: Woodruff, 1913.

————. *The Forged Note*. Lincoln, Neb.: Western Book Supply, 1915.

————. *The Homesteader*. Sioux City, Ia.: Western Book Supply, 1917.

————. *The Wind from Nowhere*. New York: Book Supply, 1941.

————. *The Case of Mrs. Wingate*. New York: Book Supply, 1944.

————. *The Story of Dorothy Stanfield*. New York: Book Supply, 1946.

————. *The Masquerade*. New York: Book Supply, 1947.

Ashby, William M. *Redder Blood*. New York: Cosmopolitan Press, 1915.

Gilmore, F. Grant. *The Problem, a Military Novel*. Rochester, N. Y.: Henry, Conolly, 1915.

Shackelford, Otis M. *Lillian Simmons*. Kansas City: R. M. Rigby, 1915.

Bruce, John Edward. *The Awakening of Hezekiah Jones*. Hopkinsville, Ky.: Philip H. Brown, 1916.

Adams, Clayton (Charles H. Holmes). *Ethiopia, the Land of Promise*. New York: Cosmopolitan Press, 1917.

Downing, Henry F. *The American Cavalryman*. New York: Neale, 1917.

Ellis, George W. *The Leopard's Claw*. New York: International Authors' Association, 1917.

Rogers, Joel A. *From Superman to Man*. Chicago: M. A. Donahue, 1917.

Fleming, S. L. B. *Hope's Highway*. New York: Neale, 1918.

Brown, Charlotte H. *"Morning," an Appeal to the Heart of the South*. Boston: Pilgrim Press, 1919.

Dreer, Herman. *The Immediate Jewel of His Soul*. St. Louis: St. Louis Argus, 1919.

Tracy, Robert A. *The Sword of Nemesis*. New York: Neale, 1919.

Johnson, Fenton. *Tales of Darkest America*. Chicago: Favorite Magazine Publishers, 1920.

Wright, Zara. *Black and White Tangled Threads*. Chicago: The Author, 1920.

Spencer, Mary Etta. *The Resentment*. Philadelphia: A. M. E. Book Concern, 1921.

Pickens, William. *The Vengeance of the Gods and Three Other Stories of Real American Color Line Life*. Philadelphia: A. M. E. Book Concern, 1922.

———. *American Aesop, Negro and Other Humor*. Boston: Jordan and Moore, 1926.

Jordan, Moses. *The Meat Man*. Chicago: Jody, 1923.

Toomer, Jean. *Cane*. New York: Boni and Liveright, 1923.

Braithwaite, William S. *Going Over Tindel*. Boston: Brimmer, 1924.

Dorsey, John T. *The Lion of Judah*. Chicago: Fauche, 1924.

Fauset, Jessie R. *There Is Confusion*. New York: Boni and Liveright, 1924.

————. *Plum Bun*. New York: Stokes, 1929.

————. *The Chinaberry Tree*. New York: Stokes, 1931.

————. *Comedy American Style*. New York: Stokes, 1933.

Jones, Joshua Henry. *By Sanction of Law*. Boston: Brimmer, 1924.

White, Walter. *The Fire in the Flint*. New York: Knopf, 1924.

————. *Flight*. New York: Knopf, 1926.

Liscomb, Harry F. *The Prince of Washington Square*. New York: Stokes, 1925.

Brocket, Joshua A. *Zipporah, the Maid of Midian*. Zion, Ill.: Zion Printing, 1926.

Roberts, Walter A. *The Haunting Hand*. New York: Macaulay, 1926.

————. *Mayor Harding of New York*. New York: Mohawk, 1931.

————. *The Moralist*. New York: Mohawk, 1931.

————. *The Top Floor Killer*. London: Nicholson and Watson, 1935.

————. *The Pomegranate*. Indianapolis: Bobbs-Merrill, 1941.

————. *Royal Street*. Indianapolis: Bobbs-Merrill, 1944.

————. *Creole Dusk*. Indianapolis: Bobbs-Merrill, 1948.

————. *The Single Star*. Indianapolis: Bobbs-Merrill, 1949.

Walrond, Eric. *Tropic Death*. New York: Boni and Liveright, 1926.

Durant, E. Elliot and Cuthbert M. Roach. *The Princess of Naragpur; or a Daughter of Allah*. New York: Grafton, 1928.

Fisher, Rudolph. *The Walls of Jericho*. New York and London: Knopf, 1928.

————. *The Conjure Man Dies*. New York: Convici, Friede, 1932.

Larsen, Nella. *Quicksand*. New York and London: Knopf, 1928.

————. *Passing. New York: Knopf, 1929.*

McKay, Claude. *Home to Harlem*. New York and London: Harper, 1928.

————. *Banjo*. New York: Harper, 1929.

————. *Gingertown*. New York: Harper, 1932.

————. *Banana Bottom*. New York: Harper, 1933.

Coleman, Albert E. *The Romantic Adventures of Rosy the Octoroon*. Boston: Meador, 1929.

Thurman, Wallace. *The Blacker the Berry*. New York: Macaulay, 1929.

————. *Infants of the Spring*. New York: Macaulay, 1932.

———— (with A. L. Furman). *The Interne*. New York: Macaulay, 1932.

Huffman, Eugene H. *Now I Am Civilized*. Los Angeles: Wetzel, 1930.

Hughes, Langston. *Not Without Laughter*. New York: Knopf, 1930.

————. *The Ways of White Folks*. New York: Knopf, 1934.

————. *Simple Speaks His Mind*. New York: Simon and Schuster, 1950.

————. *Laughing to Keep from Crying*. New York: Henry Holt, 1952.

————. *Simple Takes a Wife*. New York: Simon and Schuster, 1953.

————. *Simple Stakes a Claim*. New York: Rinehart, 1957.

————. *Tambourines to Glory*. New York: John Day, 1958.

————. *The Best of Simple*. New York: Hill and Wang, 1961.

————. *Something in Common*. New York: Hill and Wang, 1963.

————. *Simple's Uncle Sam*. New York: Hill and Wang, 1965.

Lubin, Gilbert. *The Promised Land*. Boston: Christopher, 1930.

Paynter, John H. *Fugitives of the Pearl*. Washington, ·D.C.: Associated Publishing, 1930.

Bontemps, Arna. *God Sends Sunday*. New York: Harcourt, Brace, 1931.

————. *Black Thunder*. New York: Macmillan, 1936.

————. *Drums at Dusk*. New York: Macmillan, 1939.

Henry, William S. *Out of Wedlock*. Boston: Badger, the Golden Press, 1931.

Imbert, Dennis I. *The Colored Gentlemen*. New Orleans: Williams, 1931.

Schuyler, George. *Black No More*. New York: Macaulay, 1931.

————. *Slaves Today*. New York: Brewer, Warren, and Putnam, 1931.

Cullen, Countee. *One Way to Heaven*. New York and London: Harper, 1932.

Hill, John H. *Princess Malah*. Washington, D. C.: Associated Publishers, 1933.

Miller, E. H. *The Protestant*. Boston: Christopher, 1933.

Hurston, Zora Neale. *Jonah's Gourd Vine*. Philadelphia: Lippincott, 1934.

————. *Mules and Men*. Philadelphia: Lippincott, 1935.

————. *Their Eyes Were Watching God*. Philadelphia and London: Lippincott, 1937.

————. *Moses, Man of the Mountain*. Philadelphia: Lippincott, 1939.

————. *Seraph on the Suwanee*. New York: Scribner's, 1948.

Henderson, George. *Ollie Miss*. New York: Stokes, 1935.

————. *Jule*. New York: Creative Age Press, 1946.

Waterman, Charles E. *Carib Queens*. Boston: Bruce Humphries, 1935.

Shaw, O'Wendell. *Greater Need Below*. Columbus, Ohio: Bi-Monthly Negro Book Club, 1936.

Lee, George W. *River George*. New York: Macaulay, 1937.

————. *Beale Street Sundown*. New York: Field, 1942.

Patton, Lew. *Did Adam Sin? And Other Stories*. Los Angeles: n.p., 1937.

Turpin, Waters E. *These Low Grounds*. New York and London: Harper, 1937.

———. *O Canaan!* New York: Doubleday, Doran, 1939.

———. *The Rootless*. New York: Vantage, 1957.

Gilbert, Mercedes. *Aunt Sara's Wooden God*. Boston: Christopher, 1938.

Ross, G. H. *Beyond the River*. Boston: Meador, 1938.

Wright, Richard. *Uncle Tom's Children*. New York: Harper, 1938.

———. *Native Son*. New York: Harper, 1940.

———. *The Outsider*. New York: Harper, 1953.

———. *Savage Holiday*. New York: Harper, 1954.

———. *The Long Dream*. New York: Doubleday, 1958.

———. *Eight Men*. New York: World, 1961.

———. *Lawd Today*. New York: Walker, 1963.

Attaway, William. *Let Me Breathe Thunder*. New York: Doubleday, Doran, 1939.

———. *Blood on the Forge*. New York: Doubleday, Doran, 1941.

Pitts, Gertrude. *Tragedies of Life*. Newark, N. J.: The Author, 1939.

Scott, Anne. *George Sampson Brite*. Boston: Meador, 1939.

Garner, Carlyle W. *It Wasn't Fair*. New York: Fortuny's, 1940.

Lee, John M. *Counter Clockwise*. New York: Wendell Malliet, 1940.

Graham, K. C. *Under the Cottonwood*. New York: Wendell Malliet, 1941.

Swados, Felice. *House of Fury*. New York: Doubleday, Doran, 1941.

Jenkins. D. F. *It Was Not My World*. Los Angeles: The Author, 1942.

Nelson, Annie G. *After the Storm*. Columbia, S. C.: Hampton, 1942.

———. *The Dawn Appears*. Columbia, S. C.: Hampton, 1944.

Powell, Adam Clayton, Sr. *Picketing Hell*. New York: Wendell Malliet, 1942.

Bernard, R. T. *What's Wrong with Lottery?* Boston: Meador, 1943.

Gholson, Edward. *From Jerusalem to Jericho*. Boston: Chapman and Grimes, 1943.

Lucas, Curtis. *Flour Is Dusty*. Philadelphia: Dorrance, 1943.

————. *Third Ward Newark*. New York and Chicago: Ziff Davis, 1946.

————. *Forbidden Fruit*. New York: Universal, 1953.

Offord, C. R. *The White Face*. New York: McBride, 1943.

————. *The Naked Fear*. New York: Ace Books, 1954.

Roach, Thomas E. *Victor*. Boston: Meador, 1943.

————. *Samson*. Boston: Meador, 1952.

Williams, Chancellor. *The Raven*. Philadelphia: Dorrance, 1943.

————. *Have You Been to the River?* New York: Exposition Press, 1952.

Dean, Corinne. *Cocoanut Suite*. Boston: Meador, 1944.

Gray, W. S. *Her Last Performance*. Omaha, Neb.: Rapid Printing, 1944.

Burnham, Frederick R. *Taking Chances*. Los Angeles: Haynes, 1945.

Caldwell, L. A. H. *The Policy King*. Chicago: New Vista, 1945.

Himes, Chester B. *If He Hollers Let Him Go*. New York: Doubleday, Doran, 1945.

————. *Lonely Crusade*. New York: Knopf, 1947.

————. *Cast the First Stone*. New York: Coward- McCann, 1952.

————. *Third Generation*. New York: World, 1954.

————. *The Primitive*. New York: New American Library, 1955.

————. *For Love of Imabelle*. New York: Fawcett, 1957.

————. *The Crazy Kill*. New York: Berkeley, 1959.

————. *The Real Cool Killers*. New York: Berkeley, 1959.

————. *All Shot Up*. New York: Berkeley. 1960.

————. *The Big Gold Dream*. New York: Berkeley, 1960.

————. *Cotton Comes to Harlem*. New York: Putnam, 1965.

————. *A Rage in Harlem*. New York: Avon, 1965.

————. *Pinktoes*. New York: Putnam, 1965.

————. *The Heat's On*. New York: Putnam, 1966.

————. *Run Man Run*. New York: Putnam, 1966.

Wood, O. P. *High Ground*. New York: Exposition Press, 1945.

Gross, Werter L. *The Golden Recovery*. Reno, Nev.: The Author, 1946.

Petry, Ann. *The Street*. Boston: Houghton Mifflin, 1946.

————. *Country Place*. Boston: Houghton Mifflin, 1947.

————. *The Narrows*. Boston: Houghton Mifflin, 1953.

————. *Tituba of Salem Village*. New York: Crowell, 1964.

————. *Miss Muriel and Other Stories*. Boston: Houghton Mifflin, 1971.

Yerby, Frank. *The Foxes of Harrow*. New York: Dial, 1946.

————. *The Vixens*. New York: Dial, 1947.

————. *The Golden Hawk*. New York: Dial, 1948.

————. *Pride's Castle*. New York: Dial, 1949.

————. *Flood Tide*. New York: Dial, 1950.

————. *A Woman Called Fancy*. New York: Dial, 1951.

————. *The Saracen Blade*. New York: Dial, 1952.

————. *The Devil's Laughter*. New York: Dial, 1953.

————. *Benton's Row*. New York: Dial, 1954.

————. *Bride of Liberty*. New York: Doubleday, 1954.

————. *The Treasure of Pleasant Valley*. New York: Dial, 1955.

————. *Captain Rebel*. New York: Dial, 1956.

————. *Fairoaks*. New York: Dial, 1957.

————. *The Serpent and the Staff*. New York: Dial, 1958.

————. *Jarrett's Jade*. New York: Dial, 1959.

————. *Gillian*. New York: Dial, 1960.

————. *The Garfield Honor*. New York: Dial, 1961.

————. *Griffin's Way*. New York: Dial, 1962.

————. *The Old Gods Laugh*. New York: Dial, 1964.

————. *An Odor of Sanctity*. New York: Dial, 1965.

————. *Goat Song*. New York: Dial, 1967.

————. *Judas, My Brother*. New York: Dial, 1968.

————. *Speak Now: A Modern Novel*. New York: Dial, 1969.

Blair, J. P. *Democracy Reborn*. New York: The Author, 1947.

Bland, Alden. *Behold A Cry*. New York: Scribner's, 1947.

Motley, Willard. *Knock on Any Door*. New York: Appleton-Century, 1947.

————. *We Fished All Night*. New York: Appleton-Century-Crofts, 1951.

————. *Let No Man Write My Epitaph*. New York: Random House, 1958.

————. *Let Noon Be Fair*. New York: Putnam, 1966.

Rasmussen, E. M. *The First Night*. New York: Wendell Malliet, 1947.

Thomas, Will. *God Is for White Folks*. New York: Creative Age Press, 1947.

————. *Love Knows No Barriers (God is for White Folks* reprinted). New York: New American Library, 1951.

Smith, William Gardner, *Last of the Conquerors*. New York: Farrar, Straus, 1948.

————. *Anger at Innocence*. New York: Farrar, Straus, 1950.

————. *South Street*. New York: Farrar, Straus, 1954.

————. *The Stone Face*. New York: Farrar, Straus, 1963.

West, Dorothy. *The Living Is Easy*. Boston: Houghton Mifflin, 1948.

Cooper, Alvin C. *Stroke of Midnight*. Nashville: Counterpoise, 1949.

Hunter, H. L. *The Miracles of the Red Altar Cloth*. New York: Exposition Press, 1949.

Jarrette, A. Q. *Beneath the Sky*. New York: Weinberg Book Supply, 1949.

Savoy, Willard. *Alien Land*. New York: Dutton, 1949.

Demby, William. *Bettlecreek*. New York: Rinehart, 1950.

————. *The Catacombs*. New York: Pantheon, 1965.

Kaye, Philip B. *Taffy*. New York: Crown, 1950.

Redding, J. Saunders. *Stranger and Alone*. New York: Harcourt, Brace, 1950.

Bridgeforth, Med. *Another Chance*. New York: Exposition Press, 1951.

Brown, Lloyd. *Iron City*. New York: Masses and Mainstream, 1951.

Dodson, Owen. *Boy at the Window*. New York: Farrar, Straus and Young, 1951.

————. *When Trees Were Green*. New York: Popular Library, 1967.

Finch, Amanda. *Back Trail*. New York: William-Frederick Press, 1951.

Morris, E. J. *The Cop*. New York: Exposition Press, 1951.

Dickens, Dorothy Lee. *Black on the Rainbow*. New York: Pageant Press, 1952.

Ellison, Ralph. *Invisible Man*. New York: Random House, 1952.

Arnold, Ethel Nishua. *She Knew No Evil*. New York: Vantage, 1953.

Baldwin, James. *Go Tell It on the Mountain*. New York: Knopf, 1953.

————. *Giovanni's Room*. New York: Dial, 1956.

————. *Another Country*. New York: Dial, 1962.

————. *Going to Meet the Man*. New York: Dial, 1965.

————. *Tell Me How Long the Train's Been Gone*. New York: Dial, 1968.

————. *No Name in the Street*. New York: Dial, 1972.

Brooks, Gwendolyn. *Maud Martha*. New York: Harper, 1953.

Fisher, William. *The Waiters*. New York: World, 1953.

Groves, John Wesley. *Pyrrhic Victory, A Collection of Short Stories*. Philadelphia: United Publishers, 1953.

————. *Shellbreak*. New York: Paperback Library, 1970.

Hough, Florenz H. *Black Paradise*. Philadelphia: Dorrance, 1953.

Kennedy, Mark. *The Pecking Order*. New York: Appleton, 1953.

Lamming, George. *In the Castle of My Skin*. New York: McGraw-Hill, 1953.

Jordan, Elsie. *Strange Sinner*. New York: Pageant, 1954.

Killens, John O. *Youngblood*. New York: Dial, 1954.

———. *And Then We Heard the Thunder*. New York: Knopf, 1963.

———. *'Sippi*. New York: Simon and Schuster, 1967.

———. *Slaves*. New York: Pyramid, 1969.

———. *The Cotilliin; or One Good Bull is Half the Herd*. New York: Trident, 1971.

Smythwick, Charles A., Jr. *False Measure*. New York: William-Frederick, 1954.

Tarter, Charles L. *Family of Destiny*. New York: Vantage, 1954.

Wallace, Elizabeth West. *Scandal at Daybreak*. New York: Pageant, 1954.

Ward, Thomas Playfair. *The Clutches of Circumstances*. New York: Pageant, 1954.

———. *The Truth That Makes Men Free*. New York: Pageant, 1955.

Wiggins, Walter, Jr. *Dreams in Reality of the Undersea Craft*. New York: Pageant, 1954.

Browne, Theodore. *The Band Will Not Play Dixie*. New York: Exposition, 1955.

Breechwood, Mary. *Memphis Jackson's Son*. Boston: Houghton Mifflin, 1956.

Carrere, Mentis. *Man in the Cane*. New York: Vantage, 1956.

Childress, Alice. *Like One of the Family*. Brooklyn, N. Y.: Independence, 1956.

Coolidge, Fay Liddle. *Black is White*. New York: Vantage, 1956.

Sydnor, W. Leon. *Veronica*. New York: Exposition, 1956.

English, Rubynn M. *Citizen U. S. A*. New York: Pageant, 1957.

Jackson, W. Warner. *The Birth of the Martyr's Ghost*. New York: Comet, 1957.

Mayfield, Julian. *The Hit*. New York: Vanguard, 1957.

———. *The Long Night*. New York: Vanguard, 1958.

———. *The Grand Parade*. New York: Vanguard, 1961.

Shaw, Letty M. *Angel Mink*. New York: Comel, 1957.

Simmons, Herbert. *Corner Boy*. Boston: Houghton Mifflin, 1957.

———. *Man Walking on Eggshells*. Boston: Houghton Mifflin, 1962.

Austin, Edmund C. *The Black Challenge*. New York: Vantage, 1958.

Gibson, Richard A. *A Mirror for Magistrates*. London: Anthony Blond, 1958.

Williams, Jerome Ardell. *The Tin Box*. New York: Vantage, 1958.

Anderson, Alston. *Lover Man*. Garden City, N.Y.: Doubleday, 1959.

———. *All God's Children*. Indianapolis: Bobbs-Merrill, 1965.

Beaumont, Charles. *The Intruder*. New York: Putnam, 1959.

Brown, Frank London. *Trumbull Park*. Chicago: Regnery, 1959.

Davis, Joseph A. *Black Bondage*. New York: Exposition, 1959.

Fenderson, Harold. *The Phony and Other Stories*. New York: Exposition, 1959.

Holder, Geoffrey. *Black Gods, Green Islands*. Garden City, N.Y.: Doubleday, 1959.

Hooks, Nathaniel. *Town on Trial*. New York: Exposition, 1959.

Lee, James F. *The Victims*. New York: Vantage, 1959.

Marshall, Paule. *Brown Girl, Brownstones*. New York: Random House, 1959.

———. *Soul Clap Hands and Sing*. New York: Atheneum, 1961.

———. *The Chosen Place, the Timeless People*. New York: Harcourt, Brace and World, 1969.

Pollard, Freeman. *Seeds of Turmoil*. New York: Exposition, 1959.

West, John. *Cobra Venom*. New York: New American Library, 1959.

———. *An Eye for an Eye*. New York: New American Library, 1959.

———. *A Taste for Blood*. New York: New American Library, 1960.

———. *Bullets Are My Business*. New York: New American Library, 1960.

———. *Death on the Rocks*. New York: New American Library, 1961.

Cooper, Clarence L. *The Scene*. New York: Crown, 1960.

———. *Weed*. Evanston, Ill.: Regency, 1961.

———. *The Dark Messenger*. Evanston, Ill.: Regency, 1962.

———. *The Farm*. New York: Crown, 1967.

Pitcher, Oliver. *Dust of Silence*. San Francisco: Troubador, 1960.

Shores, Minnie T. *Publicans and Sinners*. New York: Comet, 1960.

———. *Americans in America*. Boston: Christopher, 1966.

Williams, John A. *The Angry Ones*. New York: Ace Books, 1960.

———. *Night Song*. New York: Farrar, Straus, 1961.

———. *Sissie*. New York: Farrar, Straus, 1963.

———. *The Man Who Cried I Am*. Boston: Little, Brown, 1967.

———. *Sons of Darkness, Sons of Light*. Boston: Little, Brown, 1969.

———. *Captain Blackman*. Garden City, N.Y.: Doubleday, 1972.

Anderson, Henry L. *No Use Cryin'*. Los Angeles: Western Publishers, 1961.

Davis, Christopher. *First Family*. New York: Coward-McCann, 1961.

Hercules, Frank. *Where the Hummingbird Flies*. New York: Harcourt, 1961.

———. *I Want a Black Doll*. New York: Simon and Schuster, 1967.

Madden, Will A. *Two and One*. New York: Exposition, 1961.

————. *Five More Short Stories*. New York: Exposition, 1963.

Broaders, Robert. *Spokes for the Wheel*. Amherst, N.Y.: Kingdom Press, 1962.

Brown, Mattye J. *The Reign of Terror*. Washington, D. C.: Vantage, 1962.

Cooper, William A. *Thank God for a Song*. New York: Exposition, 1962.

Crump, Paul. *Burn, Killer, Burn*. Chicago: Johnson, 1962.

Farrell, John T. *The Naked Truth*. Washington, D.C.: Vantage, 1962.

Kelley, William M. *A Different Drummer*. Garden City, N.Y.: Doubleday, 1962.

————. *Dancers on the Shore*. Garden City, N.Y.: Doubleday, 1964.

————. *A Drop of Patience*. Garden City, N.Y.: Doubleday, 1965.

————. *Dem*. Garden City, N.Y.: Doubleday, 1967.

————. *Dunfords Travels Everywhere*. New York: Doubleday, 1970.

Skinner, Theodosia B. *Ice Cream from Heaven*. Washington, D.C.: Vantage 1962.

Teague, Robert L. *The Climate of Candor*. New York: Pageant, 1962.

Davis, Russell F. *Anything for a Friend*. New York: Crown, 1963.

Delaney, Samuel R. *Captives of the Flame*. New York: Avon, 1963.

————. *The Tomorrow of Taron*. New York: Avon, 1964.

————. *City of a Thousand Suns*. New York: Ace, 1965.

————. *Babel-17*. New York: Ace, 1966.

————. *The Einstein Intersection*. New York: Ace, 1967.

————. *Nova*. Garden City, N.Y.: Doubleday, 1968.

————. *The Jewels of Aptor*. New York: Ace, 1968.

Edward, Junius. *If We Must Die*. Garden City, N.Y.: Doubleday, 1963.

Parks, Gordon. *The Learning Tree*. New York: Harper, 1963.

Perry, Charles. *Portrait of a Young Man Drowning*. New York: Simon and Schuster, 1963.

Roberson, Sadie. *Killer of the Dream*. New York: Carlton, 1963.

Rogers, Joel. *She Walks in Beauty*. Los Angeles: Western, 1963.

Vroman, Mary E. *Esther*. New York: Bantam, 1963.

———. *Harlem Summer*. New York: Berkeley, 1968.

Wells, Moses Peter. *Three Adventurous Men*. New York: Carlton, 1963.

Wright, Charles. *The Messenger*. New York: Farrar, Straus, 1963.

———. *The Wig, a Mirror Image*. New York: Farrar, Straus, 1966.

Edwards, S. W. *Go Now in Darkness*. Chicago: Baker, 1964.

Flemister, John T. *Furlough from Hell*. New York: Exposition, 1964.

Gaines, Ernest J. *Catharine Carmier*. New York: Atheneum, 1964.

———. *Of Love and Dust*. New York: Dial, 1967.

———. *Bloodline*. New York: Dial, 1968.

———. *The Autobiography of Miss Jane Pittman*. New York: Dial, 1971.

Gunn, Bill. *All the Rest Have Died*. New York: Delacorte, 1964.

Hunter, Helen. *Magnificent White Men*. New York: Vantage, 1964.

Hunter, Kristin. *God Bless the Child*. New York: Scribner's, 1964.

———. *The Landlord*. New York: Scribner's, 1966.

West, William. *Cornered*. New York: Carlton, 1964.

Boles, Robert. *The People One Knows*. Boston: Houghton Mifflin, 1965.

———. *Curling*. Boston: Houghton Mifflin, 1967.

Braithwaite, E. R. *Choice of Straws*. London: Bodley Head, 1965.

Carew, Jan. *Green Winter*. New York: Stein and Day, 1965.

Fair, Ronald. *Many Thousand Gone*. New York: Harcourt, Brace, 1965.

———. *Hog Butcher*. New York: Harcourt, Brace, 1966.

————· *World of Nothing: Two Novellas.* New York: Harper and Row, 1970.

Jones, LeRoi (Imamu Amiri Baraka). *The System of Dante's Hell.* New York: Grove, 1965.

————. *Tales.* New York: Grove, 1967.

Ottley, Roi. *White Marble Lady.* New York: Farrar, Straus and Giroux, 1965.

Paulding, James E. *Sometime Tomorrow.* New York: Carlton, 1965.

Rhodes, Hari. *A Chosen Few.* New York: Bantam, 1965.

Robinson, John Terry. *White Horse in Harlem.* New York: Pageant Press, 1965.

Rollins, Lamen. *The Human Race a Gang.* New York: Carlton, 1965.

Van Dyke, Henry. *Ladies with the Rachmaninoff Eyes.* New York: Farrar, Straus and Giroux, 1965.

————. *Blood of Strawberries.* New York: Farrar, Straus and Giroux, 1968.

Barrett, Nathan. *Bars of Adamant.* New York: Fleet, 1966.

Battles, Jesse Moore. *Somebody Please Help Me.* New York: Pageant, 1966.

Bennett, Hal. *A Wilderness of Vines.* Garden City, N.Y.: Doubleday, 1966.

————. *The Black Wine.* Garden City, N.Y.: Doubleday, 1968.

————. *Lord of Dark Places.* New York: Norton, 1970.

Guy, Rosa B. *Bird at My Window.* Philadelphia: Lippincott, 1966.

Phillips, Jane. *Mojo Hand.* New York: Simon and Schuster, 1966.

Walker, Margaret. *Jubilee.* Boston: Houghton Mifflin, 1966.

Johnson, William M. *The House on Corbett Street.* New York: William Frederick, 1967.

Kirk, Paul. *No Need to Cry.* New York: Carlton, 1967.

Moreau, Julian. *The Black Commandos.* Atlanta: Cultural Institute, 1967.

Parrish, Clarence R. *Images of Democracy*. New York: Carlton, 1967.

Polite, Carlene H. *The Flagellants*. New York: Farrar, Straus and Giroux, 1967.

Ramsey, Leroy L. *The Trial and the Fire*. New York: Exposition, 1967.

Reed, Ishmael. *The Free-Lance Pallbearers*. Garden City, N.Y.: Doubleday, 1967.

————. *Yellow Back Radio Broke-Down*. Garden City. N.Y.: Doubleday, 1969.

Rollins, Bryant. *Danger Song*. Garden City, N.Y.: Doubleday, 1967.

Stevens, Shane. *Go Down Dead*. New York: Morrow, 1967.

Wideman, John Edgar, *A Glance Away*. New York: Harcourt, Brace and World, 1967.

Bates, Arthenia. *Seeds beneath the Snow*. New York: Greenwich, 1968.

Heard, Nathan C. *Howard Street*. New York: Dial, 1968.

Lee, Audrey. *The Clarion People*. New York: McGraw-Hill, 1968.

————. *The Workers*. New York: McGraw-Hill, 1969.

Morrison, C. T. *The Flame in the Icebox: An Episode of the Vietnam War*. New York: Exposition, 1968.

Pharr, Robert D. *Book of Numbers*. Garden City, N.Y.: Doubleday, 1968.

————. *S. R. O.* Garden City, N.Y.: Doubleday, 1971.

Van Peebles, Melvin. *A Bear for the F. B. I.* New York: Trident, 1968.

Beckham, Barry. *My Main Mother*. New York: Walker, 1969.

Brown, Cecil. *The Life and Loves of Mr. Jiveass Nigger*. New York: Farrar, Straus and Giroux, 1969.

Cannon, Steve. *Groove, Bang and Jive Around*. New York: Ophelia Press, 1969.

Carvalho, Grimaldo. *The Negro Messiah*. New York: Vantage, 1969.

Farmer, Clarence. *Soul on Fire*. New York: Belmont, 1969.

Ferguson, Ira Lunan. *Which One of You is Interracial?* San Francisco: Lunan-Ferguson, 1969.

Greenlee, Sam. *The Spook Who Sat by the Door*. London: Allison and Busby, 1969.

Johnson, Joe. *Courtin', Sportin', and Non-Supportin'*. New York: Vantage, 1969.

Mahoney, William. *Black Jacob*. New York: Macmillan, 1969.

Major, Clarence. *The All-Night Visitors*. New York: Olympia, 1969.

McPherson, James Alan. *Hue and Cry*. Boston: Little, Brown, 1969.

Rhodes, Hari. *A Chosen Few*. New York: Bantam, 1969.

Wright, Sarah E. *This Child's Gonna Live*. New York: Seymour Lawrence, 1969.

Cain, George. *Blueschild Baby*. New York: McGraw-Hill, 1970.

Carson, Lular L. *The Priceless Gift*. New York: Vantage, 1970.

Colter, Cyrus. *The Beach Umbrella*. Iowa City: Univ. of Iowa Press, 1970.

Fairley, Ruth A. *Rocks and Roses*. New York: Vantage, 1970.

Jackson, Emma Lou. *The Veil of Nancy*. New York: Carlton, 1970.

Jarry, Hawke. *Black Schoolmaster*. New York: Exposition, 1970.

Morrison, Toni. *The Bluest Eye*. New York: Holt, Rinehart and Winston, 1970.

Royal, A. Bertrand. *Which Way to Heaven?* New York: Carlton, 1970.

Russ. George B. *Over Edom, I Lost My Shoe*. New York: Carlton, 1970.

Scott-Heron, Gil. *The Vulture*. New York: World, 1970.

————. *The Nigger Factory*. New York: Dial, 1972.

Stone, Chuck. *King Strut*. Indianapolis: Bobbs-Merrill, 1970.

Turner, Peter. *Black Heat*. New York: Belmont, 1970.

Walker, Alice. *The Third Life of Grange Copeland*. New York: Harcourt, Brace and World, 1970.

Young, Al. *Snakes*. New York: Holt, Rinehart and Winston, 1970.

Davis, George. *Coming Home*. New York: Random House, 1971.

Hamilton, Virginia. *The Planet of Junior Brown*. New York: Macmillan, 1971.

Harrison, Deloris. *Journey All Alone*. New York: Dial, 1971.

Haskins, LeRoi Rossetti. *The Weak Arm of Justice*. New York: Vantage, 1971.

Johnson, B. B. (Joe Greene). *Blues for a Black Sister*. New York: Paperback Library, 1971.

Mungin, Horace. *How Many Niggers Make Half a Dozen: Short Stories*. New York: Brothers Distributing, 1971.

Goines, Donald. *Whoreson: The Story of a Ghetto Pimp*. Los Angeles: Holloway, 1972.

Kemp, Arnold. *Eat of Me, I Am the Savior*. New York: Morrow, 1972.

Drama

Brown, William Wells. *Miralda: Or the Beautiful Quadroon*. Boston: n.p., 1855.

————. *Experience: Or How to Give a Northern Man a Backbone*. n.p., 1856.

————. *The Escape: Or a Leap for Freedom*. Boston: R. F. Wallcut, 1858.

Dunbar, Paul Laurence, and Marion Cook. *Clorindy*. n.p., 1898.

————. *Jes' Lak White Folks.* n.p., 1900.

Dunbar, Paul Laurence. *Uncle Eph's Christmas.* n.p., 1900.

Dunbar, Paul Laurence, Alex Rogers, and J. A. Shipp. *In Dahomey.* n.p., 1902.

Cotter, Joseph Seamon. *Caleb the Degenerate.* Louisville: Bradley and Gilbert, 1903.

————. *Paradox. Saturday Evening Quill Magazine*, June, 1913.

————. *On the Fields of France. Crisis Magazine*, June, 1920.

Johnson, James Weldon, Bob Cole, and John McNally. *In Newport.* New York: n.p., 1904.

Johnson, James Weldon, and Bob Cole. *The Shoo-Fly Regiment.* n.p., 1907.

Downing, Henry F. *The Arabian Lioness.* London: F. Griffiths, 1913.

————. *Human Nature.* London: F. Griffiths, 1913.

————. *Lord Eldred's Other Daughter.* London: F. Griffiths, 1913.

————. *Placing Paul's Play.* London: F. Griffiths, 1913.

————. *The Shuttlecock.* London: F. Griffiths, 1913.

————. *Incentive.* London: F. Griffiths, 1914.

————. *A New Coon in Town.* London: F. Griffiths, 1914.

————. *Voodoo.* London: F. Griffiths, 1914.

————. *The Racial Tangle.* n.p., 1920.

DuBois, W. E. B. *The Star of Ethiopia.* New York: Horizon Guild, 1913.

Aldridge, Ira Frederick. *A Glance at the Life of Ira Frederick Aldridge.* Washington, D. C.: R. L. Pendleton, 1917.

Nelson, Alice Dunbar. *Mine Eyes Have Seen. Crisis Magazine,* April, 1918.

Grimke, Angelina. *Rachel.* Boston: Cornhill, 1920.

Richardson, Willis. *The Deacon's Awakening. Crisis Magazine,* Nov., 1920.

————. *The Chip Woman's Fortune.* (In Patterson's *Anthology of the American Negro in the Theatre*), 1923.

————. *Mortgaged.* (In Cromwell, Dykes, and Fuller's *Readings from Negro Authors*), 1924.

————. *The Broken Banjo.* (In Locke and Montgomery's *Plays of Negro Life*), 1925.

————. *Compromise.* (In Locke's *The New Negro*), 1925.

————. *The Flight of the Natives.* (In *Plays of Negro Life*), 1927.

————. *The House of Sham.* (In Richardson's *Plays and Pageants from the Life of the Negro*), 1928.

————. *The Peacock's Feathers.* n.p., 1928.

————. *The Black Horseman.* (In *Plays and Pageants*), 1929.

————. *The Idle Head. Carolina Magazine*, April, 1929.

————. *The King's Dilemma.* (In Richardson's *The King's Dilemma and Other Plays for Children*), 1929.

————. *Plays and Pageants from the Life of the Negro.* Washington, D.C.: Associated Pub., 1930.

————. *Antonio Maceo.* (In Richardson and Miller's *Negro History in Thirteen Plays*), 1935.

————. *Attucks the Martyr.* (In *Negro History*), 1935.

————. *The Elder Dumas.* (In *Negro History*), 1935.

————. *In Menelik's Court.* (In *Negro History*), 1935.

————. *Near Calvary.* (In *Negro History*), 1935.

————. *The Gypsy's Finger Ring.* (In *The King's Dilemma*), 1956.

————. *The King's Dilemma and Other Plays for Children.* New York: Exposition Press, 1956.

————. *Man of Magic.* (In *The King's Dilemma*), 1956.

————. *The New Santa Claus.* (In *The King's Dilemma*), 1956.

Busey, DeReath Byrd. *The Yellow Tree.* Washington, D.C.: n.p., 1922.

Edmonds, Randolph. *Job Hunting.* n.p., 1922.

————. *The Highwayman.* n.p., 1925.

————. *Rocky Roads*. n.p., 1926.

————. *Silas Brown*. (In Edmonds' *Land of Cotton and Other Plays*), 1927.

————. *The Devil's Price*. (In Edmonds' *Shades and Shadows*), 1930.

————. *Everyman's Land*. (In *Shades and Shadows*), 1930.

————. *Hewers of Wood*. (In *Shades and Shadows*), 1930.

————. *The Phantom Treasure*. (In *Shades and Shadows*), 1930.

————. *Shades and Shadows*. Boston: Meador, 1930.

————. *The Tribal Chief*. (In *Shades and Shadows*), 1930.

————. *Bad Man* (In Edmonds' *Six Plays for a Negro Theatre*), 1934.

————. *Bleeding Hearts*. (In *Six Plays*), 1934.

————. *The Breeders*. (In *Six Plays*), 1934.

————. *Nat Turner*. (In *Six Plays*), 1934.

————. *The New Window*. (In *Six Plays*), 1934.

————. *Old Man Pete*. (In *Six Plays*), 1934.

————. *Six Plays for a Negro Theatre*. Boston: W. H. Baker, 1934.

————. *Yellow Death*. (In *Land of Cotton*), 1935.

————. *Gangsters over Harlem*. (In *Land of Cotton*), 1939.

————. *The High Court of Historia*. (In *Land of Cotton*), 1939.

————. *G. I. Rhapsode*. n.p., 1943.

————. *The Shape of Wars to Come*. n.p., 1943.

————. *Land of Cotton and Other Plays*. Washington, D.C.: Associated Pub., 1944.

————. *The Trial and Banishment of Uncle Tom*. n.p., 1945.

————. *Prometheus and the Atom*. n.p., 1955.

————. *Earth and Stars*. Tallahassee: Florida A. and M. University, 1962.

Thompson, Eloise Bibb. *Africannus*. Los Angeles: n.p., 1922.

————. *Caught*. Chicago: n.p., 1925.

————. *Cooped Up*. New York: n.p., 1925.

Wilson, Frank. *Confidence.* n.p., 1922.

———. *Sugar Cane. Opportunity Magazine,* June, 1926.

———. *Meek Mose.* (In Mantle's *Best Plays of 1927-28*), 1928.

———. *Brother Mose: A Comedy of Negro Life with Music and Spirituals.* U.S. National Archives, National Service Bureau, 1934.

———. *Walk Together, Chillun.* n.p., 1936.

Toomer, Jean. *Kabnis.* (In Toomer's *Cane*), 1923.

———. *Balo.* (In Locke and Montgomery's *Plays of Negro Life*), 1924.

Anderson, Garland. *Appearances.* New York: n.p., 1925.

Johnson, Fenton. *The Cabaret Girl.* Chicago: n.p., 1925.

McDonald, T. *Frances. Opportunity Magazine,* 1925.

Hurston, Zora Neale. *Great Day.* n.p., 1927.

Hurston, Zora Neale, Clinton Fletcher, and Tim Moore. *Fast and Furious.* (In Mantle's *Best Plays of 1931-32*), 1931.

Hurston, Zora Neale and Dorothy Waring. *Polk County, a Comedy of Negro Life in a Sawmill Camp.* n.p., 1944.

Johnson, Georgia Douglas. *Blue Blood.* (In Shay's *Fifty More Contemporary One-Act Plays*), 1927.

———. *Plumes.* (In Locke and Montgomery's *Plays of Negro Life*), 1927.

———. *Frederick Douglass.* (In Richardson and Miller's *Negro History in Thirteen Plays*), 1935.

———. *William and Ellen Craft.* (In *Negro History*), 1935.

Spence, Eulalie. *Fool's Errand.* New York: French, 1927.

———. *Foreign Mail.* New York: French, 1927.

———. *The Hunch. Opportunity Magazine,* 1927.

———. *The Starter.* (In Locke and Montgomery's *Plays of Negro Life*), 1927.

———. *Undertow. Carolina Magazine,* April, 1929.

Hill, Leslie P. *Toussaint L'Ouverture: A Dramatic History.* Boston: Christopher, 1928.

Miller, May. *Graven Images*. (In Richardson's *Plays and Pageants from the Life of the Negro*), 1929.

―――. *Riding the Goat*. (In *Plays and Pageants*), 1929.

―――. *Christophe's Daughters*. (In Richardson and Miller's *Negro History in Thirteen Plays*), 1935.

―――. *Harriet Tubman*. (In *Negro History*), 1935.

―――. *Samory*. (In *Negro History*), 1935.

―――. *Sojourner Truth*. (In *Negro History*), 1935.

Thurman, Wallace, and William J. Rapp. *Harlem*. New York: n.p., 1929.

―――. *Jeremiah, the Magnificent*. New York: n.p., 1930.

Gilbert, Mercedes. *Environment*. (In Gilbert's *Selected Gems*), 1931.

Hughes, Langston. *Scottsboro Limited*. New York: Golden Stair, 1932.

―――. *Little Ham*. (In Smalley's *Five Plays by Langston Hughes*), 1935.

―――. *Mulatto*. (In *Five Plays*), 1935.

―――. *Joy to My Soul*. n.p., 1937.

―――. *Soul Gone Home*. (In *Five Plays*), 1937.

―――. *Don't You Want to Be Free? A Negro History Play*. One Act Play Magazine, 1938.

―――. *The Sun Do Move*. n.p., 1942.

―――. *Simply Heavenly*. New York: Dramatists Play Service, 1953. (Also in *Five Plays*.)

―――. *Tambourines to Glory*. New York: Day, 1958. (Also in *Five Plays*.)

―――. *Black Nativity*. n.p., 1961.

―――. *The Gospel Glory*. n.p., 1962.

―――. *Five Plays*. Edited by Webster Smalley. Bloomington: Indiana Univ. Press, 1963.

―――. *Jerico-Jim Crow*. n.p., 1964.

Johnson, Hall. *Run, Little Chillun*. New York: n.p., 1933.

Smith, J. Augustus. *Louisiana*. (In Mantle's *Best Plays of 1932-1933*), 1933.

————. *Turpentine*. n.p., 1936.

Richardson, Willis, and May Miller. *Negro History in Thirteen Plays*. Washington, D.C.: Associated Pub., 1935.

Ross, John M. *Rho Kappa Epsilon*. Nashville: Fisk Univ. Press, 1935.

————. *One Clear Call*. Nashville: Fisk Univ. Press, 1936.

————. *The Sword*. n.p., 1948.

————. *Wanga Doll*. New Orleans: Dillard Univ. Press, 1954.

————. *I Will Repay*. n.p., 1963.

————. *House Or No House*. n.p., 1967.

Browne, Theodore. *The Natural Man*. New York: n.p., 1936.

————. *The Gravy Train*. n.p., 1940.

Dodson, Owen. *Gargoyles in Florida*. n.p., 1936.

————. *Divine Comedy*. n.p., 1938.

————. *Amistad*. n.p., 1939.

————. *Everybody Join Hands*. Theatre Arts Magazine, 1942.

————. *The Christmas Miracle*. n.p., 1955.

————. *Till Victory Is Won*. n.p., 1967.

Fisher, Rudolph. *The Conjure Man Dies*. New York: n.p., 1936.

Allison, Hughes. *The Trial of Dr. Beck*. (In Mantle's *Best Plays of 1937-1938*), 1938.

Hill, Abram. *Stealing Lightning*. n.p., 1937.

————. *Hell's Half Acre*. n.p., 1938.

————. *On Striver's Row; A Comedy About Sophisticated Harlem*. New York: n.p., 1945.

————. *Power of Darkness*. n.p., 1948.

————. *Split Down the Middle*. New York: Simon and Schuster, 1970.

Ward, Theodore. *Big White Fog*. New York: n.p., 1937.

————. *Our Lan'*. (In Rowe's *A Theatre In Your Head*), 1941.

————. *John Brown*. n.p., 1950.

————. *Candle in the Wind*. n.p., 1967.

Pawley, Thomas D. *Jedgement Day.* (In Brown, Davis, and Lee's *The Negro Caravan*), 1938.

———. *Smokey.* n.p., 1939.

———. *Crispus Attucks.* n.p., 1947.

———. *Messiah.* n.p., 1948.

———. *The Tumult and the Shouting.* n.p., 1969.

Butcher, James W. *The Seer.* (In Brown, Davis, and Lee's *The Negro Caravan*), 1941.

Wright, Richard, and Paul Green. *Native Son; A Biography of a Young American.* New York: Harper, 1941.

Bontemps, Arna, and Countee Cullen. *St. Louis Woman.* (In Patterson's *Black Theater*), 1946.

Cullen, Countee, and Owen Dodson. *The Third Fourth of July. Theatre Arts Magazine,* 1946.

Davis, Ossie. *Alexis Is Fallen.* n.p., 1947.

———. *They Seek a City.* n.p., 1947.

———. *The Mayor of Harlem.* n.p., 1949

———. *Point Blank.* n.p., 1949.

———. *The Big Deal.* n.p., 1953.

———. *Montgomery Footprints.* n.p., 1956.

———. *Purlie Victorious.* New York: French, 1961.

———. *Curtain Call, Mr. Aldrich Sir.* (In Reardon and Pawley's *The Black Teacher and the Dramatic Arts*), 1963.

———. *What Can You Say to Mississippi?* n.p., 1965.

Hughes, Langston, and Elmer L. Rice. *Street Scene: A Folk Opera.* n.p., 1947.

Mitchell, Loften. *The Bancroft Dynasty.* n.p., 1948.

———. *The Cellar.* n.p., 1952.

———. *A Land Beyond the River.* Cody, Wyo.: Pioneer Drama Service, 1963.

———. *Ballad of a Blackbird.* n.p., 1968.

———. *The World of a Harlem Playwright.* n.p., 1968.

———. *Tell Pharoah.* New York: Negro Universities Press, 1970.

Childress, Alice. *Florence*. New York: Masses and Mainstream, 1950.

————. *Just a Little Simple*. n.p., 1950.

————. *Gold Through the Trees*. n.p., 1952.

————. *Trouble in Mind*. (In Patterson's *Black Theater*), 1955.

————. *Wedding Band*. n.p., 1963.

————. *Strings*. n.p., 1969.

————. *Young Martin Luther King, Jr*. n.p., 1969.

Shine, Ted. *Cold Day in August*. n.p., 1950.

————. *The Bats Out of Hell*. n.p., 1955.

————. *Epitaph for a Bluebird*. n.p., 1958.

————. *A Rat's Revolt*. n.p., 1959.

————. *Morning, Noon, and Night*. (In Reardon and Pawley's *The Black Teacher and the Dramatic Arts*), 1964.

————. *Sho' Is Hot in the Cotton Patch*. *Encore Magazine*, 1967.

————. *The Coca-Cola Boys*. n.p., 1969.

————. *Contribution*. (In Brasmer and Consolo's *Black Drama*), 1969.

————. *Flora's Kisses*. n.p., 1969.

————. *Shoes*. *Encore Magazine*, 1969.

————. *Plantation*. n.p., 1970.

Branch, William B. *A Medal for Willie*. New York: n.p., 1951.

————. *In Splendid Error*. (In Patterson's *Black Theater*), 1954.

————. *Light in the Southern Sky*. n.p., 1958.

————. *Fifty Steps Toward Freedom*. New York: n.p., 1959.

————. *To Follow the Phoenix*. n.p., 1960.

Mayfield, Julian. *The Other Foot*. n.p., 1952.

————. *A World Full of Men*. n.p., 1952.

Peterson, Louis S. *Take a Giant Step*. New York: French, 1954.

————. *Entertain a Ghost*. n.p., 1962.

————. *Count Me for a Stranger*. n.p., n.d.

Huntley, Elizabeth Maddox. *What Ye Sow*. New York: Court, 1955.

Harris, Tom. *The Dark Years*. n.p., 1958.

————. *Daddy Hugs and Kisses*. n.p., 1963.

————. *Divorce Negro Style*. n.p., 1968.

————. *Cleaning Day*. n.p., 1969.

————. *Moving Day*. n.p., 1969.

————. *Shopping Day*. n.p., 1969.

Hansberry, Lorraine. *A Raisin in the Sun*. New York: Random House, 1959.

————. *The Sign in Sidney Brustein's Window*. New York: Random House, 1964.

————. *To Be Young, Gifted, and Black*. Englewood Cliffs, N.J.: Prentice-Hall, 1969.

Hughes, Langston, and Robert Glenn. *Shakespeare in Harlem*. n.p., 1959.

Gunn, Bill. *Marcus in the High Grass*. n.p., 1960.

————. *Johnnas*. *Drama Review*, Summer, 1960.

Walker, Evan. *Dark Light in May*. n.p., 1960.

————. *Coda for the Blues*. n.p., 1968.

————. *East of Jordan*. n.p., 1969.

Elder, Lonne, III. *Hysterical Turtle in a Rabbit Race*. n.p., 1961.

————. *Kissin' Rattlesnakes Can Be Fun*. n.p., 1966.

————. *Seven Comes Up, Seven Comes Down*. n.p., 1966.

————. *Charades on East Fourth Street*. n.p., 1967.

————. *Ceremonies in Dark Old Men*. New York: Farrar, Straus, and Giroux, 1969.

Burgie, Irving, and Loften Mitchell. *Ballad for Bimshire*. n.p., 1963.

Kennedy, Adrienne. *The Owl Answers*. n.p., 1963.

————. *Funnyhouse of a Negro*. New York: Publisher's Company, 1964.

————. *A Lesson in a Dead Language*. n.p., 1964.

————. *A Beast's Story*. n.p., 1966.

————. *A Rat's Mass.* (In Couch's *New Black Playwrights*), 1966.

————. *Cities of Bezique.* n.p., 1969.

Baldwin, James . *Blues for Mister Charlie.* New York: Dial, 1964.

————. *Amen Corner.* New York: Dial, 1967.

Jones, LeRoi (Imamu Amiri Baraka). *Dutchman and The Slave.* New York: Morrow, 1964.

————. *A Recent Killing.* n.p., 1964.

————. *Experimental Death Unit No. 1.* (In Jones' *Four Black Revolutionary Plays*), 1965.

————. *The Baptism and The Toilet.* New York: Evergreen, 1966.

————. *A Black Mass.* (In *Revolutionary Plays*), 1966.

————. *Madheart.* (In *Revolutionary Plays*), 1966.

————. *Great Goodness of Life.* (In Richards' *Best Short Plays of the World Theatre, 1958-1967*), 1967.

————. *Board of Education.* n.p., 1968.

————. *Home on the Range. Drama Review*, Summer, 1968.

————. *Insurrection.* n.p., 1968.

————. *Police. Drama Review*, Summer, 1968.

————. *The Death of Malcolm X.* (In Bullins' *New Plays from the Black Theatre*), 1969.

————. *Four Black Revolutionary Plays: All Praises to the Black Man.* Indianapolis: Bobbs-Merrill, 1969.

————. *Junkies Are Full of Shhhh.* n.p., 1969.

————. *The Slave Ship.* Newark: Jihad, 1969.

————. *J-E-L-L-O.* Newark: Jihad, 1970.

Amis, Lola Jones. *Helen.* (In Amis's *Three Plays*), 1965.

————. *The Other Side of the Wall.* (In *Three Plays*), 1965.

————. *The Places of Wrath.* (In *Three Plays*), 1965.

————. *Three Plays.* New York: Exposition Press, 1965.

Bullins, Ed. *Clara's Ole Man.* (In Bullins' *Five Plays*), 1965.

————. *The Electronic Nigger.* (In *Five Plays*), 1966.

————. *The Gentleman Caller.* (In Oliver and Sills' *Contemporary Black Drama*), 1966.

————. *Goin' a Buffalo.* (In *Five Plays*), 1966.

————. *In the Wine Time*. (In *Five Plays*), 1966.

————. *It Has No Choice*. n.p., 1966.

————. *The Corner*. n.p., 1967.

————. *How Do You Do? A Nonsense Drama*. Mill Valley, Calif.: Illuminations Press, 1967.

————. *In New England Winter*. (In Bullins' *New Plays from the Black Theatre*), 1967.

————. *The Man Who Dug Fish*. n.p., 1967.

————. *A Son, Come Home*. (In *Five Plays*), 1968.

————. *The Duplex*. n.p., 1969.

————. *Five Plays*. Indianapolis: Bobbs-Merrill, 1969.

————. *The Pig Pen*. n.p., 1970.

Killens, John O. *Lower Than the Angels*. n.p., 1965.

Killens, John O. and Loften Mitchell. *Ballad of the Winter Soldiers*. n.p., 1965.

Ward, Douglas Turner. *Happy Ending and Day of Absence*. New York: Dramatists Play Service, 1965.

————. *The Reckoning*. n.p., 1969.

Brown, James N. *Tomorrow Is Yesterday*. New York: Exposition Press, 1966.

Caldwell, Ben. *Hypnotism*. n.p., 1966.

————. *Family Portrait; Or My Son the Black Nationalist*. (In Bullins' *New Plays from the Black Theatre*), 1967.

————. *The King of Soul; Or the Devil and Otis Redding*. (In *New Plays*), 1967.

————. *The Wall*. n.p., 1967.

————. *The Fanatic*. n.p., 1968.

————. *The Job*. *Drama Review,* Summer, 1968.

————. *Mission Accomplished*. *Drama Review,* Summer, 1968.

————. *Prayer Meeting; Or the First Militant Minister*. (In Jones and Neal's *Black Fire*), 1968.

————. *Recognition*. n.p., 1968.

————. *Riot Sale Or Dollar Psyche*. *Drama Review,* Summer, 1968.

————. *Top Secret*. *Drama Review,* Summer, 1968.

————. *Unpresidented.* n.p., 1968.

MacKey, William W. *Behold! Cometh the Vanderkellans.* New York: Azazel, 1966.

Milner, Ronald. *Who's Got His Own.* n.p., 1966.

————. *The Monster. Drama Review,* Summer, 1968.

————. *The Warning: A Theme for Linda.* n.p., 1969.

Strong, Jack Romaner. *Metamorphisms.* n.p., 1966.

————. *Mesmerism of a Maniac.* n.p., 1967.

————. *A Direct Confrontation in Black.* n.p., 1968.

Fuller, Charles H., Jr. *The Rise.* (In Bullins' *New Plays from the Black Theatre*), 1967.

————. *The Layout.* n.p., 1968

————. *Love Song for Robert Lee.* n.p., 1968.

————. *Cabin.* n.p., 1969.

————. *Indian Giver.* n.p., 1969.

————. *Perfect Party.* n.p., 1969.

Garrett, Jimmy. *We Own the Night; A Play of Blackness.* (In Jones and Neal's *Black Fire*), 1967.

Miller, Laura Ann. *The Cricket Cries.* n.p., 1967.

————. *The Echo of a Sound.* n.p., 1968.

————. *Git Away from Here, Irvine, Now Git.* n.p., 1969.

Shepp, Archie. *June Bug Graduates Tonight.* n.p., 1967.

————. *Revolution.* n.p., 1968.

Bass, Kingsley B., Jr. *We Righteous Bombers.* (In Bullins' *New Plays from the Black Theatre*), 1968.

Davidson, N. R., Jr. *El Hajj Malik.* (In Bullins' *New Plays from the Black Theatre*), 1968.

Drayton, Ronald. *Nocturne on the Rhine.* (In Jones and Neal's *Black Fire*), 1968.

————. *Notes from a Savage God.* (In *Black Fire*), 1968.

Ferdinand, Val. *Cop Killer.* n.p., 1968.

————. *Happy Birthday, Jesus.* n.p., 1968.

————. *Black Liberation Army.* n.p., 1969.

————. *Homecoming.* n.p., *1969.*

Freeman, Carol. *The Suicide.* (In Jones and Neal's *Black Fire*), 1968.

Jackmon, Marvin E. *Flowers for the Trashman.* (In Jones and Neal's *Black Fire*), 1968.

Marvin X. *Take Care of Business. Drama Review*, Summer, 1968.

————. *The Black Bird.* (In Bullins' *New Plays from the Black Theatre*), 1969.

McIver, Ray. *God Is a (Guess What?)* n.p., 1968.

Patterson, Charles. *Black Ice.* (In Jones and Neal's *Black Fire*), 1968.

Sanchez, Sonia. *The Bronx Is Next. Drama Review*, Summer, 1968.

————. *Sister Sonlji.* (In Bullins' *New Plays from the Black Theatre*), 1969.

Stokes, Herbert (Damu). *The Uncle Toms. Drama Review,* Summer, 1968.

————. *The Man Who Trusted the Devil Twice.* (In Bullins', *New Plays from the Black Theatre*), 1969.

White, Joseph. *The Leader.* (In Jones and Neal's *Black Fire*), 1968.

————. *Old Judge Mose Is Dead. Drama Review,* Summer, 1968.

Wilson, Alice T. *How an American Poet Made Money and Forget-me-not.* New York: Pageant, 1968.

Gordone, Charles. *No Place to Be Somebody.* Indianapolis: Bobbs-Merrill, 1969.

————. *Worl's Champeen Lip Dansuh an' Wahtah Mellon Jooglah.* n.p., 1969.

Hughes, Langston, and Bob Teague. *Soul, Yesterday and Today.* n.p., 1969.

McCray, Nettie (Salimu). *Growin' into Blackness.* (In Bullins' *New Plays from the Black Theatre*), 1969.

Anderson, Thomas. *Crispus Attucks.* New York: New Dimensions, 1970.

Harris, Clarence. *The Trip.* (In Knight's *Black Voices from Prison*), 1970.

Hines, John. *In Memory of Jerry*. New York: New Dimensions, 1970.

Randolph, Jeremy. *Blow Up in a Major; A Satirical Comedy in One Act*. New York: Rannick Playwrights, 1971.

Van Peebles, Melvin. *Sweet Sweetback's Baadasssss Song*. New York: Lancer, 1971.

———. *Ain't Supposed to Die a Natural Death*. New York: n.p., 1972.

———. *Don't Play Us Cheap*. New York: n.p., 1972.

Anthologies

Adams, William, Peter Conn, and Barry Slepian. *Afro-American Literature: Fiction*. Boston: Houghton Mifflin, 1970.

———. *Afro-American Literature: Nonfiction*. Boston: Houghton Mifflin, 1970.

———. *Afro-American Literature: Poetry*. Boston: Houghton Mifflin, 1970.

———. *Afro-American Literature: Drama*. Boston: Houghton Mifflin, 1970.

Adoff, Arnold. *I Am the Darker Brother*. New York: Macmillan, 1968.

———. *Black on Black*. New York: Macmillan, 1968.

Alhamisi, Ahmed, and Harun K. Wangara. *Black Arts: Anthology of Black Creations*. Hartford, Conn.: Broadside, 1970.

Austin, Lettie J., Lewis H. Fenderson, and Sophia P. Nelson. *The Black Man and the Promise of America*. Glenview, Ill.: Scott, Foresman, 1970.

Bambara, Toni Cade. *Tales and Stories for Black Folks*. Garden City, N.Y.: Doubleday, 1971.

Barbour, Floyd B. *The Black Power Revolt*. Boston: Sargent, 1968.

Barksdale, Richard, and Keneth Kinnamon. *Black Writers of America*. New York: Macmillan, 1972.

Barton, Rebecca C. *Witnesses for Freedom: Negro Americans in Autobiography.* New York: Harper, 1948.

Bayliss, John F. *Black Slave Narratives.* New York: Macmillan, 1970.

Bontemps, Arna. *American Negro Poetry.* New York: Hill and Wang, 1963.

————. *Great Slave Narratives* (Narratives of Gustavus Vassa, James W. C. Pennington, and William and Ellen Craft). Boston: Beacon, 1969.

Brasmer, William, and Dominick Consolo. *Black Drama: An Anthology.* Columbus, Ohio: Merrill, 1970.

Brawley, Benjamin. *Early Negro American Writers.* Chapel Hill: Univ. of North Carolina Press, 1935.

Breman, Paul. *Sixes and Sevens: An Anthology of New Negro Poetry.* London: Breman, 1962.

Brewer, J. Mason. *Heralding Dawn: An Anthology of Verse.* Dallas, Texas: Thomason, 1936.

Brooks, Gwendolyn. *Jump Bad: A New Chicago Anthology.* Detroit: Broadside, 1971.

Brown, Sterling A. *American Stuff.* New York: Viking, 1937.

Brown, Sterling A., Arthur P. Davis, and Ulysses Lee. *The Negro Caravan.* New York: Dryden, 1941.

Bullins, Ed. *New Plays from the Black Theatre.* New York: Bantam, 1969.

Cade, Toni. *The Black Woman: An Anthology.* New York: New American Library, 1970.

Calverton, V. F. *Anthology of American Negro Literature.* New York: Random House, 1929.

Chapman, Abraham. *Black Voices.* New York: New American Library, 1968.

————. *Afro-American Slave Narratives.* New York: Praeger, 1970.

————. *New Black Voices.* New York: New American Library, 1971.

Charters, Samuel. *The Poetry of the Blues.* New York: Oak, 1963.

Clarke, John H. *American Negro Short Stories.* New York: Hill and Wang, 1966.

————. *Harlem: Voices from the Soul of Black America.* New York: New American Library, 1970.

Coombs, Orde. *We Speak As Liberators: Young Black Poets.* New York: Apollo, 1970.

Couch, William, Jr. *New Black Playwrights.* Baton Rouge: Louisiana State Univ. Press, 1968.

Cromwell, Otelia, Lorenzo Turner, and Eva B. Dykes. *Readings from Negro Authors.* New York: Harcourt, Brace, 1931.

Cullen, Countee. *Caroling Dusk.* New York: Harper, 1927.

Culp, Daniel. *Twentieth Century Negro Literature; or a Cyclopedia of Thought.* Naperville, Ill.: J. L. Nichols, 1902.

Cunard, Nancy. *Negro Anthology.* London: Wishart, 1934.

David, Jay. *Growing Up Black* (autobiographical excerpts). New York: Morrow, 1968.

Davis, Arthur P., and Saunders Redding. *Cavalcade: Negro American Writing from 1760 to the Present.* Boston: Houghton Mifflin, 1971.

Davis, Charles T., and Daniel Walden. *On Being Black.* New York: Fawcett World, 1970.

Dreer, Herman. *American Literature by Negro Authors.* New York: Macmillan, 1950.

Emanuel, James A., and Theodore Gross. *Dark Symphony: Negro Literature in America.* New York: Free Press, 1968.

Faderman, Lillian, and Barbara Bradshaw. *Speaking for Ourselves: American Ethnic Writing.* Glenview, Ill.: Scott, Foresman, 1969.

Ford, Nick Aaron, and H. L. Faggett. *Best Short Stories by Afro-American Writers, 1925-1950.* Boston: Meador, 1950.

Gayle, Addison, Jr. *Bondage, Freedom and Beyond: The Prose of Black Americans.* Garden City, N.Y.: Doubleday, 1971.

Gibson, Donald B., and Carol Anselment. *Black and White: Stories of American Life*. New York: Washington Square, 1971.

Hayden, Robert. *Kaleidoscope, Poems by American Negro Poets*. New York: Harcourt, Brace and World, 1967.

Hill, Herbert. *Soon One Morning, New Writings by American Negroes, 1940-62*. New York: Knopf, 1963.

Hughes, Langston. *An African Treasury*. New York: Crown, 1960.

―――. *Poems from Black Africa*. Bloomington: Indiana Univ. Press, 1963.

―――. *New Negro Poets U.S.A.* Bloomington: Indiana Univ. Press, 1964.

―――. *The Book of Negro Humor*. New York: Dodd, Mead, 1966.

―――. *Best Short Stories by Negro Writers*. Boston and Toronto: Little, Brown, 1967.

Hughes, Langston, and Arna Bontemps. *The Poetry of the Negro*. Garden City, N.Y.: Doubleday, 1949.

―――. *The Book of Negro Folklore*. New York: Dodd, Mead, 1959.

James, Charles L. *From the Roots: Short Stories by Black Americans*. New York: Dodd, Mead, 1970.

Johnson, Charles S. *Ebony and Topaz*. New York: National Urban League, 1927.

Johnson, James Weldon. *The Book of American Negro Poetry*. New York: Harcourt, Brace, 1922; rev. 1931.

Jones, LeRoi (Imamu Amiri Baraka), and Larry Neal. *Black Fire*. New York: Morrow, 1968.

Jordan, June. *Soulscript: Afro-American Poetry*. Garden City, N.Y.: Doubleday, 1970.

Kerlin, Robert T. *Contemporary Poetry of the Negro*. Hampton, Va.: Hampton Institute Press, 1923.

Kearns, Francis E. *The Black Experience*. New York: Viking, 1970.

King, Woodie, and Ron Milner. *Black Drama Anthology*. New York: New American Library, 1971.

Knight, Etheridge. *Black Voices from Prison*. New York: Pathfinder, 1970.

Lanusse, Armand. *Creole Voices: Poems in French by Free Men of Color*. Washington, D.C.: Associated Pub., 1845.

Lester, Julius. *To Be a Slave*. New York: Dell, 1970.

Locke, Alain L., and Montgomery Gregory. *Plays of Negro Life*. New York: Harper, 1927.

Locke, Alain L. *The New Negro*. New York: Boni and Liveright, 1925.

————. *Four Negro Poets*. New York: Simon and Schuster, 1927.

Lomax, Alan, and Raoul Abdul. *Three Thousand Years of Black Poetry*. New York: Dodd, Mead, 1970.

Major, Clarence. *The New Black Poetry*. New York: International Pubs., 1969.

Marcus, Samuel. *Anthology of Revolutionary Poetry*. New York: Active, 1929.

Margolies, Edward. *A Native Sons Reader*. Philadelphia: Lippincott, 1970.

Miller, Adam David. *Dices or Black Bones: Black Voices of the Seventies*. Boston: Houghton Mifflin, 1970.

Miller, Ruth. *Blackamerican Literature*. Beverly Hills: Glencoe Press, 1971.

Moon, Bucklin. *The Primer for White Folks*. Garden City, N.Y.: Doubleday, 1945.

Murphy, Beatrice. *Negro Voices: An Anthology of Contemporary Verse*. New York: Harrison, 1938.

————. *Ebony Rhythm*. New York: Exposition, 1948.

Nicholas, Xavier. *Poetry of Soul*. New York: Bantam, 1971.

Oliver, Clinton, and Stephanie Sills. *Contemporary Black Drama*. New York: Scribner's, 1971.

Osofsky, Gilbert. *Puttin' on Ole Massa*. (Slave Narratives of Henry

Bibb, William Wells Brown, and Solomon Northup). New York: Harper, 1969.

Patterson, Lindsay. *Anthology of the American Negro in the Theatre*. Washington, D.C.: Association for the Study of Negro Life and History, 1967.

————. *Black Theater*. New York: Dodd, Mead, 1971.

Perkins, Eugene. *Black Expressions: An Anthology of New Black Poets*. Chicago: Conda, 1967.

Pool, Rosey E. *Black and Unknown Bards*. n.p., 1958.

————. *Beyond the Blues*. Lympne, Kent, England: Hand and Flower, 1962.

Randall, Dudley, and Margaret Burroughs. *For Malcolm: Poems on the Life and the Death of Malcolm X*. Hartford, Conn.: Broadside, 1967.

Reardon, William, and Thomas D. Pawley. *The Black Teacher and the Dramatic Arts*. Westport, Conn.: Negro Universities Press, 1970.

Robinson, William H. *Early Black American Poets*. Dubuque, Ia.: Wm. C. Brown, 1969.

————. *Early Black American Prose*. Dubuque, Ia.: Wm. C. Brown, 1971.

Rollins, Charlemae Hill. *Famous American Negro Poets*. New York: Dodd, Mead, 1965.

Schulmann, R. Baird. *Nine Black Poets*. Durham, N.C.: Moore, 1968.

Singh, Raman K., and Peter Fellowes. *Black Literature in America: A Casebook*. New York: Crowell, 1970.

Smith, Arthur L. *Rhetoric of Black Revolution*. Boston: Allyn and Bacon, 1969.

Turner, Darwin T. *Black American Literature: Fiction*. Columbus, Ohio: Merrill, 1969.

————. *Black American Literature: Poetry*. Columbus, Ohio: Merrill, 1969.

————. *Black American Literature: Essays*. Columbus, Ohio: Merrill, 1969.

————. *Black Drama in America: An Anthology*. Greenwich, Conn.: Fawcett, 1971.

Watkins, Sylvester. *Anthology of American Negro Literature*. New York: Random House, 1944.

White, N.I., and W. C. Jackson. *An Anthology of Verse by American Negroes*. Durham, N. C.: Moore, 1968.

Williams, John A. *The Angry Black*. New York: Lancer, 1962.

————. *Beyond the Angry Black*. New York: Cooper, 1966.

Woodson, Carter G. *Negro Orators and Their Orations*. Washington, D. C.: Associated Pub., 1925.

Literary Criticism and Bibliography

Abramson, Doris E. *Negro Playwrights in the American Theatre 1925-1959*. New York: Columbia Univ. Press, 1969.

Amos, Preston E. *100 Years of Freedom: Bibliography of Books about the American Negro*. Washington, D. C.: Association for Study of Negro Life and History, 1963.

Barton, Rebecca C. *Race Consciousness and the American Negro . . . The Correlation between the Group Experience and the Fiction of 1900-1930*. Copenhagen: Busck, 1934.

————. *Witness for Freedom, Negro Americans in Autobiography*. New York: Harper, 1948.

Bigsby, C. W. E. *The Black American Writer: Fiction*. Deland, Fla.: Everett/Edwards, 1969.

————. *The Black American Writer: Poetry and Drama*. Deland, Fla.: Everett/Edwards, 1969.

Bond, Frederick W. *The Negro and the Drama*. Washington, D.C.: Associated Pub., 1941.

Bone, Robert A. *The Negro Novel in America*. New Haven: Yale Univ. Press, 1958.

Brawley, Benjamin. *The Negro in Literature and Art*. New York: Dodd, Mead, 1929.

————. *Paul Laurence Dunbar: Poet of His People*. Chapel Hill: Univ. of North Carolina Press, 1936.

Bronz, Stephen H. *Roots of Negro Racial Consciousness: The 1920's*. Roslyn Heights, L. I., N. Y.: Libra, 1964.

Brown, Sterling A. *Negro in American Fiction*. Washington, D.C.: Associates in Negro Folk Education, 1937.

————. *Negro Poetry and Drama*. Washington, D.C.: Associates in Negro Folk Education, 1937.

Brown, Sterling A., Arthur P. Davis, and Ulysses Lee. *The Negro Caravan*. New York: Dryden, 1941.

Butcher, Margaret J. *The Negro in American Culture*. New York: Knopf, 1956.

Calverton, V. F. *The Liberation of American Literature*. New York: Scribner's, 1932.

Chapman, Abraham. *The Negro in American Literature and a Bibliography of Literature by and about Negro Americans*. Stevens Point, Wis.: Wisconsin State Univ., 1966.

Cunningham, Virginia. *Paul Laurence Dunbar and His Song*. Toronto: Dodd, Mead, 1947.

Deodene, Frank, and William P. French. *Black American Fiction Since 1952: A Preliminary Check List*. Chatham, N.J.: Chatham Bookseller, 1970.

Dickinson, Donald C. *A Bio-Bibliography of Langston Hughes, 1902-1967*. Hamden, Conn.: Archon Books, 1967.

Dillard, J. L. *Black English: Its History and Usage in the United States*. New York: Random House, 1972.

Dodds, Barbara. *Negro Literature for High School Students*. Champaign, Ill.: National Council of Teachers of English, 1968.

Eckman, Fern M. *The Furious Passage of James Baldwin*. New York: Popular Library, 1967.

Emanuel, James A. *Langston Hughes.* New York: Twayne, 1967.

Ferguson, Blanche E. *Countee Cullen and the Negro Renaissance.* New York: Dodd, Mead, 1966.

Ford, Nick Aaron. *The Contemporary Negro Novel.* Boston: Meador, 1936.

Gayle, Addison, Jr. *Black Expression: Essays by and about Black Americans in the Creative Arts.* New York: Weybright and Talley, 1969.

———. *The Black Aesthetic.* Garden City, N.Y.: Doubleday, 1971.

Gibson, Donald B. *Five Black Writers: Essays on Wright, Ellison, Baldwin, Hughes and LeRoi Jones.* New York: New York Univ. Press, 1970.

Gloster, Hugh M. *Negro Voices in American Fiction.* Chapel Hill: Univ. of North Carolina Press, 1948.

Graham, Shirley. *The Story of Phillis Wheatley: Poetess of the American Revolution.* New York: Julian Messner, 1949.

Green, Elizabeth L. *The Negro in Contemporary American Literature: An Outline for Individual and Group Study.* Chapel Hill: Univ. of North Carolina Press, 1928.

Gross, Seymour, and John E. Hardy. *Images of the Negro in American Literature.* Chicago: Univ. of Chicago Press, 1966.

Hatch, James V. *Black Images on the American Stage: A Bibliography of Plays and Musicals 1770-1970.* New York: Drama Book Specialists, 1970.

Heartman, Charles F. *Phillis Wheatley (Phillis Peters): A Critical Attempt and a Bibliography of Her Writings.* New York: The Author, 1915.

Hemenway, Robert. *The Black Novelist.* Columbus, Ohio: Merrill, 1970.

Hill, Herbert. *Anger and Beyond: The Negro Writer in the United States.* New York: Harper and Row, 1966.

Homer, Dorothy, and Ann Swartout. *Books on the Negro*. New York: Praeger, 1966.

Huggins, Nathan I. *Harlem Renaissance*. New York: Oxford Univ. Press, 1971.

Hughes, Carl Milton. *The Negro Novelist, a Discussion of the Writings of American Negro Novelists, 1940-50*. New York: Citadel, 1953.

Hughes, Langston, and Milton Meltzer. *Black Magic . . . The Negro in American Entertainment*. Englewood Cliffs, N.J.: Prentice-Hall, 1967.

Isaacs, Edith. *The Negro in the American Theatre*. New York: Theatre Arts Books, 1947.

Jahn, Janheinz. *Neo-African Literature: A History of Black Writing*. New York: Grove, 1968.

Johnson, Harry A. *Multimedia Materials for Black Studies*. New York: Bowker, 1971.

Johnson, James Weldon. *Black Manhattan*. New York: Knopf, 1930.

Kerlin, Robert T. *A Decade of Negro Self-Expression*. Charlottesville, Va.: Michie, 1928.

Lawson, Victor. *Dunbar Critically Examined*. Washington, D.C.: Associated Pub., 1941.

Lincoln, C. Eric. *Sounds of the Struggle: Poems and Perspectives in Civil Rights*. New York: Apollo, 1967.

Littlejohn, David. *Black on White, a Critical Survey of Writing by American Negroes*. New York: Grossman, 1966.

Locke, Alain L. *The New Negro*. New York: Boni and Liveright, 1925.

Loggins, Vernon. *The Negro Author, His Development in America to 1900*. New York: Columbia Univ. Press, 1931; 1964.

Margolies, Edward. *Native Sons: A Critical Study of 20th Century Negro American Authors*. Philadelphia: Lippincott, 1968.

————. *The Art of Richard Wright*. Carbondale: Southern Illinois Univ. Press, 1969.

Mason, Julian D. *The Critical Reception of American Negro Authors in American Magazines 1800-1885*. Ann Arbor: University Microfilms (unpublished dissertation), 1963.

Mays, Benjamin. *The Negro's God, as Reflected in His Literature*. Boston: Chapman and Grimes, 1938.

McCall, Dan. *The Example of Richard Wright*. New York: Harcourt, Brace and World, 1969.

Miller, Elizabeth W. *The Negro in America: A Bibliography*. Cambridge: Harvard Univ. Press, 1966.

Mitchell, Loften. *Black Drama*. New York: Hawthorne, 1967.

Nelson, John H. *The Negro Character in American Literature*. Lawrence: Univ. of Kansas Press, 1926.

Nichols, Charles H. *Many Thousand Gone (Study of Slave Narratives)*. Leiden, Netherlands: Brill, 1963.

Noble, Peter. *The Negro in Films*. London: Skelton Robinson, 1948.

Porter, Dorothy B. *North American Negro Poets: A Bibliographical Checklist 1760-1944*. New York: Franklin, 1944; 1963.

Redding, J. Saunders. *To Make a Poet Black*. Chapel Hill: Univ. of North Carolina Press, 1939.

Renfro, G. Herbert. *Life and Works of Phillis Wheatley*. Washington, D.C.: R. L. Pendleton, 1916.

Rousseve, Charles B. *The Negro in Louisiana: Aspects of His History and His Literature*. New Orleans: Xavier Univ. Press, 1927.

Starke, Catherine J. *Black Portraiture in American Fiction: Stock Characters, Archetypes, and Individuals*. New York: Basic Books, 1971.

Tarry, Ellen. *Young Jim: The Early Years of James Weldon Johnson*. New York: Dodd, Mead, 1967.

Tischler, Nancy M. *Black Masks: Negro Characters in Modern*

Southern Fiction. University Park, Pa.: Pennsylvania State Univ. Press, 1969.

Toomer, Jean. *Essentials: Definitions and Aphorisms.* Chicago: Dupee, 1931.

Walser, Richard. *The Black Poet.* New York: Philosophical Library, 1967.

Wegelin, Oscar. *Jupiter Hammon, American Negro Poet.* New York: Heartman, 1915.

Welsch, Erwin K. *The Negro in the United States: A Research Guide.* Bloomington: Indiana Univ. Press, 1965.

Whiteman, Maxwell. *A Century of Fiction by American Negroes, 1853-1952: A Descriptive Bibliography.* Philadelphia: Jacobs, 1955.

Whitlow, Roger. *Black American Literature: A Critical History of the Major Periods, Movements, Themes, Works, and Authors.* Chicago: Nelson-Hall, 1973.

Williams, Kenny J. *They Also Spoke: An Essay on Negro Literature in America, 1787-1930.* Nashville: Townsend, 1970.

Yellin, Jean Fagan. *The Intricate Knot: The Negro in American Literature 1776-1863.* New York: New York Univ. Press, 1971.

Social and Historical Comment

Aptheker, Herbert, ed. *A Documentary History of the Negro People in the United States.* New York: Citadel, 1951.

————. *Nat Turner's Slave Rebellion.* New York: Humanities, 1966.

Bailey, Harry A., Jr., ed. *Negro Politics in America.* Columbus, Ohio: Merrill, 1967.

Baldwin, James. *Notes of a Native Son.* Boston: Beacon, 1955.

————. *Nobody Knows My Name.* New York: Dial, 1961.

————. *The Fire Next Time*. New York: Dial, 1963.

Bennett, Lerone, Jr. *Before the Mayflower: A History of the Negro 1619-1962*. Chicago: Johnson, 1962.

————. *The Negro Mood*. Chicago: Johnson, 1965.

————. *Black Power U.S.A.: The Human Side of Reconstruction 1867-1877*. Chicago: Johnson, 1967.

Bernard, Jessie. *Marriage and Family Among Negroes*. Englewood Cliffs, N.J.: Prentice-Hall, 1966.

Berrian, Albert H., and Richard A. Long. *Negritude: Essays and Studies*. Hampton, Va.: Hampton Institute Press, 1967.

Bond, Horace Mann. *The Education of the Negro in the American Social Order*. New York: Octagon, 1934.

Brawley, Benjamin. *A Social History of the American Negro*. New York: Macmillan, 1921.

————. *The Negro in Literature and Art*. New York: Duffield, 1929.

————. *The Negro Genius*. Toronto: McClelland-Stewart, 1937.

————. *Negro Builders and Heroes*. Chapel Hill: Univ. of North Carolina Press, 1937.

Broderick, Francis, and August Meier, eds. *Negro Protest Thought in the Twentieth Century*. Indianapolis: Bobbs-Merrill, 1965.

Broom, Leonard, and Norval D. Glenn. *Transformation of the Negro American*. New York: Harper and Row, 1965.

Brown, William Wells, *Three Years in Europe*. London: n.p., 1852.

————. *The American Fugitive in Europe*. Boston: Wallcut, 1855.

————. *The Black Man: His Antecedents, His Genius, and His Achievements*. New York: Thomas Hamilton; Boston: Wallcut, 1863.

————. *My Southern Home*. n.p., 1880.

Bullock, Henry A. *A History of Negro Education in the South: From 1619 to the Present*. Cambridge: Harvard Univ. Press, 1968.

Butcher, Margaret. *The Negro in American Culture*. New York: Knopf, 1956.

Cable, George W. *The Silent South*. New York: Scribner's, 1885.

————. *The Negro Question*. Garden City, N.Y.: Doubleday, 1958.

Carmichael, Stokely, and Charles V. Hamilton. *Black Power: The Politics of Liberation*. New York: Random House, 1967.

Clark, Kenneth. *The Negro Protest (Conversations with Baldwin, King, and Malcolm X)*. Boston: Beacon, 1963.

————. *Dark Ghetto*. New York: Harper and Row, 1965.

Clark, Thomas D. *The Emerging South*. New York: Oxford Univ. Press, 1961.

Clayton, Edward. *The Negro Politician*. Chicago: Johnson, 1965.

Cleaver, Eldridge. *Soul on Ice*. New York: McGraw-Hill, 1968.

Cook, Mercer, and Stephen E. Henderson. *The Militant Black Writer in Africa and the United States*. Madison: Univ. of Wisconsin Press, 1969.

Cronon, E. D. *Black Moses: The Story of Marcus Garvey and the Universal Negro Improvement Association*. Madison: Univ. of Wisconsin Press, 1955.

Cruse, Harold. *The Crisis of the Negro Intellectual*. New York: Morrow, 1967.

————. *Rebellion or Revolution*. New York: Morrow, 1968.

Davie, Maurice. *Negroes in American Society*. New York: McGraw-Hill, 1949.

Demarest, David P., and Lois S. Lamdin, eds. *The Ghetto Reader*. New York: Random House, 1970.

Duberman, Martin B. *In White America: A Documentary Play*. Boston: Houghton Mifflin, 1964.

DuBois, W. E. B. *The Negro Church*. Atlanta, Ga.: Atlanta Univ., 1903.

————. *The Souls of Black Folk*. Chicago: McClurg, 1903.

————. *Darkwater*. New York: Harcourt and Brace, 1920.

————. *The Gifts of Black Folk*. Boston: Stratford, 1924.

Edwards, Harry. *Black Students*. New York: Free Press, 1970.

Elkins, Stanley M. *Slavery: A Problem in American Institutional and Intellectual Life*. New York: Universal, 1963.

Ellison, Ralph. *Shadow and Act*. Toronto: Random House, 1964.

Embree, Edwin R. *Brown America: The Story of a New Race*. New York: Viking, 1931.

Epps, Archie, ed. *The Speeches of Malcolm X at Harvard*. New York: Morrow, 1968.

Essien-Udom, Essien U. *Black Nationalism: A Search for an Identity in America*. Chicago: Univ. of Chicago Press, 1962.

Fanon, Frantz. *Black Skin, White Masks*. New York: Grove, 1967.

Franklin, John Hope. *From Slavery to Freedom*. New York: Knopf, 1956.

————. *Reconstruction after the Civil War*. Chicago: Univ. of Chicago Press, 1961.

————. *The Emancipation Proclamation*. Garden City, N.Y.: Doubleday, 1963.

Frazier, E. Franklin. *The Negro Family in the United States*. Chicago: Univ. of Chicago Press, 1939; 1966.

————. *Black Bourgeoisie*. Glencoe, Ill.: Free Press, 1957; 1962.

————. *The Negro Church in America*. New York: Schocken, 1963.

Furnas, J. C. *Goodbye to Uncle Tom*. New York: Sloane, 1956.

Fry, John R. *Fire and Blackstone*. Philadelphia: Lippincott, 1969.

Gayle, Addison, ed. *Black Expression: Essays by and About Black Americans in the Creative Arts*. New York: Weybright and Talley, 1969.

Goldston, Robert. *The Negro Revolution*. New York: Macmillan, 1968.

Grant, Joanne. *Confrontation on Campus: The Columbia Pattern of the New Protest.* New York: New American Library, 1969.

Greene, Lorenzo J. *The Negro in Colonial New England, 1620-1776.* New York: Columbia Univ. Press, 1942.

Grier, William, and Price Cobbs. *Black Rage.* New York: Basic Books, 1968.

Halasz, Nicholas. *The Rattling Chain.* New York: McKay, 1966.

Hawkins, Hugh. *Booker T. Washington and His Critics: The Problem of Negro Leadership.* Boston: Heath, 1962.

Hernton, Calvin C. *Sex and Racism in America.* Toronto: Doubleday, 1965.

———. *White Papers for White Americans.* Toronto: Doubleday, 1967.

Herskovits, Melville J. *The Myth of the Negro Past.* New York: Harper, 1941.

———. *The New World Negro.* Bloomington: Indiana Univ. Press, 1966.

Holmes, Dwight O. W. *The Evolution of the Negro College.* New York: Teachers College, Columbia Univ., 1934.

Hughes, Douglas A., ed. *From a Black Perspective: Contemporary Black Essays.* New York: Holt, Rinehart and Winston, 1970.

Hughes, Langston. *Fight for Freedom: The Story of the NAACP.* New York: Norton, 1962.

Isaacs, Harold R. *The New World of Negro Americans.* New York: Day, 1963.

Johnson, James Weldon. *Black Manhattan.* New York: Knopf, 1930.

Jones, LeRoi (Imamu Amiri Baraka). *Blues People.* New York: Morrow, 1963.

———. *Home: Essays Written Since 1960.* New York: Morrow, 1966.

———. *Black Music.* New York: Morrow, 1967.

Karon, Bertram P. *The Negro Personality: A Rigorous Investigation of the Effects of Culture*. New York: Springer, 1963.

Killens, John O. *Black Man's Burden*. New York: Simon and Schuster, 1965.

King, Martin Luther, Jr. *Stride Toward Freedom: The Montgomery Story*. New York: Harper, 1958.

―――. *Strength to Love*. New York: Harper, 1963.

―――. *Why We Can't Wait*. New York: Harper, 1964.

―――. *Where Do We Go from Here: Chaos or Community?* New York: Harper and Row, 1967.

Lapides, Frederick R., and David Burrows, eds. *Racism: A Casebook*. New York: Crowell, 1971.

Lester, Julius. *Look Out, Whitey! Black Power's Gon' Get Your Mama!* New York: Dial, 1968.

Lincoln, C. Eric. *Sounds of the Struggle: Poems and Perspectives in Civil Rights*. New York: Morrow, 1967.

Logan, Rayford. *The Betrayal of the Negro*. New York: Collier, 1965.

Lomax, Louis E. *The Negro Revolt*. New York: Harper, 1962.

Marine, Gene. *The Black Panthers*. New York: New American Library, 1969.

Marx, Gary T. *Protest and Prejudice: A Study of Belief in the Black Community*. New York: Harper and Row, 1968.

Mays, Benjamin. *The Negro's God, as Reflected in His Literature*. Boston: Chapman and Grimes, 1938.

McCord, William, et al. *Life Styles in the Black Ghetto*. New York: Norton, 1969.

Meier, August. *Negro Thought in America, 1880-1915: Racial Ideologies in the Age of Booker T. Washington*. Ann Arbor: Univ. of Michigan Press, 1963.

Meredith, James. *Three Years in Mississippi*. Bloomington: Indiana Univ. Press, 1966.

Miller, Abie. *The Negro and the Great Society.* New York: Vantage, 1965.

Miller, Kelly. *Race Adjustment.* New York: Schocken, 1908.

————. *Out of the House of Bondage.* New York: Neale, 1914.

————. *An Appeal to Conscience.* New York: Macmillan, 1918.

————. *The Everlasting Stain.* Washington: Associated Pub., 1924.

Miller, William R. *Martin Luther King, Jr.: His Life, Martyrdom and Meaning for the World.* New York: Weybright and Talley, 1968.

Moon, Bucklin. *Primer for White Folks.* Garden City, N.Y.: Doubleday, 1945.

Muhammad, Elijah. *Message to the Black Man in America.* Chicago, n.p., 1965.

Muse, Benjamin. *The American Negro Revolution: From Non-Violence to Black Power, 1963-1967.* Bloomington: Indiana Univ. Press, 1969.

Myrdal, Gunnar. *An American Dilemma.* New York and London: Harper, 1944.

Osofsky, Gilbert. *The Burden of Race: A Documentary History of Negro-White Relations in America.* New York: Harper and Row, 1967.

Ottley, Roi. *New World A'Coming: Inside Black America.* Boston: Houghton Mifflin, 1943.

Pettigrew, Thomas. *A Profile of the Negro American.* Princeton, N.J.: Van Nostrand, 1964.

Proudfoot, Merrill. *Diary of a Sit-In.* Chapel Hill: Univ. of North Carolina Press, 1962.

Quarles, Benjamin. *The Negro in the Civil War.* Boston: Little, Brown, 1953.

————. *The Negro in the American Revolution.* Chapel Hill: Univ. of North Carolina Press, 1961.

————. *The Negro in the Making of America.* New York: Collier, 1964.

Redding, Saunders. *They Came in Chains.* Philadelphia: Lippincott, 1950.

————. *On Being Negro in America.* Indianapolis: Bobbs-Merrill, 1951; 1962.

————. *The Lonesome Road: The Story of the Negro's Part in America.* Garden City, N.Y.: Doubleday, 1958.

————. *The Negro.* Washington, D.C.: Potomac Books, 1967.

Reuter, Edward Byron. *The Mulatto in the United States.* Boston: Badger, 1918.

Richardson, Ben. *Great American Negroes.* New York: Crowell, 1956.

Rogers, Joel A. *The World's Great Men of Color, 3000 B.C. to 1946 A.D.* New York: The Author, 1946-47.

————. *Africa's Gift to America.* New York: The Author, 1961.

Scott, Nathan A., Jr. *Rehearsals of Discomposure: Alienation and Reconciliation in Modern Literature.* Toronto: King's Crown Press, 1952.

————. *Modern Literature and the Religious Frontier.* New York: Harper, 1958.

————. *The Broken Center: Studies in the Theological Horizon of Modern Literature.* New Haven: Yale Univ. Press, 1966.

————. *Negative Capability: Studies in the New Literature and the Religious Situation.* New Haven: Yale Univ. Press, 1969.

Shade, William, and Roy C. Herrenkohl, eds. *Seven on Black.* Philadelphia: Lippincott, 1969.

Silberman, Charles E. *Crisis in Black and White.* New York: Random House, 1964.

Stampp, Kenneth M. *The Peculiar Institution: Slavery in the Ante-Bellum South.* New York: Knopf, 1956.

Taylor, Julius H., ed. *The Negro in Science.* Baltimore: Morgan State College Press, 1955.

Teague, Bob. *Letters to a Black Boy.* New York: Lancer, 1969.

Thompson, Daniel C. *The Negro Leadership Class.* Englewood Cliffs, N.J.: Prentice-Hall, 1963.

Thorpe, Earl E. *Negro Historians in the United States.* Baton Rouge, La.: Fraternal, 1958.

―――. *The Mind of the Negro: An Intellectual History of Afro-Americans.* Baton Rouge, La.: Ortlieb, 1961.

Warren, Robert Penn. *Who Speaks for the Negro?* New York: Random House, 1965.

Washington, Booker T. *The Future of the American Negro.* Cambridge, Mass.: Small, Maynard, 1899.

Wesley, Charles H., and Patricia W. Romero. *Negro Americans in the Civil War.* Washington, D.C.: United Publishing, 1968.

Williams, John A. *This is My Country Too.* New York: New American Library, 1965.

Woodson, Carter G. *The History of the Negro Church.* Washington, D.C.: Associated Pub., 1921.

―――. *Negro Orators and Their Orations.* Washington, D.C.: Associated Pub., 1925.

―――. *The Negro Professional Man and the Community.* Washington, D.C.: Association for the Study of Negro Life and History, 1934.

―――. *The Story of the Negro Retold.* Washington, D.C.: Associated Pub., 1959.

Woodward, C. Vann. *The Strange Career of Jim Crow.* New York: Oxford Univ. Press, 1966.

Wright, Nathan. *Black Power and Urban Unrest: Creative Possibilities.* New York: Hawthorne, 1967.

―――. *Ready to Riot.* New York: Holt, Rinehart and Winston, 1968.

Wright, Richard. *12 Million Black Voices.* New York: Viking, 1941.

―――. *Black Power,* New York: Harper, 1954.

―――. *White Man, Listen.* Toronto: Doubleday, 1957.

―――. *Pagan Spain.* New York: Harper, 1957.

Index

Abolitionist newspapers, 29

Abramson, Doris E., 192, 194

"Address to Miss Phillis Wheatley, An" (Hammon), 19-20

"Address to Negroes in the State of New York, An" (Hammon), 20

Afro-American Literature: An Introduction (Hayden, et al.), 134

Afro-American Literature: Drama (Adams, Conn, and Slepian), 195-196

Alien Land (Savoy), 115

All God's Chillun Got Wings (O'Neill), 73

Along This Way (Johnson), 65, 67

Amen Corner, The (Baldwin), 127

America and Other Poems (Whitfield), 33, 36

American Cavalryman, The (Downing), 59

American Negro Folktales (Dorson), 2

American Negro Poetry (Bontemps), 101

American Slave-Trade, The (Spears), 195

Amistad (ship), 134

Amsterdam News, 117

Anderson, Garland, 89

Anderson, Sherwood, 73, 116

Anglo-African Magazine, 49

Angry Ones, The (Williams), 180

Annie Allen (Brooks), 130

Another Country (Baldwin), 128

Anyplace But Here (Bontemps), 101

Appearances (Anderson), 89

Armageddon, themes of, 167-183

Atlantic Monthly, 60
Attaway, William, 116
Attucks, Crispus, 17
"Autiobiographical Notes" (Baldwin), 129-130
Autobiography of a Fugitive Slave (Ward), 39
Autobiography of an Ex-Colored Man, The (Johnson), 65-67
Autobiography of W. E. B. DuBois, 69

"Bad nigger" stereotype, 7, 110
Baldwin, James, 11, 120; life and works of, 127-130; 145
Ballad of Remembrance, A (Hayden), 134
Banana Bottom (McKay), 79-80
Banjo (McKay), 79
Baraka, Imamu Amiri (LeRoi Jones), 167; life and works of, 170-176; 185, 187
"Bars Fight" (Terry), 15-16
Bean Eaters, The (Brooks), 132
"Bear in the Mudhole, The" (anonymous folktale), 9-10
Beautiful Days, The (Spellman), 170
Beetlecreek (Demby), 120, 122-124
Bell, James Madison, 33
Bennett, Hal, 162
Bergman, Peter M., 189, 193-194
Best of Simple, The (Hughes), 190
"Between the World and Me" (Wright), 113-115
Bible, The, 27
Big Sea, The (Hughes), 88
Black Boy (Wright), 107-108

Black Christ and Other Poems, The (Cullen), 85
Black codes, 54, 98
Black Dialogue (periodical), 177
Black Drama: An Anthology (Brasmer and Consolo), 194-195
Black Feeling, Black Talk (Giovanni), 177
Black Feeling, Black Talk/Black Judgement (Giovanni), 177
Black Fire (Baraka and Neal), 170
Black Flame, The (DuBois), 68-69
Black Judgement (Giovanni), 177
Black Magic Poetry (Baraka), 170
Black Manhattan (Johnson), 67
Black Man's Verse (Davis), 96
Black Music (Baraka), 171-172
Black No More (Schuyler), 97-100
Black Opals, 72
Black Renaissance. See Harlem Renaissance
Black Thunder (Bontemps), 101-103
Black Voices from Prison (Knight), 168
Blacker the Berry, The (Thurman), 89
Blake; or The Huts of America (Delany), 48-51
Blake, William, 23
Blood on the Forge (Attaway), 116
Blue Vein Society, 63-64
Blues for Mister Charlie (Baldwin), 129
Blues People (Baraka), 171
Boas, Franz, 103

Bolshevism: and Claude McKay, 76

Bone, Robert A., 59, 81, 116-117

Bontemps, Arna, 1; life and works of, 100-103; 192

Book of Negro Folklore (Bontemps and Hughes), 1-2, 101

Book of Negro Humor, The (Hughes), 190

Book of Numbers, The (Pharr), 162, 165-167

Boone, Daniel, 43

Boxley, George, 28-29

Branch, William, 142

Br'er Rabbit and other folk animals, 8-10

Bronzeville Boys and Girls (Brooks), 132

Brooks, Gwendolyn, (Blakely), 11,106,120; life and works of, 130-133; 168, 185

Brown, Henry Box, 39

Brown, John, 29, 41

Brown, Lloyd, 115

Brown, Sterling A., 96, 191-192

Brown, Wells (Quaker), 44

Brown, William Wells, 24, 39; life and works of, 42-46; 49, 185

Brown Girl, Brownstones (Marshall), 139-141

Bullins, Ed, 174

Burn, Baby, Burn! The Los Angeles Race Riot, August 1965 (Cohen and Murphy), 196

Cambridge, Godfrey, 13

Cane (Toomer), 81-83, 106

Captain Blackman (Williams), 182

Catacombs, The (Demby), 122

Catechism of D Neo-American Hoodoo Church (Reed), 154

Challenge (magazine), 121

Chesnutt, Charles W., 11, 54; life and works of, 60-64; 95

Chosen Place, the Timeless People, The (Marshall), 139

Christianity: early writers' attitudes toward, 17-28; Christian justification of slavery, 25, 27-28; and Countee Cullen, 84-85; and James Baldwin, 127-128; the ghetto church, 128

Chronological History of the Negro in America, The (Bergman), 189, 193-194

Cincinnati Black Arts Festival of 1967, 177

Cities Burning (Randall), 170

Civil Rights Act of 1875, 42, 54

Civil Rights Movement of the 1960's, 147, 167, 174

Civil War, The, 42, 49, 53-54, 61, 75, 139

Clara's Ole Man (Bullins), 174

Clotel; or, The President's Daughter (Brown), 42, 44-46; later versions, 45

Clotelle; or, A Tale of the Southern States (Brown), 45

Clotelle; or, The Colored Heroine (Brown), 45

Cohen, Jerry, 196

Colonel's Dream, The (Chesnutt), 64

Color (Cullen), 84

Communist Party, The: and
    W. E. B. DuBois, 68; and
    Claude McKay, 76; and
    Richard Wright, 109, 111; and
    Dorothy West, 121; in *Invisible
    Man*, 126
*Complete Poems of Paul
    Laurence Dunbar, The*, 55
*Condition, Elevation, Emigration
    and Destiny of the Colored
    People of the United States,
    Politically Considered, The*
    (Delany), 49
Confessions of Nat Turner, The
    (Styron), 191
Conjure Woman, The (Chesnutt),
    60-63
Conquest, The (Micheaux), 59-
    60
Constab Ballads (McKay), 76
Constitutional Convention of
    1787, 17
Contending Forces (Hopkins), 65
Cosby, Bill, 13
Country Place (Petry), 117
Craft, William and Ellen, 39
Crisis (magazine), 68, 86, 100,
    136
Cullen, Countee: life and works
    of, 83-86; 96, 133

Daily Worker (Communist news-
    paper), 109
Dancers on the Shore (Kelley),
    158
Dark Laughter (Anderson), 73
Dark Princess (DuBois), 68
Davis, Arthur P., 191-192
Davis, Frank Marshall, 96, 134

Davis, Ossie, 145, 148; life and
    works of, 148-151; 185
Day of Absence (Ward), 174-175
Dead Lecturer, The (Baraka), 170
"Death of Malcolm X, The"
    (Baraka), 172
DeLaine, Rev. Joseph, 142
Delany, Martin R., 33; life and
    works of, 48-51
Dem (Kelley), 148, 158-161
Demby, William, 120; life and
    works of, 122-125
*Dices or Black Bones; Black
    Voices of the Seventies* (Miller),
    154
Different Drummer, A (Kelley),
    158-159
Dodson, Owen, 133-134
Don't Cry! Scream (Lee), 167
Dorson, Richard M., 1-2
"Double Standard, A" (Harper),
    38
Douglass, Frederick, 24, 39; life
    and works of, 40-42; 44, 48,
    63, 185
Downing Henry F., 59
Drama, black: earliest plays, 44-
    45; first Broadway plays, 88-
    89; important plays of the
    1940's and 1950's, 141-142;
    Harlem Black Arts Theatre,
    170; important plays of the
    1960's, 172-175; Doris E.
    Abramson's *Negro Playwrights
    in the American Theatre 1925-
    1959*, 192, 194
Drop of Patience, A (Kelley),
    158
Drums at Dusk (Bontemps), 101

DuBois, W. E. B., 53-54, 63; life and works of, 67-70; 77

Dunbar, Paul Laurence, 11; life and works of, 54-59

Dunfords Travels Everywhere (Kelley), 158

Dust Tracks on a Road (Hurston), 103

Dutchman (Baraka), 172-173

Early Black American Poets (Robinson), 190-191

Eastman, Max, 76

Ebony (magazine), 180

"Echoes of the Jazz Age" (Fitzgerald), 96

Electronic Nigger, The (Bullins), 174

Ellison, Ralph, 120; life and works of, 125-127; 185-186

Emancipation Proclamation, 42

Emperor Jones, The (O'Neill), 73

Escape; or, A Leap for Freedom, The (Brown), 44, 88

Essays; Including Biographies and Miscellaneous Pieces, in Prose and Poetry (Plato), 33

Evans, Mari, 170

"Evening Thought: Salvation by Christ with Penetential Cries, An" (Hammon), 18-19

Experience; or, How to Give a Northern Man a Backbone (Brown), 44, 88

Fabio, Sarah Webster, 170

Family Pictures (Brooks), 132

Farnsworth, Robert M., 60-61

Fauset, Jessie R., 95

Federal Writers' Project: and Richard Wright, 109; and Dorothy West, 121; and Ralph Ellison, 125; and Margaret Walker, 136

"Feet Live Their Own Life" (Hughes), 11-13

"Fern" (Toomer), 81-82

Fifty Years and Other Poems (Johnson), 67

Fight for Freedom (Hughes), 88

Fine Clothes to the Jew (Hughes), 87

Fire Next Time, The (Baldwin), 129

First World African Festival of Arts, 134

First World War, 71

Fitzgerald, F. Scott, 72, 96

Folklore, 1-14; origins of, 1-2; Bontemps and Hughes' *Book of Negro Folklore*, 1; Dorson's *American Negro Folktales*, 2; Joel Chandler Harris, 2; Uncle Remus, 2; Hurston's *Mules and Men*, 3, 103-104; tales of exaggeration, 3-5; blues and spirituals, 5; Odum and Johnson's *The Negro and His Songs*, 5; work songs, 5-7; legendary-men tales, 7-8; slave stories, 8-9; animal tales, 9-10; minstrel shows and vaudeville, 10-11; folk tradition in black literature, 11-13; contemporary folk forms, 13-14

"For My People" (Walker), 137-138

For My People (collection) (Walker), 136-138

Ford Foundation awards, 134, 139

47th Street (Davis), 134

Foster and Ford Committee, 85-86

Four Black Revolutionary Plays (Baraka), 172

Four Negro Poets (Locke), 74

Franklin, John Hope, 69

Freedmen's Bureau, 49

Freedom's Journal (newspaper), 29

Free-Lance Pallbearers, The (Reed), 148, 154-157

Fugitive Slave Law, The (Rogers), 33

Fund for the Republic Award, 151-152

Future of the American Negro, The (Washington), 193

Gaines, Ernest J., 11

Garies and Their Friends, The (Webb), 46-48

Garrett, Jimmy, 175

Garrison, William Lloyd, 29

Genius of Universal Emancipation (abolitionist newspaper), 29, 44

Gingertown (McKay), 79

Giovanni, Nikki, 167; life and works of, 177-179

Giovanni's Room (Baldwin), 128

Go Tell It on the Mountain (Baldwin), 120, 127-128

God Bless the Child (Hunter), 151

God Sends Sunday (Bontemps), 101

God's Trombones: Seven Negro Sermons in Verse (Johnson), 67

Goin' a' Buffalo (Bullins), 174

Going to Meet the Man (Baldwin), 128-129

Golden Slippers (Bontemps), 101

Gone with the Wind (Mitchell), 138-139

Goodness of St. Rocque and Other Stories, The (Moore), 55

"Goophered Grapevine, The" (Chesnutt), 61-63

Great Migration, 72, 75

Great Slave Narratives (Bontemps), 192

Green, Paul, 73, 141

Greenlee, Sam, 167

Gregory, Dick, 13

Griggs, Sutton, 65

Growin' into Blackness (McCray), 175

Guggenheim fellowships, 92, 130 139, 170

Gurdjieff, Georges Ivanovitch, 83

"Hammer Song" (anonymous folk song), 6-7

Hammon, Briton, 24

Hammon, Jupiter: life and works of, 18-20; 24-25, 31, 35, 185

Hansberry, Lorraine, 88; life and works of, 141-145; 185

Hansberry v. Lee, 142

Happy Ending (Ward), 174

Harlem (Rapp and Thurman), 89

"Harlem Dancer, The" (McKay), 71

Harlem Renaissance, 53, 65, 70-106; beginning of, 71-73; black culture organizations, 72;

J. W. Johnson's *Black Manhattan*, 72; white contributions to, 73; Alain Locke and "the new Negro," 73-76; major writers of, 75; Claude McKay, 76-80; Jean Toomer, 80-83; Countee Cullen, 83-86; Langston Hughes, 86-92; Nella Larsen, 92-95; end of the Renaissance, 96; Arna Bontemps, 100-103; Zora Neale Hurston, 103-106; Dorothy West, 121

"Harlem Shadows" (McKay), 78-79

Harlem Shadows (McKay collection), 79

Harmon Award for Literature, 87, 92

Harper, Fenton, 36

Harper, Frances E. W., 29, 33; life and works of, 36-39

Harriet Tubman: Conductor on the Underground Railway (Petry), 117

Harris, Joel Chandler, 2

Hayden, Robert: life and works of, 133-136

Haynes, Lemuel, 17

Heard, Nathan, 116

Heart Shape in the Dust (Hayden), 134

Henderson, George W., 104

Henry, John, 7

Henson, Josiah, 39

Heyward, DuBose, 73

Himes, Chester, 115

"Historical Footnote to Consider Only When All Else Fails (For Barbara Crosby), A" (Giovanni), 177

Holiday (magazine), 180

Home (Baraka), 171

Home to Harlem (McKay), 76-77, 165

Hope of Liberty (Horton), 30

Hopkins, Pauline, 65

Horatio Alger thesis, 59

Horton, George Moses, 29; life and works of, 30-33; 35

House Behind the Cedars, The (Chesnutt), 64

Howard Street (Heard), 116

Howells, William Dean, 55, 57

Hughes, Langston, 2, 11; life and works of, 86-92; on the end of the Harlem Renaissance, 96; 134, 141, 185

Hunter, Kristin, 148; life and works of, 151-154

Hurston, Zora Neale, 3-5, 11; life and works of, 103-106; 162

"I Am a Cowboy in the Boat of Ra" (Reed), 154-155

I Am the American Negro (Davis), 96

"I Shall Return" (McKay), 77

I Wonder as I Wander (Hughes), 88

If He Hollers Let Him Go (Himes), 115

"If We Must Die" (McKay), 71

Imes, Dr. Elmer, 92

Imperium in Imperio (Griggs), 65

In Abraham's Bosom (Green), 73

In the Mecca (Brooks), 132

Infant mortality, black and white, 109

Infants of the Spring (Thurman), 89

Interesting Narrative of the Life of Olaudah Equiano, or Gustavus Vassa, the African, The (Vassa), 24-25
Invisible Man (Ellison), 120, 125-127
Iola Leroy; or, Shadows Uplifted (Harper), 39
Iron City (Brown), 115
It's Nation Time (Baraka), 170

James, Frank and Jesse, 7-8
Jazz Age, 71-73
Jeb (Broadway play), 148
Jefferson, Thomas, 45
Jim Crow restrictions, 54, 108, 125
"Joe Louis Story, The" (movie), 148
John Hay Whitney fellowships, 152, 158, 170
Johnson, Guy B., 5
Johnson, James Weldon, 54; life and works of, 65-67; 96, 185
Jonah's Gourd Vine (Hurston), 104
Jones, Casey, 7
Jones, Eddy, 7
Jones, LeRoi. *See* Imamu Amiri Baraka
Jubilee (Walker), 136, 138-139
Jupiter Hammon, American Negro Poet (Wegelin), 190-191

Kaleidoscope (Hayden), 134
Kaye, Philip B., 115
"Keep A-Pluggin' Away" (Dunbar), 57-59

Kelley, William Melvin, 148; life and works of, 158-161; 187
King Alfred Plan: in Williams' *The Man Who Cried I Am*, 181-182
Knight, Etheridge: life and works of, 167-170
Knock on Any Door (Motley), 116
Ku Klux Klan, 54, 72, 123, 139

Land Beyond the River, A (Mitchell), 142
Landlord, The (Hunter), 148, 151-154
Larsen, Nella: life and works of, 92-96; 98
Lawd Today (Wright), 112-113
Learning Tree, The (Parks), 162
Lee, Don L., 167
Lee, Ulysses, 191-192
Lester, Julius, 192
Liberator (abolitionist newspaper), 29
Liberator (socialist periodical), 76
"Liberty and Peace" (Wheatley), 21
Life and Times of Frederick Douglass (Douglass), 39
Life and Works of Phillis Wheatley (Renfro), 191
Life expectancy, black and white, 109
Life of Josiah Henson, The (Henson), 39
"Lift Every Voice and Sing" (Johnson), 65

Lincoln, Abraham, 40, 42, 87
"Little Black Boy, The" (Blake), 23
"Little Cindy Ella" (Mabley), 14
Living Is Easy, The (West), 95-96, 121-122
Lloyd, Henry, 18
Locke, Alain L.: life and works of, 73-75
Lonely Crusade (Himes), 115
Long Way from Home, A (McKay), 79
Lost Zoo, The (Cullen), 86
Lovejoy, Elijah P., 43
Lucas, Curtis, 115
Lundy, Benjamin, 29, 44
Lynching, 55, 72, 113-115, 159
"Lynching of Jube Benson, The" (Dunbar), 55
Lyrics of Lowly Life (Dunbar), 57

Mabley, Jackie "Moms," 13-14
McCray, Nettie, 175
McKay, Claude, 71, 73; life and works of, 76-80; 165
Majors and Minors (Dunbar), 55
Mamba's Daughters (Heyward), 73
Man Who Cried I Am, The (Williams), 167, 180-182
Manumission Intelligencer (newspaper), 29
Marrant, John, 24
Marrow of Tradition, The (Chesnutt), 64
"Mars Jeems's Nightmare" (Chesnutt), 61
Marshall, Paule: life and works of, 139-141

Massachusetts Anti-Slavery Society, 44
Maud Martha (Brooks), 106, 120, 131-132
May Day Riots, 71
Medal for Willie, A (Branch), 142
Medea and Other Poems, The (Cullen), 86
Micheaux, Oscar, 59-60
"Middle Passage" (Hayden), 134-136
Miller, Adam David, 196
Miller, Floyd J., 192-193
Miller, Kelly, 69, 193
"Millinery" (Brooks), 131-132
Mine Eyes Have Seen (Moore-Nelson), 55
"Minority of One" (television documentary), 151-152
Miralda; or, The Beautiful Quadroon (Brown), 44-45, 49, 88
Mirror: A Soul, A (Fabio), 170
"Miscellaneous Verses; or, Reflections . . . " (Vassa), 25
Miss Muriel and Other Stories (Petry), 117
Mitchell, Loften, 142
Mitchell, Margaret, 138-139
Monologue comedy, contemporary, 13-14
Monroe, James, 101
Montage of a Dream Deferred (Hughes), 87-88, 134
Moore, Alice Ruth (Mrs. Paul L. Dunbar), 55
Moses: A Story of the Nile (Harper), 39
Moses, Man of the Mountain (Hurston), 104

Motley, Willard, 116
Mulatto (Hughes), 87-92, 141
Mules and Men (Hurston), 3-5, 104
Murphy, William S., 196
Murray, Anna, 40
Music Journal, 168
My Bondage and My Freedom (Douglass), 39
"My Poem" (Giovanni), 179

NAACP, 65, 68, 88
Naked Genius (Horton), 30
Narrative (Henry Box Brown), 39
Narrative (Truth), 39
Narrative of the Lord's Wonderful Dealings with J. Marrant, a Black, A (Marrant), 24
Narrative of the Uncommon Sufferings and Surprising Deliverance of Briton Hammon, a Negro Man, A (B. Hammon), 24
Narrative of William Wells Brown, The (W. Brown), 39, 43-44
Narrows, The (Petry), 117
Nation (magazine), 97, 170
National Book Award, 125
Native Son (Wright), 107, 109-112
Native Son: A Biography of a Young American (Wright and Green), 141
Neal, Larry, 170
Negro and His Music, The (Locke), 74
Negro and His Songs, The (Odum and Johnson), 5

"Negro-Art Hokum, The" (Schuyler), 97-98
Negro Caravan, The (Brown, Davis, and Lee), 191-192
Negro Digest, 158, 168, 177, 180
Negro in America, The (Locke), 74
Negro in Art, The (Locke), 74
Negro in Our History, The (Woodson), 190
Negro in the Making of America, The (Quarles), 190
Negro Novel in America, The (Bone), 59, 81
Negro Playwrights in the American Theatre 1925-1959 (Abramson), 192, 194
Negro Renaissance. *See* Harlem Renaissance
"Negro Speaks of Rivers, The" (Hughes), 86-87
Neither Bond nor Free (Pryor), 65
Nelson, Alice Dunbar. *See* Moore, Alice Ruth
Nemiroff, Robert, 142, 145
New Challenge (periodical), 125
New Frontier (Kennedy years), 147-148
New Masses (periodical), 125
"New Negro, The" (Locke), 74-75
New Negro, The (Locke), 73-75
New York Drama Critics Circle Award: granted to Lorraine Hansberry, 142
Niagara Movement, The, 68
Nigger Heaven (Van Vechten), 73
"Nikki-Rosa" (Giovanni), 178-179

No Name in the Street (Baldwin), 128

Nobody Knows My Name (Baldwin), 129

North Star (abolitionist newspaper), 48

Northup, Solomon, 39

Not a Man and Yet a Man (Whitman), 33

Not Without Laughter (Hughes), 87

Notes of a Native Son (Baldwin), 127-130

Oak and Ivy (Dunbar), 55

Obie Award: granted to Imamu Baraka for *Dutchman*, 172

Odum, H. W., 5

Old John (folk character), 8-9, 62

Ollie Miss (Henderson), 104

"On Being Brought from Africa to America" (Wheatley), 23

O'Neill, Eugene, 73

"On Liberty and Slavery" (Horton), 31-33

"On the Death of the Rev. Mr. George Whitefield" (Wheatley), 21-22

On These I Stand (Cullen), 86

"One Hundred and One 'Final' Performances of *Sidney Brustein*, The" (Nemiroff), 145

One Hundred Years of Negro Freedom (Bontemps), 101

One Way to Heaven (Cullen), 85

Opportunity (magazine), 100, 121

Osborn, Charles, 29

Osofsky, Gilbert, 192

"Our Detroit Conference (For Don L. Lee)" (Giovanni), 177

Our Lan' (Ward), 141

Our World (magazine), 139

Out of the House of Bondage (Miller), 193

Pan-African Congress, 68

Parks, Gordon, 162

Passing (Larsen), 92

Payne, Daniel A., 33

Peace Information Service, 68

"People Who Have No Children Can Be Hard" (Brooks), 133

People's Voice (newspaper), 117

"Personae Poem (For Sylvia Henderson)" (Giovanni), 177

Personals (Bontemps), 101

Peters, John, 21

Peterson, Louis, 142

Petry, Ann, 115; life and works of, 117-120

Pharr, Robert Deane, 162; life and works of 165-167

Philanthropist (newspaper), 29

Phylon (magazine), 68

Pinchback, P. B. S., 81

Pitts, Helen, 40

Pittsburgh Courier (newspaper), 96-97, 151

"Plantation" stereotypes, 55, 75

Plato, Ann, 33

Pleasures and Other Miscellaneous Poems (Payne), 33

Plessy v. Ferguson, 54

Plum Bun (Fauset), 95

"Po' Sandy" (Chesnutt), 61

"Poem (For Dudley Randall)"
   (Giovanni), 177
Poems (Harper), 39
Poems (Ray), 33
Poems by a Slave (Horton), 30
Poems from Prison (Knight), 168
Poems on Miscellaneous Subjects
   (Harper), 33, 36
Poems on Various Subjects,
   Religious and Moral (Wheat-
   ley), 21
Poetical Works of George M.
   Horton, the Colored Bard of
   North Carolina (Horton), 30
Poetry (magazine), 130, 137, 170
Poetry of the Negro, The (Bon-
   temps and Hughes), 101, 154
Pope, Alexander, 21-23
Porgy (Heyward), 73
Powerful Long Ladder (Dod-
   son), 134
Preface to a Twenty Volume
   Suicide Note (Baraka), 170-
   171
Prince, Abijah, 16
Prophets for a New Day (Walker),
   136
Prosser, Gabriel, 28, 101-103
"Protest" (Dunbar), 56-57
Pryor, G. Langhorne, 65
Public education costs, black and
   white, 109
Pulitzer Prize for Poetry:
   awarded to Gwendolyn Brooks,
   130
Purlie Victorious (Davis), 148-
   151
Puttin' on Ole Massa (Osofsky),
   192

Quarles, Benjamin, 190
Quest of the Silver Fleece, The
   (DuBois), 68
Quicksand (Larsen), 92-95

Race Adjustment (Miller), 193
Raisin in the Sun, A (Hansberry),
   141-144, 148
Randall, Dudley, 170
Rapp, William J., 89
Ray, Henrietta C., 33
Re: Creation (Giovanni), 177
Reconstruction period, 17, 49,
   54, 60-61, 63, 75, 138
Reed, Ishmael, 148; life and
   works of, 154-157
Rendezvous with America (Tol-
   son), 133
Renfro, G. Herbert, 191
Resentment, The (Spencer), 59
Revolutionary War period, 17,
   35-36
Riot (Brooks), 132
Robinson, William H., 190-191
Rogers, Elymas P., 33
Rosenwald fellowship, 134
Running a Thousand Miles for
   Freedom (Craft), 39

St. Peter Relates an Incident
   (Johnson), 67
Sanchez, Sonia, 167, 175
Satire: George Schuyler, 97; of
   the 1960's, 147-161
Saturday Evening Quill Club, 72
Saturday Review, 170, 180
Savoy, Willard, 115
Schuyler, George S.: life and
   works of, 96-100; 185

Science: used to justify slavery, 27

Secession, the Southern, 42

Selected Poems (Brooks), 132

Selected Poems (Hayden), 134

Selected Poems (Hughes), 87

Seraph on the Suwanee (Hurston), 104

Shadow and Act (Ellison), 186

"Sheriff's Children, The" (Chesnutt), 63

"Shroud of Color" (Cullen), 83-84

Sign in Sidney Brustein's Window, The (Hansberry), 144-145

Simple, Jesse B. (Hughes' creation), 11-13

"Sis Becky's Pickaninny" (Chesnutt), 61

Sister Sonji (Sanchez), 175

Sketches of Southern Life (Harper), 39

Slave, The (Baraka), 173, 182

"Slave Auction, The" (Harper), 36-37

Slave insurrections, 28-29, 49-50, 101; Joseph C. Carroll's *Slave Insurrections in the United States 1800-1865*, 191

Slavery: attitudes of early writers toward, 17-25; the slave narrative, 24, 39-41, 43-44; slave insurrections, 28-29, 49-50, 101; abolitionist newspapers, 29; nineteenth-century protest writing, 29-51; John Spears' *The American Slave Trade*, 195

"Slave's Complaint, The" (Horton), 30-31

Songs of Jamaica (McKay), 76

Sons of Darkness, Sons of Light (Williams), 167, 182-183

Soul Clap Hands and Sing (Marshall), 139

Souls of Black Folk, The (DuBois), 68-70

Southern Road (Brown), 96

Spears, John, 195

Spellman, A. B., 170

Spencer, Mary Etta, 59

Spin a Soft Black Song (Giovanni), 177

Spook Who Sat by the Door, The (Greenlee), 167

Sport of the Gods, The (Dunbar), 55

Spring in New Hampshire (McKay), 79

Stagolee (also Stackolee), 7

Stowe, Harriet Beecher, 36, 39, 41, 46-47

Street, The (Petry), 115, 117-120, 162

Street in Bronzeville, A (Brooks), 130

Styron, William, 191

System of Dante's Hell, The (Baraka), 175-176

Taffy (Kaye), 115

Take a Giant Step (Peterson), 142

Talented tenth (coined by (DuBois), 63

Tales (Baraka), 175

Tambourines to Glory (Hughes), 87

"Teacher, Teacher" (television play), 148

Tell Me How Long the Train's Been Gone (Baldwin), 128

Tell My Horse (Hurston), 104

Terry, Lucy, 15 - 16

Their Eyes Were Watching God (Hurston), 104-106

There Is Confusion (Fauset), 95

Third Ward Newark (Lucas), 115

This Child's Gonna Live (Wright), 162-165

This Is My Country Too (Williams), 180

Thurman, Wallace, 89

Tituba of Salem Village (Petry), 117

To Be a Slave (Lester), 192

"To Certain Critics" (Cullen), 85-86

"To His Excellency General Washington" (Wheatley), 21

Tolson, Melvin B., 133

Toomer, Jean, 11, 73; life and works of, 80-83; 98, 106, 185

"Tragic mulatto" theme, 66

Triumph of Liberty (Bell), 33

"True Import of Present Dialogue, Black vs. Negro, The (For Peppe, Who Will Ultimately Judge Our Efforts)" (Giovanni), 177-178

Truth, Sojourner, 39, 41-42

Turner, Nat, 29, 45

Twelve Million Black Voices (Wright), 112

Twelve Years a Slave (Northup), 39

Uncle Remus: His Songs and His Sayings (Harris), 2

Uncle Tom's Cabin (Stowe), 39

Up from Slavery (Washington), 193

Urban realism, 107-120; authors of, 115-117

Van Vechten, Carl, 73

Vassa, Gustavus (Olaudah Equiano): life and works of, 24-25; 35

Vesey, Denmark, 29, 168

Violet and Other Tales (Moore), 55

"Voodoo of Hell's Half-Acre, The" (Wright), 108

Walker, Margaret, 11; life and works of, 136-139

Ward, Douglas Turner, 174-175

Ward, Samuel Ringgold, 39

Ward, Theodore, 141

Washington, Booker T., 48, 68-69, 193

"WASP Woman Visits a Black Junkie in Prison, A" (Knight), 168-170

Watkins, William, 36

Watts riot of 1965, 167

We a Badddd People (Sanchez), 167

We Own the Night (Garrett), 175

Weary Blues, The (Hughes), 87

"Web of Circumstance, The" (Chesnutt), 63

Webb, Frank J., 46-48

Weekly Anglo-African (periodical), 49

Wegelin, Oscar, 190-191
Wells, Ebenezer, 16
West, Dorothy, 95-96, 120; life and works of, 121-122
Wheatley, John, 20-21
Wheatley, Phillis, 18; life and works of, 20-23; 24-25, 35
Where Is All the Music? (Evans), 170
White Man, Listen! (Wright), 112
Whitfield, James M., 29-30, 33; life and work of, 33-36; 49
Whitman, Albery A., 33
Wife of His Youth and Other Stories of the Color Line, The (Chesnutt), 63-64, 95
Wilderness of Vines, A (Bennett), 162
Williams, John A., 167; life and works of, 179-183; 185, 187
Wilson, Flip, 13

Women's Christian Temperance Union, 36
Woodson, Carter G., 190
Words in the Mourning Time (Hayden), 134
Wright, Richard: life and works of, 107-117; as poet, 113-115; as playwright, 141; 185
Wright, Sarah E., 11, 162; life and works of, 162-165
Wright School, The: authors of, 115-117; Robert Bone on, 116-117
Writers' Guild, 72

Yale University Younger Poets Award: granted to Margaret Walker, 137
Yellow Back Radio Broke-Down (Reed), 154
"Yet Do I Marvel" (Cullen), 84
Yugen (magazine), 170